Book Synopsis: The entire Bible reveals ungodly acts occurring in God's temple. Sexual abuse, sexual acts, desecration of the temple, money laundering, conflicts, etc. From the Old Testament to the New Testament, challenges occurred within the church and among God's people. When these challenging experiences occur, they can be very traumatic as there is a perception that bad things should not happen in the church. Though this is an understandable perception, we are an imperfect people being perfected by a perfect God. We have choices, free will, our own uniqueness, and ideologies. We will conflict on matters. From time to time, we will hurt one another. God is in pursuit of a church without spot and wrinkle, however, he never promised us that challenges would not occur in the church. He did provide us with standards to avoid church hurt and applicable tools of how to handle it when it occurs.

"Annihilating The Powers of Church Hurt," is a manual designed to explore the truth and myths regarding church hurt, define church hurt, and provide applicable strategies for avoiding, resolving and healing from church hurt. It will posture believers and the church in recognizing that church hurt is real, but we can be healed. This manual will also equip the body of Christ with the ability to reconcile and restore those who have left the church, rectify wrongs that have been done within the church, and to make healthy disciples of those who reside in the church. Your perception and fellowship with God, the church, the body of Christ, and your fellow believers will be transformed as you embody the revelation in this manual. SHIFT!

(Website) Kingdomshifters.com
(Email) kingdomshifters@gmail.com
Connect with Taquetta via Email, Facebook or YouTube

Copyright 2017 – Kingdom Shifters Ministries
All rights reserved. This book is protected by the copyright laws of the United States of America. This book may not be reprinted for commercial gain or profit. The use of occasional page copying for personal or group study is permitted and encouraged. Permission will be granted upon request.

Taquetta's Bio

Taquetta Baker is the founder of Kingdom Shifters Ministries (KSM). She has authored sixteen books and two decree CD's. Taquetta has a Master's Degree in Community Counseling with an emphasis on Marriage, Children and Family Counseling, a Bachelor's Degree in Psychology and Associates Degree in Business Administration. In addition, Taquetta has a Therapon Belief Therapist Certification from Therapon Institute and has over 20 years of professional and Christian Counseling experience.

Taquetta is also gifted at empowering and assisting people with launching ministries, businesses and books and provides mentoring, counseling and vision casting through Kingdom Shifters Kingdom Wellness Program. Taquetta serves on the Board of Directors for New Day Community Ministries, Inc. of Muncie, IN. In October 2008, Taquetta graduated from the Eagles Dance Institute under Dr. Pamela Hardy and received her license in liturgical dance. Before launching into her own ministry, Taquetta served at her previous church for 12 years. She was a prophet, pioneer and leader of Shekinah Expressions Dance Ministry, teacher, member of the presbytery board, and overseer of the Altar Workers Ministry. Taquetta receives mentoring and ministry covering from Bishop Jackie Green, Founder of JGM-National PrayerLife Institute (Phoenix, AZ), and was ordained as an Apostle on June 7, 2014.

Taquetta flows through the wells of warfare and worship and mantles an apostolic mandate of judging and establishing God's kingdom in people, ministries, communities, and regions. Taquetta travels in foreign missions and throughout the United States. She has mentored and established dance, altar workers, deliverance, and prophetic ministries. Taquetta ministers in the areas of fine arts, all manners of prayer, fivefold ministry, deliverance, healing, miracles, atmospheric worship, and empowers and train people in their destiny and life's vision.

Connect with Taquetta and KSM at kingdomshifters.com or via Facebook. For more information regarding Bishop Jackie Green at Jgmenternational.org.

Table of Contents

FOREWORD 1
FOREWORD 2
DECREEING KINGDOM ENLIGHTENMENT 3
TAQUETTA'S TESTIMONY 4
THE TRUE PURPOSE OF THE CHURCH 11
PURE RELIGION 16
WHAT IS CHURCH HURT 19
DISMANTLING THE TRAUMA OF CHURCH HURT 45
THE HIGHER STANDARD OF LEADERSHIP 53
SPIRITUAL CLEANSING! MAINTAINING DELIVERANCE! 58
BIBLICALLY RESOLVING CONFLICT 73
CONFLICT RESOLUTION STRATEGIES & QUESTIONS 83
CANNIBAL SPIRIT OPERATING IN CHURCHES 90
IDOLATROUS CANNIBALISM! THE SACRIFICE OF PREACHERS KIDS & CHURCH KIDS 97
LEADERSHIP & PARENTAL STRATEGIES FOR HEALING PREACHER & CHURCH KIDS & FAMILIES 101
STRATEGIES FOR HEALING PREACHERS' KIDS & 105
HEALING PREACHERS' KIDS OF FALSE IDENTITIES & LABELS 109
HEALING PRAYER FOR PREACHER'S KIDS 114
HURTS LEADERS ENDURE 116
HEALING PRAYER FOR LEADERS 118
DISMANTLING THE PAIN OF BETRAYAL 120
GUARDING YOUR HEART 135
WHEN THE GLORY HAS DEPARTED 140
GLORY VERSUS WITCHRAFT 144
CULT LIKE BEHAVIORS IN MINISTRIES 164
THE DIFFERENCE BETWEEN OFFENSE VERSUS CHURCH ABUSE 169
HINDERANCES TO RECONCILIATION 177
SPIRITUAL STOCKHOLM SYNDROME KIDNAPPED DESTINIES 179
WOULDA SHOULDA COULDA DEALING WITH REGRETS 181

RECKLESS WISDOM!_DISPLACING THE SHEEP!	*187*
HOW TO LEAVE A MINISTRY	*191*
FORSAKE NOT THE ASSEMBLY	*202*
WHY DO WE GATHER AS THE CHURCH?	*208*
IS SPIRITUAL COVERING IMPORTANT?	*210*
POSSESSING MINISTERIAL VISION	*214*
HEAL THEN RELEASE	*218*
SURVIVAL IS NOT HEALING	*221*
HOW DO I KNOW IF I AM REALLY HEALED?	*224*
NUGGETS FOR DETERRING CHURCH HURT	*225*
ANNIHILATING THE POWERS OF CHURCH HURT CHARGE	*227*

FOREWORD

We can all identify with the uncomfortable conversations that life requires. Do you remember your Mom or Dad having "the" sex talk with you? What about the first time you wanted to break up with a boyfriend or girlfriend? The list goes on, but we have all experienced both the discomfort of such a conversation and the sense of relief afterward that you survived it! This book is "that" conversation about church hurt. Thank goodness that Apostle Taquetta Baker has a spiritual Star Trek commitment to "going where no man (or woman) has gone before." She holds nothing back and leaves us nowhere to hide. Whether you are the one that has caused church hurt or you have been the recipient of church hurt, this book will embrace you and walk you step-by-step to a place of healing.

May I share a personal story? I experienced a deep, personal hurt that happened a long time ago but had impacted the course of my life in a major way. A few years ago, I came face-to-face with the person who caused the offense. I was stunned at the sense of peace that allowed me to walk right up to the person, extend my hand, and say sincerely, "It is good to see you again. How are you?" A couple of days later, I was driving to work, and I heard the Lord speak to me, "Don't act like you did something big because you forgave that guy." With the most innocent response, I said, "Lord? What do you mean?" The next question from the Lord, "Do I need to bring out your list?" The simple truth is that all of us have been the cause of hurting someone else. We all need healing, and we all need repentance.

Apostle Taquetta brings more than two decades of professional expertise as a counselor, extensive understanding from ministry, and most of all, personal experience to the table as she invites the reader to the journey of healing from church hurt. This book reaches across generations, cultures, gender, and other factors of diversity to say, "We are in this together." Apostle Baker educates the reader on how to use church hurt as a catalyst for destiny. It is my privilege to contribute a foreword to this essential work. I foresee a support group guide coming because those of you who work to the end of this book will want to share your victory by reaching a helping hand out to others. May God bless and tremendously use you as you heal from church hurt, while bringing healing and wellness to the body of Christ and to the world.

Dr. Kathy E. Williams
Founder of New Day Ministries,
Muncie, Indiana

FOREWORD

I needed this book on **Annihilating the Powers of Church Hurt** *twenty-five years ago, when I was traumatized and crushed by the rejection of my calling through those that I had trusted with my life in the Baptist church. My calling in the Body of Christ as a woman, preacher, apostle and later, as a consecrated bishop left me bitter and bleeding for a long time. I finally was able through years of deliverance and forgiveness as a process, to get free and set others free of the same cancer called Church Hurt.*

I loved this book and could not put it down. It of course should be called an "ENCYCLOPEDIA ON CHURCH HURTS." Apostle Taquetta amazes the reader with her depth, insight, and revelatory healing message. It does explore truths and myths on every level of church hurt. It is a tremendous counseling tool for pastors and lay persons.

Annihilating the Powers of Church Hurt is a weapon of mass destruction to the enemy. It will annihilate his tactics and plans on every level that the church is dealing with today.

I was most fascinated with the chapter on the cannibalism spirit in the churches and internet cannibalism, which she defines as spirits that devour a person or ministry and sacrifice preachers' kids. But all along the way, even the other contributing writers to this book give solutions and practical ways to walk in total deliverance and healing from church hurts. The author calls for "total reformation" to the way we handle church hurts.

I highly recommend this book in local churches and universities and for professional counselors, saved and unsaved. It is full of the Word of God and dripping with wisdom. It will get the church back on track to HEAL AND RELEASE THE BODY OF CHRIST INTO DESTINY.

Bishop Jackie Green,
Founder of JGM Prayerlife Enternational Institute
Redlands, California

DECREEING KINGDOM ENLIGHTENMENT

One challenge we have within the body of Christ is people leaving ministries mostly because of the issues and dynamics within the system more so than sin. Many are tired of the lack of progress in their personal lives, not experiencing the God that is preached in their personal lives, having to jump through systems and deal with challenging people, in hopes of being equipped, empowered, and released in destiny. Many people feel judged by doctrines that are not grounded in biblical truth or that have biblical truth, but no deliverance power, practical guidance, and accountability that promotes transformation and sustainability. Many are weary and have lost faith in a system designed to be a faith walk. This is indeed a challenge and even a crisis that the church must awaken to and SHIFT into addressing. Transformation in people, ministries, and in the body of Christ is essential, such that we restore faith in God's bride - the church, restore faith in leaders and members, and restore faith in the power of God that should be tangible within our ministries and God's people.

Please understand that this is not a church bashing manual, neither is it a leadership bashing manual. This manual is not intended to negate church hurt, but bring enlightenment to it. Your painful experiences and challenges within the church are valid and real. Hurtful experiences within the church are very real and need to be exposed and addressed. There are a lot of generalizations, myths, and falsehoods surrounding church hurt that need to be exposed, addressed, and dismantled. This manual will address truths and lies regarding church hurt, while providing applicable biblical wisdom to address, resolve and heal conflicts within the church.

As you embark upon the revelation in this manual, I decree the eyes of your understanding will be enlightened to receive the truth about your experiences, truth regarding yourself, and truth concerning those who hurt you. I decree further enlightenment will enable you to retain truth regarding the character and purpose of the church, of believers, and the body of Christ at large. I decree that clarity and understanding will dismantle trauma, confusion, generalizations, and fears that often accompany being hurt in the church. I decree sustaining deliverance and healing will be your portion as you allow God to enlighten, empower, and SHIFT you from hurt to wellness. SHIFT!

TAQUETTA'S TESTIMONY

I am equipped to write this manual because I have not only experienced church hurt, I have overcome it again and again and again. I know what it is like to be hurt within the church and feel like you will never get over it. I was raised in the church and my first experience of church hurt was when I was a teenager. My aunt adopted me at two weeks old. She drug my brothers and me to church almost every time the doors opened. I was a member of many of the children's ministries. By the time I was a teenager, I was the president of the usher board, a leader among the youth at my church, and within the Baptist convention system. My aunt was the adult overseer of the youth usher board although she did not give me my position. I was voted in by the youth who were members of the ministry. The usher board was very successful. It was so huge that we needed several pews so that all of us could have a place to sit on second Sunday when it was our time to serve in the service.

Jealousy, discord, and messiness manifested concerning my aunt and I and the youth usher board. This resulted in my aunt being removed as overseer. I was so hurt by the betrayal, lies, and injustice, that I quit the usher board and other ministry departments. I would have quit church, but my aunt had a rule in our home that everyone was going to church no matter what. Many of the other youth members quit as well. They did not have a parent making sure they remained connected to church and to God. Unfortunately, many of them do not go to church to this day. They probably do not even realize that this hurtful experience may be a factor in the reason they do not attend church.

Though church hurt SHIFTED me into living an ungodly life of drinking, smoking, clubbing, and doing God knows what on Friday and Saturday, on Sunday, I was in church. That was the rule of the house and you were going to church whether you wanted to or not. This was so ingrained in me that even with attending college four hours away from home, I was a heathen Monday through Saturday and I was in somebodies' church on most Sundays. I lived this way from my teen years into my young adult years. I must admit that it was a very tormenting time. I loved the world, but I hated it at the same time. I hated church but loved it at the same time. I loved God and was aware that my actions were not pleasing to him. I would often become intoxicated and grieved with regret and repentance for my sinful actions. It was not until I had an experience where I passed out at a party and lost track of time, that I decided to relinquish my party life and really live for Jesus.

When making this decision, I wish I could say I went running to join a church. That is not my testimony. I was still hurt by what happened to my aunt and me as a teenager. After my rededication to the Lord, which occurred at home, I spent two years attending different churches on Sundays, while being purged, delivered, and healed in seclusion with Jesus. I was not trying to have a "me and Jesus" experience. It just occurred that way. God DID NOT tell me to separate from the church. He DID NOT tell me to join a church either. I also did not ask if I should join a church. We never ask those questions we do not want the answer too. It was obvious that I knew I needed to be in an assembly since I was church hoping every Sunday. I also studied my bible even as a heathen and knew that church was important to God.

God did require that I separate from my friends and family members for a season. This was difficult as I had the same friends since I was in seventh grade. I was also close to my current friends at that time to whom I had met in graduate school. My childhood friends and I were so close that many of them would go to church with me on Sunday mornings when I was in the world. We would be in church with hangovers, but we were there. My family is quite close. To this day, my family and neighborhood friends gather at my grandmother's house on Sunday. There is always good eating, laughter, and lots of love. There is also drinking and smoking, which I was being delivered from. During my time of separation, God required that I not attend these family gatherings or hang with my friends. I had a habit of getting drunk and verbally promising God that I was going to get my life together. I would be preaching and drinking and blowing everyone's high, only to return to my wretched ways at the next family or friend gathering. When I really decided to change, no one believed me. They thought I would be found drinking, smoking, and clubbing the following week, but that was not the case. I was serious this time and God was serious. For two years I would go to work, come home, and spend time in my room, praying, studying my bible, reading Christian books, listening to sermons, and searching the web.

While in my season of separation, my God mother invited me to a bible study at a church she was attending. She raved about this bible study, so I decided to go. I really enjoyed the class. It was so good that I became a regular attendee. I was the only young adult in the bible study for it was an older adult class. They allowed me to remain in the class even though there was a class with adults closer to my age. The teacher answered my questions, and if he did not know the answer, he would do research and answer my questions the following week. This was huge for me as I have had bible teachers and ministers shut me down.

They could not answer my questions and would leave me hanging in confusion and wonder while making inferences that I was asking questions to make them look bad. I truly needed answers and guidance on where to receive answers if they could not provide them to me. This teacher was not intimidated by my questions. He welcomed them and encouraged me in my quest for more of God.

After attending bible study for about six months, I decided to visit a Sunday service. Sunday services were awesome. The word was rich, the choir was anointed, God's presence was tangible, and his blessings and fruit were evident in the church and upon the lives of the saints. Everyone was nice to me and I enjoyed the fellowship and culture of the church. With all the spiritual delights, it still took me over a year to join the church. People would inquire, yet no one pressured me to become a member. Despite not being a member, I was allowed to have my poems and declarations posted in the Sunday bulletin. People were empowered through my writings and often shared them with their family members and coworkers for weekly encouragement.

One Sunday during the altar call, I stood up and started walking down to the front. Everyone in the bible study I attended, stood up and started clapping and praising the Lord. They knew a miracle was occurring right before their eyes. Even though I was faithful to bible study and to church, I was not trying to be a member of nobody's church. But God provoked me that Sunday and I became a proud faithful member. My experience at this church was great and refreshing. I, however, did not have any friends at the church and I only interacted with the saints at bible study, Sunday services, and special events. I was a part of the body of Christ but not invested or integrated with my assembly or the lives of the people. Somebody catch that in the spirit.

While still in seclusion, I would surf the web and became a regular attendee of a popular Christian chat community. People from all walks of life and from different religions and denominations were interested in this chat community. Often the dialog was fun and empowering, and sometimes it was messy and religious. I was in the chatroom frequently and was asked to be a moderator – one who helped to oversee the chatroom and the ministry's message board. My job was to pray and minister to people, provide interesting topics of discussion, and make sure people were having respectful dialogs. I had moderator features that enabled me to block and kick people out if they were disrespectful or disruptive. My experience in this chatroom was eye-opening. The same people who I would pray for and talk off the ledges one day would be telling me the next day, that I was not saved because I did not speak in tongues and other crazy crap. I was a moderator for a good three or four years. These experiences were challenging because regardless of what they said to me, I still had to minister and oversee them. I probably should have quit. As I look back, it was really the only real communication I had with the saints at that time, outside of the bible study and church events. The chatroom was safe. I could be a leader, walk in my gifts, but control my interactions within the church aka chatroom, and with the saints. Even if I was challenged by people, there was no real investment where they could really hurt me. Somebody catch that in the spirit.

Many saints do this today. They are on social media ministering, doing Facebook live videos, periscopes and on and on. They have church hurt and have separated from true fellowship with the church. They appear to be plugged in through social media interactions, but truth is, they may not even attend church. And if they do, they go to church but are not integrated within the ministry or in fellowship with the saints. Church hurt will have you doing just enough to say you are saved, love God, and comprehend your calling and destiny, but not enough to reap the full blessings of salvation, truly advance in your relationship with God and his kingdom, or freely walk in destiny without fear of being hurt again.

Truthfully, I did not even know what occurred when I was sixteen was church hurt, until later in life when I transitioned out of a church where I endured a series of challenging and hurtful experiences. So even though the church I attended when in isolation with God was a good experience, I did not know to examine my past church hurt before God, and seek to heal from it. Just being a part of an assembly did not automatically heal me. Especially since I was not truly integrated within that ministry and within the body of Christ. I learned later in life that church hurt has to be addressed like any other hurt. I had to take my hurt from experiences within the church before God, and let him deal with me and it. I believe this is the biggest mistake we make as saints. We will take every other hurt to God, but not our church hurt. And because church hurt is not discussed in the church, no one within the assembly thinks to ask if we have church hurt, or even think to address church hurt. Especially when people come from other churches. Though we make people jump through hoops before we release them in ministry, we do not ask the reason they left those churches, and whether healing and closure are necessary to them positively integrating into their new assembly.

Within a year of joining the church where I attended bible study, I moved to another state where my spiritual mother lived. When visiting her, I would go to church with her, so when I moved there, I began attending the church. My bible study church back home was nondenominational. You could wear pants, make-up, cut your hair, play sports, go to the movies, etc. As long as you were modest and not engaging in wretched behavior that conflicted with biblical standards, you were considered saved. Well, the church I began attending in my new state had recently transitioned from under the Pentecostal Assemblies of the World. Though they were SHIFTING to embracing more liberal nondenominational concepts, it would take years to gut out and break the stronghold mindsets from the Pentecostal doctrine that had been engrained in the people and within the church culture.

I came in during their transition. Many of the people did not know how to embrace me and the new liberty they were seeking personally and as an assembly, more so than intentionally trying to hurt me. This was a great church with great vision. The ministry had great leadership with a heart to be in the will and purpose of God. Most people within this ministry had sacrificed their lives for ministry and to advance the kingdom of God. I was a representation of what they said they wanted, yet they had learned to despise and be suspicious of certain liberated aspects of Christianity for so long until it caused many of them to treat me in a negative manner. I probably should have left the church, but despite what was occurring, I believed it was God's will for me to be there. Because of the Pentecostal doctrine within the culture of the church and people, I often experienced ostracism and was treated like an outsider. I constantly had to prove I was saved, heard from God, and was worth being a part of the assembly. It was such a difficult time that I refused to join the church and would refer to it as my spiritual mother's church, which was the TRUTH.

It was three years later when I finally joined the church and was because I had lost a basketball game at the church picnic. That was my perspective anyway, but God set me up. I made a bet with some guys in the church that if I won, I could keep my bootleg status as a nonmember, and if I lost I would become a member. I gathered all the bootleg members and even some sinners that did not go to church but were good basketball players to be on my squad. And the saints had their members' squad. After a hard battle on the basketball court, we lost by one point. I thought the pastor was going to be like, "she needs to want to be a member rather than lose a game to become a member." But they told him I lost, and he was like *"tell her and the bootleggers I will see them Sunday at the front of the church."* We were fellowshipped in the following Sunday. Because I had been attending for so long, many thought I was already a member until the basketball game exposed me. I might as well had been a member since I attended the church for another nine years. God knew I needed a push to join. I would not have joined on my own, so he set me up to join.

After joining the church, I slowly SHIFTED into more leadership roles. Over a nine-year span, I founded and pioneered a dance ministry and praise and worship dance on Sunday mornings. I was one of the prophets in the church and was a teacher in the prophetic schools. I occasionally taught Sunday School and bible study. I was over the altar workers ministry and a deliverance worker. I was a member of the presbytery ministry. I would oversee various events in the areas of fine arts, healing, and deliverance ministry. I was always mentoring, encouraging, and praying for somebody. I also ministered abroad and when I was not ministering, I was at a training event, reading a book, studying a book or my bible, so that I could further equip myself in my destiny and calling. I poured my life into the ministry and the body of Christ at large. I was always seeking to please God and advance his kingdom regardless of the sacrifice.

I wish I could say my church challenges lessened with having leadership positions and ministry opportunities. At times my challenges were very intense. God would use me to pioneer different and unique ministries, movements and events for the church. I often found myself having to intercede and war to really break ground, gain the favor of the people, and see the will of God come to pass for what he had granted to my hands. Change and newness can sometimes come with trial and tribulation. At times, I would cry out to God in wonder as to the reason my experiences had to be so difficult. Especially since most people were elated during and after the events. They loved the blessings and transformations that occurred and was in expectation of the next endeavor. I thought my track record of excellent work would eventually lessen the challenges. Sometimes it did and other times the challenges would heighten. It was very hurtful to have to explain myself and sometimes protect myself from people and an assembly I was faithful to, and poured my life out too. I eventually learned that some of the contentions were not just with the transition of the people or the church, but due to principalities and powers within the region that knew this church was an essential gatekeeper. These demonic entities did not want this ministry to flourish into what God had envisioned. This gave me more grace and compassion for the processing and SHIFT that was taking place. However, it did not SHIFT the challenges I endured as a trailblazer.

Despite it all, I did complete my assignment at this church. As you read this book, you will learn more about my experience and find that God eventually led me to transition out of the ministry to further plant and plow my own ministry. My SHIFT out of the church was done with Godly order but came with some hurtful events. It is with this SHIFT that I had to deal with church issues stemming from my teenage years. I was committed to being delivered and healed and God did just that. Because of my journey, I am able to take you on this journey towards personal transformation. I am looking forward to what God will do in your life as I share my experiences, revelations, skills, and strategies for annihilating the powers of church hurt! Church hurt is indeed real, but you will be healed. IT IS SO! SHIFT!

THE TRUE PURPOSE OF THE CHURCH

Let's address the purpose of the church to dissect the truths and myths of church hurt.

One factor we need to consider is often we equate the purpose of the church to doctrines and denominational systems within the church.

Religious Doctrines are religious creeds, philosophies, and standards a church abides by (e.g. We believe that Jesus is the only way to salvation, we believe in the gifts of the Holy Spirit and the evidence of speaking in tongues).

Denominational Systems are organizations that a church or ministry tend to identify themselves with to create a corporate culture with norms, rules, and expectations (e.g., Baptist, Pentecostal, Methodist, Nondenominational).

Often doctrines and systems are manmade standards men set using many biblical principles to help bring structure to a ministry vision, a church, or church body. But this is not necessarily God's purpose of the church. Especially if the doctrine or system has biblical errors, untruths, and becomes more important than God, God's people, his word, vision for that ministry and the body of Christ as a whole.

Some church doctrines and systems may include standards regarding attire, code of conduct, and activities that are more based on what that doctrine's or leader's personal perspective of being saved, holy, or modest is, rather than God's biblical perspective of salvation.

The other challenge we have with doctrines and systems is that if some people decide they believe something different than the doctrines and systems of that church, many become hurt by it. Especially if it excludes them, challenges a sin they want to compromise or engage in, or causes them to have to disconnect from that ministry. The challenge with this is, often if these perspectives are rooted in sin and compromise, a person will consider that assembly religious. The expectation of God loving all people, while recognizing that God has a standard for salvation has become distorted, confusing, and debatable, despite what the Bible says.

A lot of ideologies we call religious today are not religious. For example, if someone seeks to keep or iterate the standard of holiness that is the foundation of God and his biblical word, we automatically call that person "religious." Many often proclaim the concept of grace, or the fact that we all sin to counterattack what we deem to be "holier than though," "self-righteous jargon," regarding the need to be holy and pursue holiness. Holiness is not a doctrine or a system. It is a biblical truth of God's character and nature and is a biblical expectation he has for us as his people. God does not want his people willingly living in sin, bound by devils, and compromising his word and standards. He wants us to have a clear understanding of his holiness, and to live in pursuit of his holiness.

Because doctrines and systems have set standards to define holiness, and we have learned over the centuries that some of these religious acts and perceptions are not important to God, many have rebelled against God's standard for the church. Many want to throw God's entire purpose of the church out rather than acknowledge and correct the errors within some systems and doctrines and teach people to have a relationship with God, and honor his word so that we begin to live and morph as his true church.

As I have started my own ministry, I have learned that everyone is not going to like my church, feel comfortable at my church, or even fit at my church. My church is called Kingdom Shifters Christian Empowerment Center. Its core foundation is to save, deliver, heal, and teach people how to journey in a personal relationship with God. As the person evolves in a personal relationship with God, the ministry's vision is to equip saints in their personal destiny, and empower, release and support them as they become and do what God has called them to do in the earth. If people just want to come to church every Sunday, sit on the pews, hear a good message and go home, then my church will not be the right ministry for them. They will find me, my team, and the doctrines and systems of the church a nuisance, as we will be seeking to activate, equip, empower and release them in who they are in God. It is the culture of our ministry. If you attempt to sit down and do nothing, hide in the pews, run from your destiny, reject your destiny, etc., you will feel judged and exposed. We will not be judging you or exposing you, but the ministry vision itself and the standards that God has set for the ministry will do that. This is the reason why when I evangelize I give people options of churches to attend. My heart is to see them in the body of Christ, not be a number at my church. I give them the right to choose if they want to visit my ministry or other assemblies. I encourage them to pursue a ministry that they believe is a good fit for them, and what God is saying for their lives.

God's church is designed to save, deliver, heal, empower, and equip people to walk in their ordained destiny. That is the whole reason Jesus came to earth, was crucified, and rose for our sins.

> ***Luke 4:18*** *The Spirit of the Lord is upon me, because he hath anointed me to preach the gospel to the poor; he hath sent me to heal the brokenhearted, to preach deliverance to the captives, and recovering of sight to the blind, to set at liberty them that are bruised, to preach the acceptable year of the Lord. And he closed the book, and he gave it again to the minister, and sat down.*

The church does what it is created to do. Jesus was an embodying representation of the church. Regardless of the actions of man, implementations of denominations, doctrines, and systems, God's design of the church does not change and does not hurt anyone but the devil.

Though we have different churches all over our cities and the world, Jesus never said we were to be our own separate church. To Jesus, we are all one church and upon us all, he builds and fulfills his kingdom in the earth.

> ***Matthew 16:13-18*** *The Amplified Bible Now when Jesus went into the region of Caesarea Philippi, He asked His disciples, Who do people say that the Son of Man is? And they answered, some say John the Baptist; others say Elijah; and others Jeremiah or one of the prophets. He said to them, But who do you [yourselves] say that I am? Simon Peter replied, You are the Christ, the Son of the living God.*
>
> *Then Jesus answered him, Blessed (happy, fortunate, and to be envied) are you, Simon Bar-Jonah. For flesh and blood [men] have not revealed this to you, but My Father Who is in heaven. And I tell you, you are Peter [Greek, Petros – a large piece of rock], and on this rock [Greek, petra – a huge rock like Gibraltar] I will build My church, and the gates of Hades (the powers of the infernal region) shall not overpower it [or be strong to its detriment or hold out against it].*
>
> ***Ephesians 4:4-8*** *The Amplified Bible [There is] one body and one Spirit – just as there is also one hope [that belongs] to the calling you received – [There is] one Lord, one faith, one baptism, One God and Father of [us] all, Who is above all [Sovereign over all], pervading all and [living] in [us] all.*

> *Yet grace (God's unmerited favor) was given to each of us individually [not indiscriminately, but in different ways] in proportion to the measure of Christ's [rich and bounteous] gift. Therefore it is said, when He ascended on high, He led captivity captive [He led a train of vanquished foes] and He bestowed gifts on men.*

As a church and as a church member, to Jesus, we are one body with different gifts, visions, workings, and operations. Our vision from ministry to ministry may be different, but we are one church.

> ***1Corinthians 12:12-20*** *For just as the body is a unity and yet has many parts, and all the parts, though many, form [only] one body, so it is with Christ (the Messiah, the Anointed One). For by [means of the personal agency of] one [Holy] Spirit we were all, whether Jews or Greeks, slaves or free, baptized [and by baptism united together] into one body, and all made to drink of one [Holy] Spirit. For the body does not consist of one limb or organ but of many. If the foot should say, Because I am not the hand, I do not belong to the body, would it be therefore not [a part] of the body?*
>
> *If the ear should say, because I am not the eye, I do not belong to the body, would it be therefore not [a part] of the body? If the whole body were an eye, where [would be the sense of] hearing? If the whole body were an ear, where [would be the sense of] smell? But as it is, God has placed and arranged the limbs and organs in the body, each [particular one] of them, just as He wished and saw fit and with the best adaptation. But if [the whole] were all a single organ, where would the body be? And now there are [certainly] many limbs and organs, but a single body.*

Each church and each person has a measure of Jesus that we bring to the world to help make up his complete church.

> ***Ephesians 4:8-13*** *The Amplified Bible Therefore it is said, When He ascended on high, He led captivity captive [He led a train of vanquished foes] and He bestowed gifts on men. [But He ascended?] Now what can this, He ascended, mean but that He had previously descended from [the heights of] heaven into [the depths], the lower parts of the earth? He Who descended is the [very] same as He Who also has ascended high above all the heavens, that He [His presence] might fill all things (the whole universe, from the lowest to the highest).*
>
> *And His gifts were [varied; He Himself appointed and gave men to us] some to be apostles (special messengers), some prophets (inspired preachers and*

expounders), some evangelists (preachers of the Gospel, traveling missionaries), some pastors (shepherds of His flock) and teachers. His intention was the perfecting and the full equipping of the saints (His consecrated people), [that they should do] the work of ministering toward building up Christ's body (the church), That it might develop] until we all attain oneness in the faith and in the comprehension of the [full and accurate] knowledge of the Son of God, that [we might arrive] at really mature manhood (the completeness of personality which is nothing less than the standard height of Christ's own perfection), the measure of the stature of the fullness of the Christ and the completeness found in Him.

1Corinthians 12:21-27 *The Amplified Bible And the eye is not able to say to the hand, I have no need of you, nor again the head to the feet, I have no need of you. But instead, there is [absolute] necessity for the parts of the body that are considered the more weak. And those [parts] of the body which we consider rather ignoble are [the very parts] which we invest with additional honor, and our unseemly parts and those unsuitable for exposure are treated with seemliness (modesty and decorum),*

Which our more presentable parts do not require. But God has so adjusted (mingled, harmonized, and subtly proportioned the parts of) the whole body, giving the greater honor and richer endowment to the inferior parts which lack [apparent importance], So that there should be no division or discord or lack of adaptation [of the parts of the body to each other], but the members all alike should have a mutual interest in and care for one another. And if one member suffers, all the parts [share] the suffering; if one member is honored, all the members [share in] the enjoyment of it. Now you [collectively] are Christ's body and [individually] you are members of it, each part severally and distinct [each with his own place and function].

We were never supposed to be viewed as our own separate church. We are one church, even though we are in different locations. Our experiences within the church are not God's church hurting us. Receiving this truth will help dismantle fears, indignations, generalizations, and separations that keep us bound in hurtful church experiences.

Decreeing you are receiving truth and SHIFTING forward with enlightenment and healing. SHIFT!

PURE RELIGION
By: Minister Nina Cook
Kingdom Shifters Ministries, Muncie, IN

<u>Religion</u> in Dictionary.com means:
1. A set of beliefs concerning the cause, nature, and purpose of the universe, especially when considered as the creation of a superhuman agency or agencies, usually involving devotional and ritual observances, and often containing a moral code governing the conduct of human affairs
2. A specific fundamental set of beliefs and practices generally agreed upon by a number of persons or sects
3. The body of persons adhering to a particular set of beliefs and practices

Religion in relations to this meaning is the consensus amongst a group of people of set beliefs, practices and standards for living. Religion itself is important in relationship with God and our daily lives, however, not in the sense of what is often practiced in the world and body of Christ today. The fact that many form religious ideals based on human opinion alone without the word, will, heart, and truth of God, is what strips religion of its purity and falsely represents it. This false representation is what has been identified as the spirit of religion. A demonic spirit that demeans people by demanding that they submit to man-made ideologies void of the spirit and truth of God. It is a form of idolatry that exalts man in external works rather than inner communion with God that produces his fruit. It makes everything all about self where the focus is no longer Jesus Christ. The focus becomes what can I do and what can I say to be more righteous, when the focus should always be on how to abide more in Jesus to be made more like him. It also causes people to surrender to the opinions of man and not the heart and will of God for their lives and unique walk with the Lord. The operation of this spirit breeds hurt, confusion, rejection, rebellion, bitterness, anger and various afflictions within the affected person. It draws the person away from their own personal relationship, communication, and salvation journey with the Lord into following an external protocol that will fill them with a form of godliness that has no power to truly heal, deliver, and sustain them in a life of holiness, purity and the fruits of true salvation.

To protect people from being hurt by this spirit, we must know the truth about religion and have God's heart and intent for it rooted in us personally and in the foundations of our churches. We cannot use it to justify abuse, control, manipulation, and various other ungodly behaviors that wound people and give them a negative perspective of the church. We must begin to show the world God's heart in this matter. Religion is not meant to harm people, control people, force people or judge people. Pure religion is designed to serve God and serve others.

> ***James 1:25-27 New Living Translation*** *But the one who looks into the perfect law, the law of liberty, and perseveres, being no hearer who forgets but a doer who acts, he will be blessed in his doing. If anyone thinks he is religious and does not bridle his tongue but deceives his heart, this person's religion is worthless. Religion that is pure and undefiled before God the Father is this: to visit orphans and widows in their affliction, and to keep oneself unstained from the world.*

> ***James 1:26-27 The Voice*** *If you put yourself on a pedestal, thinking you have become a role model in all things religious, but you can't control your mouth, then think again. Your mouth exposes your heart, and your religion is useless. Real, true religion from God the Father's perspective is about caring for the orphans and widows who suffer needlessly and resisting the evil influence of the world.*

According to this scripture, pure religion is the practice of modeling the life (standards, behavior, character) of Jesus Christ by caring for the afflicted and remaining undefiled from the world. It is about being a doer of Jesus's practices where the fruit of implementing them in our own lives exhibits through how we help, serve, and interact with others. Religion is in our actions and not in our words, as it is about knowing the word of God AND doing it. The fruit of this will speak through our lives and we can empower others by not forcing them to do what we do, but by encouraging them in their relationship with Jesus. In doing so, we help them stay their own personal course with God and give room for his power to produce fruit in them that will be able to sustain and maintain. We do not put ourselves on a pedestal and make ourselves their model for religion, we keep them directed to Jesus.

This scripture says we are to bridle our tongues. Bridle means to restrain, curb, control and hold back. This expresses to us that if we choose to claim that we are religious but have no control over our mouths, the words we speak exalt ourselves and reveal what lies in our hearts. It shows that our religion is truly about us, thus making it useless. We profess holiness and righteousness based on our own opinions and personal judgments, but not through Gods spirit, truth, and heart producing through us. We deceive ourselves because we think we are pure, while also deceiving others in thinking our haughty actions is what religion is. As we desire to bring healing in this area, we must embody the true characteristics of pure religion which are meekness, humility, lowliness, and servanthood. A major key in understanding pure religion is that it is never about us, it is always about others. As we begin to take on this truth, we can annihilate the spirit of religion in us, our local assemblies, and display God's pure perspective.

> *2 Corinthians 1:12 New Living Translation We can say with confidence and a clear conscience that we have lived with a God-given holiness and sincerity in all our dealings. We have depended on God's grace, not on our own human wisdom. That is how we have conducted ourselves before the world, and especially toward you.*

- ✓ Religion is not in our human wisdom, it is within the grace (power) of God
- ✓ Religion lies within God-given holiness and sincerity in all we do

2 Corinthians 2:17 Amplified Version For we are not like many, [acting like merchants] peddling God's word [shortchanging and adulterating God's message]; but from pure [uncompromised] motives, as [commissioned and sent] from God, we speak [His message] in Christ in the sight of God.

New International Version
Unlike so many, we do not peddle the word of God for profit. On the contrary, in Christ we speak before God with sincerity, as those sent from God.

- ✓ Religion is not about pushing God's word for our personal profit and gain
- ✓ Religion is pure and uncompromised in our motives as we share the message of Jesus Christ

WHAT IS CHURCH HURT

You may experience hurt from:
- ✓ People
- ✓ Leaders
- ✓ Manmade denominations and doctrines
- ✓ Religious and traditional systems that are false representations of the church

However, the church itself did not hurt you. Even though I just shared my testimony in a previous chapter regarding church hurt, the church itself did not hurt me. Your experience happened to be at church, and I truly sympathize and apologize for your experience. I truly regret it occurred and I decree this manual delivers and heals you. I do, however, want to speak truth that despite your situation and my experiences occurring in a church or with church people, the church itself did not hurt either of us. Let me say that again, "your experience occurred in church, but the church itself did not hurt you."

In fairness, when we are hurt on the job we do not call it "*job hurt*." When a family member hurts you, you do not label it "*family hurt*." You do not stop working and never return to work because you encounter challenges on a job. You do not ostracize your entire family because a few people in the family hurt you. We do not throw away entire systems or do away with entire systems when we are hurt in other areas of life. We, therefore, must stop doing this with the church. Especially since God's church is not a building, it is not a select group of people, it is not a particular ministry. God's church is the body of Christ. We are all his church.

Church hurt can be the worst kind of hurt for several reasons:

- ✓ You are trying to process how a Godly leader or person in church can hurt you.
- ✓ You are trying to process how a place that is supposed to protect and empower you can harm you.
- ✓ You are trying to process how others can still follow that leader or attend that church, while knowing you have been hurt.
- ✓ You are trying to process why God has not revealed to the people that you have been hurt by a leader or person, or why they have not discerned your pain.

- ✓ You are trying to process how the leader or person can hurt you and still be used of God to do mighty acts.
- ✓ You are trying to process how a leader or person from a church can hurt you and still be blessed, even as the ministry continues to advance.
- ✓ You are trying to process how the leader or person can hurt you and can call everyone else out on their sin but have no conviction for their actions towards you.
- ✓ You are trying to process how that leader or person can study and seek God for mighty revelation, yet receive no insight on their actions towards you.
- ✓ You are trying to process how everyone else appears to be getting what they need from that leader or church but you only received pain.

These checkpoints are what I would label as "friendly fire." Friendly fire is defined as a weapon firing from one's own camp that causes injury or death. We expect the demons to hurt us, wicked people to hurt us, people who hate God and his word to hurt us, but we do not expect those within our own camp to harm us. We deem ministries to be our heaven on earth. They are our safe havens for being protected by the presence and power of God. The saints are our friends, our allies, our partners, and supports who help us to take the kingdom by force. Whether intentionally or unintentionally, we never expect to get hurt by those on our team. When this happens, we demand a logical explanation, but because it is within the church, and we do not expect church hurt to happen, any explanation tends to be viewed as illogical and unacceptable.

As I explored the concept of church hurt, I would have to contend that challenges within the church are inevitable. We will experience them. We are imperfect people seeking to be perfected by a perfect God. God does not promise us that we will not have challenges and trials within the church. He does expect us to be transformed by his presence, standards, strategies, and guidance so as we are SHIFTING in our transformation, we should be more loving, considerate, honoring, empowering, and unified with one another. When SHIFTING from level to level and glory to glory in and with him, God also provides us with wisdom and guidance regarding how to handle conflicts and trials. I, therefore, would first like to dismantle the myth and mindset that church hurt should not happen. It will occur. We, however, need to be trained and equipped in how to handle it. How to care for one another's emotions, hearts, souls, and identities, such that we SHIFT into the perfect church that God is in pursuit of.

The definition of church hurt in its simplest form is being wounded by the leaders and/or church that should have nurtured you as any believer should expect to be fed, protected, taught, loved, accepted, corrected, empowered, trained, etc. Church hurt violates fundamental needs, foundational needs, boundaries, and covenants, as we all have the need to be nurtured, loved, accepted, safe, encouraged, and empowered to achieve in life and sustain in destiny.

Church hurt in a more extensive concept can be defined by any of the following experiences:
- Physical, verbal, or sexual abuse.
- Neglect by leaders or church members.
- Experiencing rejection and ostracism due to being different, new, radical, sinful, defiant, messy, temperate, anointed, a perceived threat, etc. I added the not so pleasant behaviors because many claim to want people saved, but the minute they start manifesting themselves, we reject and ostracize them rather than seeking to deliver, heal and equip them to act better. Doing this can cause church hurt to the already wounded and broken.
- Experiencing offense to a level of brokenness in one's identity or soul from leadership or church members with no regard for your pain and how to be restored.
- Experiencing inordinate relationships where people fulfill roles in one another's lives or positions in the church that are not theirs to fulfill; these relationships can cause discord, strife, sin, sexual and emotional soulties and sins. Being misaligned in relationships, and our gifts and callings can cause confusion, discord, a lack of or sense of feeling under-appreciated. Especially when people are being validated by their works and/or relationships.
- Disempowerment, belittling and degrading preaching and teaching that instills fear, insecurity, unworthiness, victimization, discouragement, confusion, rejection, and pain on top of the woundedness that a person may already have.
- Experiencing betrayal by leaders and/or members.
- Being corrected or rebuked in an abusive manner that disempowers, degrades, oppresses or damages your soul; public shaming, preaching about people over the pulpit or regarding things that were shared privately, sharing private information with other saints without the person's permission.

- Using the word to manipulate and control people for personal gain or to keep them bound to your life or ministry.
- Lack of communication skills, conflict resolution skills, relationship skills, social and interpersonal skills. People are not taught applicable skills to express their thoughts and feelings and handle challenges and resolve conflict, so they communicate and interact in the church how they did in the world. Leaders lack proper skills in these areas, so they are not able to bring correction and dialog in a way that does not degrade, belittle, and harm the sheep.
- Leaders are hurt so they hurt the sheep – wounded people hurt people.

Unintentional Church Hurt

Some church hurt is not always intentional. Sometimes leaders and saints do not know they hurt you, especially if you do not tell them. We assume that church folks should know when they hurt us, or God will tell them. However, these are misconceptions as often people may not know they hurt you unless you tell them. There is also this unwritten rule within the church that we automatically forgive one another and move on. This is a horrible rule and causes saints to stuff their feelings rather than properly resolve conflict and SHIFT forward with truly forgiving and restoring fellowship.

To a certain degree, there is a religious culture and system within the church where harsh dialog, lingo, slave master leadership styles and interactions have been cultivated, accepted, and viewed as Godly chastisement, rebuke, preaching, and teaching. Therefore, some leaders and people do not recognize that they are abusive and are hurting people. This type of leadership style has been cultivated and accepted as Godly and authoritative and is not perceived as causing church hurt. We must acknowledge that this is ungodly behavior, let people know that they hurt us with this type of approach, and give grace as people weed this type of behavior out of their character and ministry style.

The Victim Mentality

Sometimes people are not healed from past hurts. They are not able to receive constructive criticism or personal examination that promotes Godly transformation. Anytime someone speaks truth to them, they feel hurt and victimized. Their past wounds cause them to misinterpret correction, rebuke, or enlightenment regarding a challenging matter, and assume they are being abused and victimized when that is not the case. They SHIFT deeper into living through their wounds and offense. Though this church hurt is not justifiable, their past hurt is, and the need for healing is. Leaders and saints must recognize the wounded and provide the necessary programs and tools, so they can be healed and empowered to decipher experiences in a healthy manner.

Abuse Of Position
Some leaders are abusive. I will say it again, "**SOME LEADERS ARE ABUSIVE!**"
- Some abuse their position.
- Some abuse their authority.
- Some are not healed so they are abusive in their communication style, demeanor, presentation; their intimidating nonverbals allow them to cower others.
- Some leaders do not have the character, nature, and/or maturity for the position they are in, so they are abusive.
- Some leaders have lived hard lives. Therefore, their personalities come across as hard and rigid. Because abrasiveness and aggressiveness have been customary within the traditions of the church, such leaders have not allowed God to deliver them in this area.

Leadership abuse is a fact that we need to acknowledge and seek to correct. Many good leaders, especially those with public platforms and authority, tend to dissociate themselves from abusive leaders, ignore or not acknowledge the abuse of a leader, help sweep it under the rug or give the impression that addressing it is a sin against that leader and God. We need good leaders to arise and be a voice for the hurting. The more good leaders contend for the hurting and provide a safe haven for the hurting to heal, the less we will have the hurting bashing God, leaders, and the church. I decree this manual will be a heart opener for leaders and that we will SHIFT to acknowledging truth within the church even as we do to the world, and we will be healers for ALL the broken-hearted. SHIFT!

Hurt By The Leader's Tribe
We assume that because leaders have other leaders in positions, that they automatically know how those leaders are treating the people. But this may not be the truth. Many leaders are very busy and some rarely have consistent meetings with those they have in charge so that they can receive updates and provide knowledge regarding what is going on in those ministerial departments. I know this is not a good excuse and proper overseeing should be done, but many leaders are so stretched until having consistent meetings is not possible. Many leaders leave it to the person overseeing that department to come to them when they have a challenge. Often that person does not go to the

leader unless it is absolutely necessary. This is because many do not want to infringe or bother the leader, especially if that leader is continuously busy. Some believe they can handle the ministry endeavors and any situations that arise, so they do not seek the leader's guidance. Because of a lack of consistent supervision or not knowing about trials until it is too late, many leave the church wounded without informing the main leader of the hurtful experiences they have endured.

Sometimes people are so protective of the main leader or the church that they will exhibit inappropriate behaviors to protect their positions and relationships with the leader and within the church. Such people tend to be validated by who they are to the leader and or the church so their behavior towards others can cause church hurt.

Some leaders have armorbearers, leaders, bodyguards, and a bandwagon of people around them, taking their calls and meeting with people rather than them doing it themselves. Leaders appear untouchable or unapproachable in public as these people crowd around them - shielding off the people from them. This can cause church hurt as people feel the main leader is inaccessible or that they have to go through an entourage of people to get to the leader. It also lends an idolatrous mentality, as it makes people feel they are not worthy to speak to the leader, or the leader is on this grand pedestal that they are not qualified to commune with.

Jesus was always accessible to the people. Even though at times his life was in jeopardy, he never cut himself off from the people. Such structures and mentalities cause church hurt, as people are rejected and cut off from the person who claims to have their key to breakthrough, or the leader that is supposed to be the keeper of their soul - the covering of their destiny.

Validation Through Ministry
Leaders and members sometimes receive self-validation through the ministry and from the people. Those who threaten their distorted or broken identity may experience church hurt.

Respect Of Person's: CLIQUES!
Many ministries and department heads are overseen by family members and it is difficult for others to align rightfully with God and help advance the ministry vision and the kingdom of God. Many leaders' children, family members, friends or those they have marked as "anointed" are given different perks, rules,

and opportunities within the ministry than other saints. Some ministries entail cliques that run the church. People feel they must change themselves, engage in certain acts or be a certain way to be included in these cliques. This results in identity theft as people lose their originality in God and misalign with destiny in hopes of aligning with cliques they deem holy and worthy.

Cliques ostracize people and make them feel they are not saved or unworthy to be among them. Many people equate this as God's approval and may even feel rejected by God when these cliques dishonor and reject them. Though we all have people who are close friends and confidants in and outside of the church, we must do better in cultivating an efficient ministry environment where all feel loved, valued, honored, empowered, regarded, celebrated, and released in destiny. We must be conscious that the spirit of rejection is forever present and cultivate a ministry culture that snuffs out its power in our ministries, while bringing complete healing to those who are susceptible to this spirit. When people are empowered in their unique identity in God and encouraged to be who God ordained them to be, it stifles rejection. Also, when leaders are conscious of rejection and covetousness and do not become participants of this by esteeming some and not all, rejection does not stand a chance. Jesus was very careful not to favor one disciple over the other and to dismantle their competing heart when they would try to get him to choose one over the other (*See Luke 9:46-49, Luke 22:24, Matthew 18:1*). Though we see in the scriptures that some are with him more than others, Jesus empowered each disciple in their unique gifts and callings. They did not receive special treatment over anyone else that walked with him in ministry or that he ministered to.

Church Hurt Due To Mixture

Sometimes our choices of mixture can position us for church hurt and slander within the church and the world. To eliminate this type of woundedness, we have to start providing clear vision to people so they will understand the purpose and intent of our actions. Without clear vision we leave people to form their own opinions. They see us mixing and mingling in endeavors that do not appear to be God or are not of God. They do not have the vision we claim to have concerning God sending us into these arenas for a purpose. We have a lot of saints saying God told them to do certain things, but their actions are not in alignment with his word, does not make sense to the onlooker, and the fruit or harvest of their actions does not demonstrate God. Therefore, contending our actions are God ordained is not enough to dismantle the backlash that can come from engaging in something controversial, radical or mixing with the world.

Matthew 9:10-13 The Amplified Bible And as Jesus reclined at table in the house, behold, many tax collectors and [especially wicked] sinners came and sat (reclined) with Him and His disciples. And when the Pharisees saw this, they said to His disciples, Why does your Master eat with tax collectors and those [preeminently] sinful? But when Jesus heard it, He replied, those who are strong and well (healthy) have no need of a physician, but those who are weak and sick. Go and learn what this means: I desire mercy [that is, readiness to help those in trouble] and not sacrifice and sacrificial victims. For I came not to call and invite [to repentance] the righteous (those who are upright and in right standing with God), but sinners (the erring ones and all those not free from sin).

The Message Version *Later when Jesus was eating supper at Matthew's house with his close followers, a lot of disreputable characters came and joined them. When the Pharisees saw him keeping this kind of company, they had a fit, and lit into Jesus' followers. "What kind of example is this from your Teacher, acting cozy with crooks and riff-raff?". Jesus, overhearing, shot back, "Who needs a doctor: the healthy or the sick? Go figure out what this Scripture means: 'I'm after mercy, not religion.' I'm here to invite outsiders, not coddle insiders."*

In this passage of scripture, Jesus appeared to be mixing with the world. Jesus did not like the insinuations that were being made regarding his actions. However, he did not leave the people without explanation or drowning in their false opinions. He brought clarity for his actions, by revealing to them that he was there to call sinners to repentance. He was not there to mingle his gifts with the sinners, to do business with them, or to partake of what they had to offer. What we tend to see is saints being cozy and mixing for personal gain in the guise of saving souls. We tend to see saints defending the sinner and their communion with them, while diminishing and desecrating the gospel of Jesus Christ. Many saints tend to view their social interactions and endeavors as work than being the gift or calling of God. We see this a lot with marketplace ministers and those called to famed platforms. But as a saint, both are one and the same. The fruit of sinners getting saved followed Jesus. This same fruit should follow those who go into worldly arenas and marketplaces. If you claim God put you there to engage in a particular partnership or endeavor to save souls, we should see the fruit of sinners being called to repentance following your ministry. The lack of this causes confusion and division within the body of Christ as some people seek to defend you while others seek to bring you into accountability and repentance. This exposes your soul to woundedness from the saints and the world because the intent of your heart and the purpose of your actions are not clear. Be clear by sharing the purpose of your endeavors, while making sure the fruit of souls being saved and God being glorified is following your marketplace ministry.

Spiritual Seduction

Sometimes people are seduced by a leader or ministry and then after being enlightened that what they have been experiencing is not God, they may experience church hurt when striving to separate, expose, or address the seduction. Spiritual seduction is essentially idolatry. Idolatry is generally the foundation as the person:
- Has exalted a leader or ministry above God.
- Is seduced and connected to the leader or ministry more than to God.
- Has misconceived notions regarding what a leader or ministry vision has to offer, or should offer them.
- Has false realities of how they will be utilized in a ministry or leader's life.

Once the eyes of the person's understanding have been enlightened, they may experience church hurt from leaders and members. Especially if the person:
- Stops idolizing the leader and ministry.
- Speaks truth regarding the leader and/or ministry.
- Attempts to make changes or request changes be made in the actions of the leader and/or the ministry.
- Request that the leader and/or ministry follow through with what they promised.
- Decide to leave the ministry.
- Enlighten the eyes of others to the realities of the leader and/or the ministry.

Denominations & Doctrines

Though we may have different visions and purposes, we were never supposed to be separated by denominations or even have denominations. We tend to view those who are of a different denomination as not like us. We ostracize ourselves from them, and even view them as the false church. Though this was man's attempt to bring order, structure, and clear foundation to their particular ministry visions, division through denominationalism and with operating as distinct ministries was never the vision of Jesus. Though there are unique parts of Jesus that we bring to the world, our foundation is to be him, and we are to work as one body to empower and equip the saints, so they can reveal Jesus to the world and not be swayed by false ministries and teachers.

This is important because a lot of times we join a church body expecting them to have and supply everything we need to be empowered and equipped in God, yet this is an unrealistic expectation that often sets us up for church hurt. We expect our pastors and leaders to be everything we need, and though they have a measure, many only focus on what they did not receive. Honor is nullified based on what was not given. We expect a church to be everything we need and desire and when it falls short, many only focus and gripe on what it was not to us. There is no regard to what was and can be given.

We also tend to make generalizations that the entire body of Christ hurt us, when it was people within the church or certain ministries that hurt us. We then ostracize ourselves from the entire body of Christ, refusing to go to church – refusing to assemble in fellowship with God's church. In addition, as ministries within the body of Christ, we tend to have rules that are a part of our denominations and doctrines that may not necessarily be biblically based or that has a measure of biblical truth, but is used inappropriately. This can cause church hurt when people feel ostracized, disempowered and unrealistic as they endeavor to follow a rule that may not be in alignment with the Bible or is a manipulation of scripture. This has caused so much confusion within the body of Christ until people no longer want to regard the foundational truths about God and his church. If someone attempts to address inappropriate behavior, they are automatically viewed as religious –"holier than thou," "self-righteous." Our balance between having clear biblical vision and understanding for the foundation and truth regarding God's church and the mixtures of denominations and doctrines has been construed. We must address hurtful experiences and bring clarity to the true purpose and identity of God and his church, so we can dismantle the confused perspective that we can do away with foundational truths that make God be God and that make us saved disciples of his kingdom.

Fear & Suspicion
Many churches instill fear and suspicion in members regarding receiving training and equipping from other ministries. Often if you did not receive your training "in the church house," then it is null and void. I even know churches who do not honor the seminary degrees of their members, yet many of these same pastors have seminary degrees and would be appalled if you told them their degree did not mean anything. Many members are made to go through the church's programs to prove they are ready for ministry, regardless of previous training from other ministries and accredited seminary and ministry schools. Rarely is there a plan in place within ministries where the leader sits

down with that person, recognizes their training and degrees from other ministry entities, provide a program they can personally work to reveal their personal deliverance and healing needs, demonstrate what their spiritual skills and knowledge is, reveal what information needs to be cleansed that may not be God, and how to further heal the person, build upon their knowledge, and release them in ministry. Generally, all is voided because it was not done "in the house." Often what is learned "in the house" is a repeat of what was already taught and in some instances, not even being taught in that ministry. People may be made to go through years of training "within the house" to advance in ministry, rather than being built up where they are, equipped and released into what God has for them to do in the earth.

False Loyalty

Some members may still have a work to do in a certain ministry body, but have outgrown the teachings of that church. They need more than what the ministry can provide to sustain and adequately pour out and complete the assignment God has granted to their hands. Often loyalty causes them to die on the inside as they operate on fumes, while they are serving and striving to complete their ministry assignments within the ministry. Many of these people are viewed as renegades if they seek training outside of the ministry and often leaders find them intimidating. Many leaders even grow suspicious of such members. The members' heart is just to grow in the matters of God, yet the leaders feel there is some ulterior motive to the reason they are seeking training elsewhere. They may feel inferior for not being able to provide the person with what they feel they need. Many leaders take it personal instead of recognizing that people outgrowing the milk and meat of a ministry is a good thing. It demonstrates that people are benefiting from what is being taught and imparted. Creating an open dialog where people can come and express what they need, and even be given suggestions for where to be fed is essential to us all growing as ONE CHURCH - as a body of Christ. If we cultivate the mindset that we are all one church just different parts, then this intimidation, suspicion, and inferiority would not seep in and cause discord, division, and church hurt, where we view one another as the enemy when we seek growth. We should be able to be equipped and trained from reputable ministries and return to 'our church house' to further complete our assignment, while further being activated and empowered in who we are in God.

False Loyalty Through A Jezebel Soultie

There is a host of people that will leave a leader or from under a ministry that hurt them, but will be stifled in their destiny, because they are bound by a false loyalty to that leader or ministry. They feel like they are dishonoring or defying that leader if they start the ministry God has given them, or operate in their gifts and callings under another ministry. They feel as if producing fruit for God is disloyalty to the leader or ministry that hurt them. This is the spirit of Ahab at work. Ahabs protect their abuser. They feel like they cannot make a decision, or engage in an action without their abusers' permission, approval, validation, or without making sure their abuser will not be challenged by their actions. They are bound to a controlling perception or a soultie they have with the leader or church they left. They rather defy God as whether they admit it or not, the Jezebelic leader or ministry is their God. The person also may possess a physical fear and anxiety of how that leader or ministry will perceive them, thus binding them to destiny stagnation.

Much of this false loyalty is oppression, false perception and displaced obligation. Sometimes these people will still interact with these leaders and ministries even though they have left the church. They are overly merciful, as though forgiveness is a commandment, they do not use healthy boundaries, discernment, or operate in reality and truth, to keep themselves from being abused again. They secretly hope the person or ministry will change, validate them, and even welcome them back into the ministry. Many people that operate in an Ahab spirit are passive and even can be passive aggressive. They care immensely about what people think about them, especially those in authority or those they want love and approval from. They fear people thinking ill of them. They will go above and beyond to be seen in a favorable light, even though most of them are very awesome and gifted people and do not need to people please. They hide behind their overly merciful, kind, and peaceful personalities, which is more of a covering for their low self-esteem and inadequacy, to avoid confrontation and conflict. If they do confront, they have a difficult time expressing their thoughts and feelings where they adequately give themselves a voice regarding a matter. They grumble inside their heart or to those who will listen to their hurts, may be aware of the changes they need to make, but will not implement the skills and actions necessary to be liberated from the oppressions of Jezebel. The spirit of Ahab and the soulties with the spirit of Jezebel must be broken, so the person can adequately heal, and SHIFT into the things of God.

Ministry Vision
Paradigms: A church paradigm is usually pastoral led with very few people carrying the vision of the church. A kingdom paradigm is team oriented where the leaders, a team, and the people carry the vision of the ministry. The vision

itself hurts the sheep when it is a church paradigm and not a kingdom paradigm. Many claim to be operating in a kingdom paradigm, but are really operating in a church paradigm.

People can experience church hurt when they are given mixed messages regarding the vision and when they are striving to operate in a kingdom paradigm when the ministry is not conducive to this vision. They appear to be imposing or trying to push themselves into ministry endeavors and positions when really their heart is to be released in who they are in God, have their gifts and callings be utilized in the ministry, and to advance God's kingdom.

It is important to discern a ministry by their fruit, not who they claim they are, acknowledge the reality of the paradigm a church is operating in, and know if God has called you to that ministry. You will experience rejection if you are striving to operate in a paradigm that is not conducive to the ministry. If God called you there, even if you experience rejection, you will not be denied. God will give you strategies to intercede and plow where the people and ministry will receive you whether they desire to or not. You also will not view your challenges as church hurt, but understand they come with the ministry assignment God has granted to your hands.

It is very easy for leaders to slip into church paradigms when:

- They started off in ministry this way then had to restructure their foundation and vision to a kingdom paradigm.
- They become impatient and just want things done versus processing with God in the vision.
- Members become fickle, inconsistent, or relaxed with helping to carry the vision.
- They become burnt-out which causes a person to be self-focused with trying to sustain in the little strength and endurance they have.

Burnout gives an illusion that it is much easier to complete the task than to waste strength directing and delegating. Instead of stopping to refresh, the person tends to take on more than they are supposed to which results in completing duties that other vision carriers should be doing. Many team members do not recognize when their leader is burnt-out and thus do not step up to assist the leader until it is too late and the vision has already reverted to a church paradigm.

It is essential for leaders to effectively equip those helping to carry the vision with Godly character and kingdom accountability, so they can trust the process of the vision and trust those helping to carry it. It is also important for leaders to discern when respite is needed for themselves and vision carriers, so burnout will not dictate the decisions they make concerning the vision. Additionally, it is necessary for those helping to carry the vision to know the character and spirit of their leader, and be open to stepping up when the leader needs a moment to refresh and recuperate.

As old church paradigms are demolished, and new kingdom paradigms are implemented, it is essential that members and leaders are patient and process with God. It will take time to gut out the old paradigm systems and mindsets, while introducing, planting, plowing, building, and establishing the kingdom paradigm. Do not bash and gripe about the body of Christ and how horrible it is if you are not willing to connect with ministries that are seeing the need for change and are making those changes, yet you are not willing to help transform the body of Christ into the true bride he desires. It is important to note that though church paradigm was manmade, some of the religious rigidness was necessary for the seasons and generations of that time. God knew what was in that generation and what they needed to sustain in holiness and focused destiny with him. Yet because God is an evolving God, we must SHIFT with him while making sure the kingdom paradigm is always at hand. It is the kingdom paradigm that will shake the world while snatching it out of darkness into the light and purpose of God. God needs us changing and evolving with him, not frustrated and murmuring about what things should be, yet not implementing the enlightenment he has given each of us to help transform ministries and the body of Christ as a whole.

Vision Misalignment: Moses was a deliverer even before he led the Israelites out of Egypt. When he killed a man, he was seeking to deliver his people from the oppressions of slavery. Many of the disciples were fisherman even before they became fishers of men. Jesus was already the savior before he became the savior of the world. The ministry vision we are called to birth in the earth is a replica of the mantle that is upon our lives. When the vision of the church house is not the vision that is on the leader's life, it can cause confusion, mayhem, and blockage to the vision of the church sufficiently flourishing. The people will not be able to productively undergird the vision, while efficiently walking and advancing in their own personal destiny and calling. The leader must be a representation of the vision of the ministry that they are building. Both go hand in hand to seeing the will of God advanced in that leader's life, the ministry, and within the people that are a part of that ministry.

Vision Insecurities: Moses often fluctuated between being confident and insecure about his ministry position. When leaders are not confident in who and what God called them to be, it causes the people to waver and instills imbalance and inconsistency within the ministry vision. This can cause people to waver and to experience wounds from being unstable in the purpose of God. It can also cause ministry wounds due to the enemy using this instability as an open door to wreak havoc in the lives of the people and within the ministry.

Misrepresentation Of The Vision Season: This is when the vision is not ready for the sheep (people) it is drawing to the ministry. Leaders, it is important to have clarity about what your ministry vision is, what stage of your vision you are in (e.g. plant, plow, build, harvest), and draw people based on where you are in the vision stage of your ministry. Often, we gather and draw people first, then we fumble through with trying to connect them to the vision. Most people connect based on the potential. They tend to do this because we often promote our ministry based on its potential rather than the reality of where we are within the current season of our vision. This can cause church hurt because people will come expecting potential and be challenged when reality manifest something different. Many people do not have a mindset or an understanding of what it takes to plant, plow, build, or advance a ministry and are not called to or want these responsibilities. Many want the harvest and to further reap from the harvest. They want potential to be right now reality. They become challenged, restless, and even feel manipulated and bamboozled when they connect from the false pretense of potential and not reality. It is important not to make promises to people based on who you and your ministry will be and be honest about where you are, as people will either grow with you, or they will go somewhere else where they can be provided with what they feel they need right now. Either way we win because we are building the body of Christ, not our personal ministries.

Lack of Equipping & Releasing

Some saints are "hurt" that their church is not able to equip them, yet they still have an assignment in that ministry or God has not told them to leave the ministry. Often such members will attempt to birth forth what they feel is needed within that ministry, or even approach leadership to ask if they could have particular events to equip themselves and others in that area. Some leaders will think this is awesome and will give the go ahead. They may reluctantly give the go ahead, but lack the revelation to further activate the church after the event is over. Other leaders will totally shun the idea. This is where knowing the vision of your church is essential. It is also important to know the timing of God regarding whether a church is ready for that area of equipping. And understanding that often such a SHIFT must occur first in the spirit realm by praying for your leaders and church to come into the revelation of the need for this particular equipping. As often we mistake the potential of a leader and a ministry for God's will when we have not considered the vision of the ministry. We just view the potential and we demand that leader or ministry operate in the potential we see.

Visiting prophets are huge with prophesying through the potential of a leader and/or ministry, and calling it God. Potential does not mean it is God's will, that the church or leader has the current capacity to operate in the potential, and have the revelation and knowledge to operate in that potential. You are expecting them to be something that they themselves have not grasped through spiritual enlightenment from God. Moreover, many leaders and ministries, have not fulfilled the capacity of what they are already doing. Which may be the reason God has not released further revelation in the areas of equipping you feel are essential at that current time. Your job may be to birth it forth in prayer rather than harp on what the church or leader is not doing. Many do not recognize that if they see it, God may be giving them a burden to intercede and birth it forth. Complaining and murmuring tends to clog the ability to hear God for the purpose to which they have that idea. Maybe it is not for the church at all and is something God desires them to pursue outside the ministry, or to birth forth through the ministry that is within them. When we are self-focused and in our feelings, we cannot discern the bigger picture. This can result in experiencing church hurt due to having expectations that have not been examined with God and trusting that if it is of him, he will provide the means to bring it to past in your life.

Lack Of Follow Through
Church hurt can occur when leaders, department heads, and ministries make promises that they do not fulfill. They will promise to be there for people or that they will do certain things, but there is no follow through. Many ministries do this in their communities. Ministries will go knocking on doors, promising certain things to people in the community, and never follow through with what was spoken. They will start organizational programs then end them with no follow up with the community. The community is not aware until they seek assistance and realize that resource is no longer available.

Saints will need help during challenging times. Often leaders or department heads are not able to or fail to walk with people through the season of their experiences, or provide needs and resources to help lighten the load during these times. Yet, saints will be told personally or over the pulpit and now on social media, that if they need anything just let the leader and ministry know. When they reach out, there is no follow through or minimal consistency with helping them. And sometimes, there is even an impression that the person is more of a burden then having the compassion to help or journey with them. Professional Social Workers and Counselors are not adequately plugged into the church's vision where they can adequately fulfill these roles, such that leaders and department heads are not stretched or striving to fulfill positions they have little knowledge and time to lend with excellence.

Often, saints leave it to the leaders and department overseers to remember their promises and to fulfill them. Especially if it is something they are supposed to receive. Some saints do not feel they have the right to inquire or follow up on a matter. Some have even been rebuked for inquiring or given the impression that they are out of line or overstepping boundaries. Many leaders are stretched in their ministry endeavors, get busy, and forget promises they have made or particular endeavors go unfulfilled. Though this is not acceptable, it is a truth we need to acknowledge and address, so leaders can implement strategies, balanced ministry duties, schedules and timelines so they can fulfill promises. Some leaders are just negligent with follow through and need to recognize that this is a character flaw that makes them, and even God look neglectful, irresponsible, and uncaring. An atmosphere within ministries and with leaders need to be cultivated where people can share their challenges when there is a lack of follow through concerning matters. This will be beneficial in rectifying situations rather than people leaving with poor perceptions of leaders and their ministries.

Misperceptions Regarding Finances

Some saints within the church and people in the community find it challenging when they go to ministries for assistance and the church is unable to help them. Many people have been told they cannot be helped because they are not a member. Some also associate all churches with the public wealthy platform ministries they see on TV. There is a perception that churches collect tithes and offerings and pocket the money, while communities and people remain impoverished. Often people do not understand the amount of money it takes to run a ministry. Many do not realize that most community ministries are funded by the leaders as many saints do not sufficiently sow into ministries. Some ministries are barely able to pay the bills and many leaders are making personal sacrifices to keep the ministry afloat. There is also this mindset that if the church is struggling financially then the leader should be impoverished. People have expectations of leaders and churches that can be unrealistic. Leaders are bashed if they have nice materialistic things, but the ministry is struggling. The ministry was never meant to be carried by one person in any area. That is a myth that needs to be dismantled. Though the leader is the head, all who are a part of that particular church, have a responsibility to help birth and cultivate the mandate of that ministry. This truth needs to be cultivated and even activated within ministries. When people are given responsibility in carrying the vision, they will be more apt to invest in it. As long as one or two people are carrying the vision as others watch, the ministries' finances will reflect this impoverished vision.

Fraudulent Finances
Being fraudulent with ministry finances has caused church hurt. Manipulating people to give has also caused people to feel swindled and not want to give. There are people who refuse to come to church because they think it is all about gimmicks and money. We need to acknowledge that there is a measure of truth to this, and really seek God for a plan on how to empower people to give through a cheerful heart rather than feeling obligated, burdened, or seduced into giving.

LEADERS MANDATE: ARISE & HEAL CHURCH HURT!
Some leaders refuse to acknowledge church hurt and some do not believe church hurt exist. This is interesting because many leaders have experienced church hurt from other leaders and those they minister to. They view this as persecution rather than what we deem to be church hurt. They view this as a part of being saved and being an ambassador of Jesus Christ. Though church hurt will occur, rejecting peoples' pain, experiences, or even misperceived perceptions will not make the challenges regarding the church and harmful treatment go away. Rejecting or misappropriating your own painful experiences, does not make a leader more enduring or anointed. This behavior just confounds and escalates the rage, anger, resentment, and rebellion that many people have against the church. LEADERS are an essential key to bringing healing to those wounded in the church even as they heal those hurt in the world.

I decree pride, deception, denial, and not wanting to address church hurt dismantles within leaders and within the church system in the name of Jesus!

SHIFT! These experiences and more should open your eyes on how church hurt occurs within a church and the body of Christ as a whole. Church hurt is real, but we SHALL be healed. SHIFT!

CHARACTERISTICS OF CHURCH HURT

Many people are so bound in shock, awe, and trauma that they are unable to identify and express their thoughts and feelings regarding church hurt. They proclaim they are hurt but cannot put words to their experiences. Let's take time to examine some of the thoughts and feelings that accompany church hurt.

You may experience thoughts and feelings in the following ways:

Betrayed - Treachery usually by someone you know, looked up to, or by someone you were not expecting to hurt you.

Slandered - Being defamed by false, malicious, measured truth, misinterpreted, distorted, gossipy information.

Accused - Being accused of something to the point of ridicule. You are viewed as the enemy, destroyed, and forgiveness and rectifying the situation does not seem possible.

Offended – Appalled, offended - irritated, annoyed, angered, resentful, and hurt by a disagreement, misunderstanding, misinterpretation. Offense is a transgression. You feel sinned against and violated.

Ridiculed - Mocked, scorned, laughed at, taken for granted, taken for a joke or viewed as unimportant.

Angry/Enraged - Hostile, animated, fiery, warlike nature, or attitude.

Resentful - Feeling ill willed, displeased or displaying indignation at some act, remark, person, etc., that injured or insulted you.

Unforgiving - Unwilling or unable to grant a pardon or grace to those that hurt you.

Confused & Baffled - Perplexed, bewildered, unclear, confounded, frustrated regarding your experience. You may struggle and be confused concerning the reason the experience occurred and how it could have happened.

Discombobulated - May not feel like yourself. May feel like you have been knocked off your game so to speak. You may feel like you have been disarranged or that your identity and life has been thrown into disorder or chaos.

Broken - Ruptured, torn, fractured, ripped a part, ripped into pieces. You may feel like you are unable to function properly or that your life is in shambles.

Vulnerable - Exposed, open, like everyone sees your issues, sees your hurts, is looking at you, gossiping about you, is judging you. You may even feel this way about people who do not know about the situation or are not connected to the situation. One of the things we dread about being vulnerable is that it makes us feel like we are open to further attack, criticism, and temptation. A lot of times, fear of being hurt again causes us to shut out people who are genuinely concerned and can help and support us. It also causes us to become the offender as we tend to be abrasive, closed off, or strike out with hurting people who hurt us.

Stupid – Feeling foolish and ignorant for not seeing that this would happen, for putting yourself in the position for it to happen, and for not preventing it from happening. Feeling taken advantage of or like others got over on you; wondering why you trusted the people, the church, and God.

Rejected – Feeling ostracized, discarded, orphaned, dehumanized, unchristian like, like an outsider; no one trust you or want you around. That you were not good enough and did/do not fit in. You feel like God is rejecting you and people are rejecting you even though it may be an issue with just one or a few people.

Unloved and Unloveable – Feeling unliked, unappreciated, underappreciated or uncared for.

Sinful – Experiencing conviction or condemnation concerning your actions or that the incident occurred, regardless of whether you were right or wrong.

Cursed - Like trials and tribulations always follow you and will always be your portion.

Abandoned - Alone, isolated, separated, and that everyone is against you or does not understand you.

Lonely - Like you are the only one that this is happening to or that is challenged in the situation.

Insecure - Have fears, doubts, feelings of worthlessness, unworthiness; not self-confident or assured in yourself, your thoughts, feelings and/or actions.

Unworthy or Worthless - Feel unworthy of redemption, feel like even if you get justice you are still nothing and cannot overcome this situation where you can succeed in life; feel like trash, a throwaway, invaluable to God and people.

Used & Dishonored - Taken advantage of: utilized for your gifts, talents, services, time and money, but not valued for who you are as a person. Some people are not just used, they are trafficked. The person is not honored, paid, or valued for their gifts, talents, services, etc. Yet they feel as if those using them own them and can use their gifts and talents whenever they want, with no regard to their feelings, worth, personal time and responsibility, etc. This type of behavior is illegal, yet scriptures, positions, control, and manipulation are used to traffick the victim whenever they want to.

Disrespected - Slapped in the face, hit in the gut, spit on, driven over, treated like a child; lack of consideration for who you are, who God is, or for your heart and soul; experiencing rudeness and contempt.

Chastised - Feel whipped by people, God, and the devil.

Bitterness – Unpleasant, angry, hostile, sour, disagreeable, defiant, resentful thoughts and feelings. Bitterness can become roots and unpleasant waters within the soul. Bitterness means that the experience has literally infiltrated your soul and physical body, has rooted itself in your foundation, while the waters infiltrate every area of your life. When this occurs, the person tends to operate through a critical well where much of what they say, even good matters, are spoken and viewed in a negative manner (*See **Exodus 15:20-26, Hebrew 12:15, Act 8:20-23***).

Rebellious - Want to leave the people, leave God, quit the team, organization, ministry; want to act out negatively, create an uprising, stir up more strife and contention.

Coward – Feel weak, like people and the devil got over on you; like you cannot protect yourself.

Victimized – Feel duped, cheat, pimped, swindled, sacrificed. Taken advantage of; stripped of your truth, your identity.

Bullied – Feel intimidated, controlled, battered, abused, beat up.

Attacked From Every Side – Feel boxed in and emotionally or physically trapped.

Attacked Spiritually & Naturally - Attacks feel like they are coming from people and the devil. Truth is, that is exactly what is occurring, as once the natural contention begins, it opens the doors for warfare in the spirit realm by principalities, territorial spirits, and powers. They lie in wait within ministries, while seeking to divide and dismantle the church and church people. These entities love to operate through religious and inordinately loyal people who can use the word and gifts of God in controlling and erred ways. They also cause further discord through gossip and by twisting information to make victims appear as offenders and betrayers. You cannot chase gossip or twisting lies. They are atmospheric and even though these entities influence people, they operate atmospherically. You also cannot get into religious bible fights that only want to web you further into malice and fighting. These entities must be dealt with through intercession and warfare. Dealing with them in the natural realm strengthens their powers, accusations, and reproach against you. This is the reason it is important to know what to address, when to address, and how to address conflict. When you have the plan of God concerning your situation, these entities become helpless and voided in their attack against you. When you operate through your wounds and need to defend yourself, these entities bind you to a cross, while seeking to crucify and kill you.

Attacked By God - May feel as if God is punishing you, judging you, or condemning you. God may convict you if you handled the situation inappropriately, but he is not going to create situations for you to be hurt, especially by his people. Situations can occur where it appears that God designed it, but usually it is because we did not adhere to God's warnings or directions, did not consult God on a matter, or people hurt us out of their own freewill.

Vengeful – You may want justice or to retaliate; want to harm or expose someone, want to take matters into your own hands.

Justified - Feel we have a right to be unforgiving, to seek justice, to harm or expose someone.

Fearful - Fear loving again, being a part of a church or organization, fear trusting God, people, leaders; fear of making decisions; fear whether you can make good decisions or discern whether people will hurt you again.

Restless & Anxious – May feel antsy, panicky, ready for the situation to be over, ready to be healed from the situation even though God may require a process to wholeness; ready for the people that hurt you to be judged and for justice to be served on your behalf; cannot sleep at night, racing thoughts, tossing and turning, cannot sit still, need to stay busy so you will not think about the situation.

Constantly Bombarded With Thoughts & Feelings – May feel uneasy, overwhelmed, feeling pressure, tension and sickness around and in the mind, heart, and stomach area.

Suspicious - Everyone and everything becomes the enemy, even people or situations that have not hurt you.
- ❖ Thinking everyone is against you
- ❖ Untrusting of everyone even God
- ❖ Untrusting of your ability to make decisions
- ❖ Untrusting of your discernment and ability to choose who to connect to
- ❖ Untrusting of covenants and bonds
- ❖ Confused and shaken in your identity and concerning who you are
- ❖ Worried if you will ever heal and trust again
- ❖ Fearful of trusting again

Dread Church - Not wanting to go to church, refusing to go to church, dreading being at church when you do go you may have thoughts that the church is a farce.

Physically Sick - May experience physical illnesses, diseases, body aches and pains, afflictions and ailments.

Appalled - Feel or overcome with horror, utter confusion, dread, awe, fear, disbelief, and dismay; just cannot believe the experience happened.

Wounded Due to Shock, Awe & Trauma - You may feel like you are continuously bleeding in your heart and soul. The pain is agonizing, nagging, paining, dull at times, but piercing, continuous, and feels like it will never end or heal.

Demonically Oppressed - Demonic spirits, demonized people, wicked people, and people who have open doors to be used by demons, seem to be drawn to you to further depress, ridicule, and wound you. You experience other challenging situations, accusations, slander, word curses from this situation, and situations in other areas of your life.

Depression & Heaviness - Because of the weight of the experience, you battle depression, heaviness, sadness, sullenness, gloominess, helplessness, hopelessness, not wanting to go out the house, eat, work, laugh, engage in activities or events; wanting to sleep all the time or cannot sleep; may even battle thoughts of suicide or not wanting to live anymore.

Wanting To Hide Or Go Into Seclusion – May not want to be around people or will want to be on a secluded island where you do not have to deal with people or the situation; wanting to hide from God and his plan for your life.

Hopeless & Helpless - Feel as there is nothing you can do to rectify the situation; feel like you can never get over the situation and like it will always be this way.

Institutionalized - Feel confined, trapped, snared, controlled by doctrine, man, and/or the religious system. Feeling like you cannot get out or if you do, God will get you, people will judge and defame you.

Rejecting Of Godly Help - Resistant, rejecting, or lacking discernment of wise counsel and accountability due to fear, insecurities, unforgiveness, shock and trauma. Remain bound to church hurt rather than seeking help to be delivered and healed.

You May Feel:
- ❖ Unloved by God
- ❖ Unsupported by God
- ❖ Led astray or misled by God
- ❖ Angry at God
- ❖ Betrayed by God

- ❖ Abused by God
- ❖ Abandoned by God
- ❖ Unprotected by God
- ❖ As if God does not care about you
- ❖ As if God is allowing or approving of the injustice - of what happened to you
- ❖ Confused by the word and God's biblical principles
- ❖ Confused about what you thought you knew about God or regarding who God is
- ❖ Untrusting of God
- ❖ Skeptical of God's existence
- ❖ Fearful of continuing a relationship with God and/or with being saved

Exploration Questions:

1. Using the list above, journal the thoughts and feelings you have experienced regarding church hurt?
2. Explore with God the root of your thoughts and feelings. Make sure they are about this situation and not past situations. If they are about past situations, journal those experiences. Journal the similarities and patterns of your pain and hurt, how you were treated, how you handled the situations, how they handled you, what they could have been done better, what you could have done better?
3. Explore your past hurts before God. Forgive where necessary, repent for ungodly actions, release any feelings and thoughts of anger, rage, resentment, offense, etc. Spend time cleansing the fruit of the hurts and pains with the blood of Jesus and the fire of God.
4. Explore your present situation before God. Talk to him about the thoughts and feelings you journaled and your present fears, insecurities and concerns regarding your experience. Ask God to reveal whether your thoughts and feelings are real or perceived impressions trying to bound you more regarding your situation. Journal whatever God reveals. Cleanse yourself using the blood of Jesus of all misperceived thoughts and feelings.
5. You may have to spend days and even months before God implementing this healing strategy, especially if you are having a difficult time forgiving, you are still resolving the situation with those that hurt you, are still in the environment where the situation occurred, or have other unresolved hurts that feed into your challenges and concerns regarding your experience. Be willing to do the work and process with God. You are worth the process and he is worth spending time with so you can be truly healed.

DISMANTLING THE TRAUMA OF CHURCH HURT

TRAUMA IS THE #1 *reason people do not get over church hurt and remain resentful and angry at the church, leaders, and even God. They think it is because "leaders fall," "Christians are judgmental hypocrites," and "the church is a farce," but it is really because they are bound in shock, awe, and trauma.*

Trauma is due to a deeply disturbing, overwhelming, appalling, distressful experience. When these experiences occur within the church, they can be even more traumatic because there is a perception that bad things should not happen in the church. Though this is an understandable perception, we are an imperfect people being perfected by a perfect God. We have choices, free wills, our own uniqueness and ideologies. We will conflict on matters. Yet, it is important to repent and correct our wrongs when they occur within the church just as we would outside the church.

We see all through the Bible that ungodly things happened in God's temple. Sexual abuse, sexual acts, desecration of the temple, money laundering, conflicts, etc. From the Old Testament to the New Testament, challenges occurred in the church. Though God is in pursuit of a church without spot and wrinkle, he never promised us that challenges would not occur in the church. He did provide us with standards to avoid church hurt and applicable tools of how to handle it when it occurs. We must acknowledge that church hurt can cause trauma and bring healing to one another when necessary.

Trauma initially begins with an injury that causes shock and awe. This injury causes a wound within a person produced by sudden physical, emotional, or mental injury. The experience hits the person with a blow that stifles them; the impact snares the person's emotional, physiological, mental, and spiritual ability to properly respond or act. They become stuck in the pain and amazement of the experience and cannot seem to move pass it. The devil knows the person's destiny is stifled and delayed when they are stuck in trauma. Demonic spirits like to oppress a person when these experiences occur. These spirits keep people bound, traumatized, and immobilized where they cannot SHIFT in their focus and drive towards reconciliation, restoration, and healing. They keep them bound in hurt, pain, disbelief, unforgiveness, anger, resentment, shock, trauma, etc., so they cannot live a fulfilled life in God.
The traumatic wound can be lodged in a person's:

- Soul
- Heart
- Mind
- Body (Body Parts, Organs, Systems)
- Memories
- Personality
- Identity
- Senses
- Will

When the wound is not healed or when the person is stuck in the shock of what happened to them, they can SHIFT into a place of being traumatized. The situation was so traumatic that it has consumed the person and becomes their identity. Most everything about the person or about anything that reminds them of that situation is filtered through their experience and through the horror, dread, or hardship of their experience. Much of how they view the world, people, or anything that reminds them of that situation, will be negative until those wounds are healed and they are delivered from trauma.

Church hurt trauma can be the result of:

- **Sexual, Physical, Verbal Abuse** – These are horrific experiences that need to be addressed within the church and within families.

- **Molestation or Rape** - This could be physical and even spiritual molestation or rape.

- **Sexual Relationships** - Having a sexual encounter or relationship with a leader or saints that may or may not result in public exposure.

- **Inordinate Affections** - Experiences where people are getting emotional needs met or playing roles in one another's lives or within the church that God did not orchestrate.

- **Control & Manipulation** - Leaders are controlling and manipulate the word to keep people tied to them and the church.

- **Cult Like Experiences** – The ministry is a cult or operates through cult like characteristics.

- **Robbery**

- There could be a misuse of church funds by leaders.
- Sometimes saints help people or the church with promises of being paid back that are never fulfilled.
- Saints can give their tithes and offerings for years to a ministry and be hurt by the lack of growth of that ministry, as there could be prophecies and financial blessings spoken over that church that never seems to come to pass.
- Some people could serve and give to a church for years, and when they are in need the church does not or is not in a position to help them. Some people do not even want to give to other ministries because of this.

- **Identity Theft** – This is spiritual and natural theft where the person's identity is being stolen. The person is being cloned or manipulated to be something they are not, or to be like someone else instead of who God created them to be.

- **Separation & Abandonment**
  - Sometimes leaders quit, leave the ministry, yield to sin, have a time of separation for restoration, die, etc. This can cause trauma to those who have been following the leader.
  - When leaders that serve in different capacities within the church leave, especially abruptly, it can cause trauma to those who relied on them. When I transitioned out of my church, people who relied on me were not ready for me to leave. Even though it was God's will for me to go, they were accustomed to depending on me. Some of them were upset and became angry with me even though it was time for me to go. Though their actions are not justifiable and reveal some areas where they relied more on me than God, for them, it caused church hurt. They felt abandoned and unfulfilled in the areas I filled in their lives. They did not know how to handle their feelings and voids of abandonment, and thus became angry, resentful, unforgiving, and resistant of my SHIFT. Instead of celebrating my SHIFT, they saw it as ungodly and as if I betrayed them. They felt hurt by me and thus hurt me by gossiping and speaking against me leaving, and severing our relationship altogether. If they could not have me in the position they wanted me in, then they did not want anything to do with me at all. They should have been provided with a clear understanding of my transition and even assistance in dealing with their thoughts and feelings of separation and abandonment.

- o Saints decide they no longer want to be friends and abruptly end relationships without conversing about it or if they do converse about it, the separation can still be a challenge to the other person depending on the extent of the relationship.

- **Cliques and/or Social Out-casting** - Many expect to be accepted and to fit in within the church. After all the famous motto is "come as you are." Yet, we find countless cliques within the church. Favoritism and respect of persons are huge within churches. People are rejected and ostracized from certain peer groups or elite groupings with the church. Those who are ostracized in the church, may also experience this in the world. Depending on their experience, this could cause traumatic church hurt; especially if it occurs over a long period of time.

- **Betrayal** - Judas experiences occur within the church all the time. Betrayal can be traumatizing, and takes great focus, surrendering to God, and time to overcome.

- **Unexpected Appalling Offenses** - These experiences can be difficult to fathom and comprehend. Conflicts about ministry, with ministry team members, misunderstandings, personality clashes, can cause traumatic church hurt, primarily if people handle them in an ungodly manner. Harsh rebukes and corrections, public rebukes, public shaming, and whippings from the pulpit can incite traumatic wounds.

SIDEBAR REVELATION: It is important that ministries begin to have workshops and trainings to deal with these traumatic experiences. Ministries need to have ongoing workshops to discuss sexual, physical, verbal abuse, molestation, rape, and sexual relationships outside of marriage. These workshops need to examine the dysfunction and detriment of abuse and inordinacy and take time to break generational cycles and strongholds, while teaching people how to express their anger in healthy ways. Sexual abuse, rape, incestuous encounters require ongoing dialog so that people can be delivered and healed as they join ministries. Social workers and Counselors need to be utilized in the church to assist with bringing abusers to justice in cases where law enforcement needs to investigate experiences. Kids play styles and how they may overstep boundaries during childhood need to be discussed. When these experiences are not delivered and cleansed from within us and the family line, they manifest in our adult lives where many victims become offenders. Addressing this issue is essential to the wellness of our church, families, and communities. The more we address these issues and rid them from our souls and lineages, the less likely they will occur in our lives, generations, and ministries.

I DECREE A PRICKING TO THE HEART WHERE THESE TOPICS BECOME A PART OF ORGANIZATIONS AND EVENTS WITHIN MINISTRIES. SHIFT!

Back to the topic at hand! When trauma is not dealt with, people live inside the shock of it. In *2Samuel 13*, we have Tamar the daughter of David, being raped by her brother Amnon. The experience was so traumatic that the Bible says Tamar lived desolate inside her other brother Absalom's house for the rest of her life.

<u>Desolate</u> in this scripture means:
1. stun (or intransitively, grow numb)
2. devastate or (figuratively) stupefy
3. make amazed, be astonied
4. astonishment, be destitute, destroy (self), (lay, lie, make) waste, wonder
5. be deserted, be appalled, awestruck

Even though Tamar was alive, her life itself was struck dead by her traumatic experience. Living in her brother's house was representative of her living inside the destitution, shame, guilt and torment of her ordeal. It does not appear that Tamar sought deliverance and healing, so the trauma became the well to which she filtered and lived her life through. She never pursued or reached destiny. Trauma became her life as she remained housed inside the trauma of what happened to her.

Many people who experience trauma build a house with their pain and devastation and reside there.

- Most need help breaking free and releasing the shock and awe they have experienced.
- Some do not know how to trust anyone again enough to be delivered and healed.
- Some are so gripped by trauma until it has become their identity.
- Though a season of sympathy is essential to their healing process, if you cuddle and enable the person for a long period of time, they will end up living inside their trauma for years and even for a lifetime.

People need to be broken free from the grip of trauma. Trauma causes the person's life to come to a halt and they remain stuck in that experience. That experience has literally arrested and imprisoned the person's life and they need help breaking free from it. When you are stuck on trauma, it is called Post Traumatic Stress Disorder (PTSD). PTSD is a mental condition that results in a series of emotional and physical symptom and reactions in people who have witnessed or experienced traumatic situations.

Signs of Church Hurt Trauma
1. The person constantly talks about the situation with no focus or ability to heal from it or move pass it.
2. The person constantly bashes leaders and the church.
3. The person wishes or waits for other leaders and ministries to fall so they can bash them for everything another leader or church member did to them.
4. The person tends to make underhanded, condescending, critical remarks about leaders and the church that derive from their wound. There may be a measure of truth to what they speak, but it is not the sum total of all leaders and churches. They may live through this well as really it is a postured wound of bitterness. Many wounded ministers do this while teaching, preaching, prophesying, etc. Their bitterness seeps through their ministry. Their Godly words are consumed by belittling and offensive jabs at the church and saints, but is due to unresolved church hurt. Even as God wants the falsehoods, error, and disorder of the church and saints exposed, he has not and will not ever give anyone a calling to disrespect the church and church people. It is amazing to watch people "Amen" this type of preaching with no discernment to the bitterness and contamination that is infiltrating their hearts and souls. Leaders and people in general need to recognize their need for healing of church hurt, and cleanse bitterness and offense out of their lives and ministries.
5. The person constantly relives the pain over and over and lives inside of the pain. You can hear the pain and hurts as they share their experiences.
6. The person does not want to go to church anymore. They may have denounced the church, contend they are doing church at home, and it is just them and Jesus.
7. The person has backslidden due to a hurtful situation in the church.
8. The person has no hope or faith in leaders, the church, or God.
9. The person fears trusting, loving, or having faith in others due to a hurtful church experience.
10. The person may hate and/or have constant insecurities regarding themselves and others because of their experience.

11. The person is appalled and in disbelief of what happened to them and speaks of the situation with shock, awe, and horror even if it happened years ago.
12. The person may waver between disbelief and denial of what happened to them.
13. The person may be numb to their feelings or in being able to express healthy emotions for themselves and for others.
14. The person may attend other churches or interact with other saints but not from a healthy well, because they fear being hurt again. They may have challenges bonding and integrating effectively into the church, with people, and in destiny.
15. The person does not make better choices or decisions. Their trauma keeps drawing them into similar situations where they are traumatized over and over again.
16. The person has challenges trusting their judgement of others and is skeptical of everyone. They exhibit continuous anxiety, suspicion, and paranoia as they think everyone is out to get them or do them harm.
17. The person cannot forgive their offender or forgive themselves.
18. The person may battle thoughts and feelings that they did something to deserve what happened to them, God is punishing them or God hates them.
19. The person is angry, enraged, resentful, bitter, negative, harsh, prideful, moody, irritable, discontent, and most of what they speak is filtered through these attributes.
20. The person is focused and committed to retaliating against their offender.
21. The person is bound by sadness, depression and/or cycles of depression, and may experience other mental health problems.
22. The person has identity problems, inferiority issues, inadequacy challenges, low self-esteem, low self-worth, and difficulty receiving complements or encouragement. They may have challenges with empowering and celebrating others. They may battle thoughts of coveting, jealousy and comparing themselves to others.
23. The person may use drugs and alcohol to numb pain.
24. The person may be promiscuous and sexually risk taking, but is not invested in committed relationships.
25. The person wanders from church to church, but is never really healed. They live their spiritual life from a place of hopelessness and destitution.
26. The person is easily panicked and fearful. They are often looking for the worst to happen, especially as they encounter believers, or make an effort to attend church.

27. The person has constant physical health issues. This could be an indication that trauma is lodged in the body.
28. The person may have trouble sleeping and may experience nightmares related to their experiences.

Strategies For Overcoming Trauma
1. Go through the list above and journal all those that apply to you.

2. Deal with the underlying root causes of the trauma. The church hurt must be dealt with. If you cannot deal with it in prayer through the steps in the manual, seek counseling. Do not remain desolate in the house of trauma.

3. Break the power and grip of shock and awe.

4. Break every way trauma is tied to your soul, heart, and mind.

5. Break every way trauma has overtaken your life, the perception of the church, saints, and relationship with God.

6. Cast out any demonic spirits of trauma, shock, and awe, and any other spirits God reveals. Demonic spirits love to take advantage of people's pain. They do not care if the hurt is not the person's fault. They just want a place to live.

7. Use the blood of Jesus and fire of God to cleanse trauma from within you. Be specific when you pray as trauma can be lodged in a person's:
   - Soul (cleanse wounds to the soul, the inner man, to the emotions)
   - Heart (cleanse where trauma has become treasures of the heart, walls of the heart, blood flow of the heart, caused the heart to become hard)
   - Mind (cleanse wounds in parts of the brain such as the processing, the memories, one's perceptions, triggers and signals in the brain)
   - Body (cleanse wounds in body parts, organs, systems)
   - Personality (cleanse wounds that cause ungodly behavioral patterns, interactions, and characteristics)
   - Identity (cleanse wounds of negative viewpoints regarding self, God, and their destiny)
   - Senses (cleanse wounds to the ability to see, hear, taste, sense, discern, understand from a Godly perspective or through a Godly well)
   - Will (cleanse their drive and wounds that dictate choices, decision making, wishes, and desires and how survival and determination drives these choices, decisions, etc.)

THE HIGHER STANDARD OF LEADERSHIP

The discretions of leaders are a huge challenge among those who have experienced church hurt, or who are challenged with being a part of church assemblies. We have had countless leaders who will contend "*I am human like everyone else,*" when their indiscretions are exposed. As sins are hidden, many leaders want the highest regard and honor, but when they are publicly revealed, they want grace without any accountability for how their actions impact those they oversee, the ministries they are affiliated with, and the entire body of Christ.

Unlike the average believer, when a leader commits a transgression, it causes wounds in the saints, and brokenness within our assemblies and ministry visions. Because there has been so much coverup or lack of addressing transgressions, and true responsibility for transformation when transgressions occur, many people have grown to mistrust leaders, God and the church. It is essential that leaders understand they are held to a higher standard, not just by the saints, but biblically by God. God has a higher accountability for leaders. It is important that we begin to recognize this truth and hold ourselves to God's standard as leaders if we are going to heal and deter some of the wounds caused by leadership indiscretions.

Leaders are judged more strictly, even to the point of being condemned.

> ***James 3:1*** *My brethren, be not many masters, knowing that we shall receive the greater condemnation.*
>
> ***New International Bible*** *Not many of you should become teachers, my fellow believers, because you know that we who teach will be judged more strictly.*

Leaders must be positioned to truly care for the flock and must take tender care of the flock. A leader's character and integral lifestyle is a part of that care. They must pay careful attention to their own lives so what they do and their leadership style, does not harm to flock.

Acts 20:28 *Pay careful attention to yourselves and to all the flock, in which the Holy Spirit has made you overseers, to care for the church of God, which he obtained with his own blood.*

Leaders must honor the platform and position God puts them in for it is a righteous position. Engaging in ungodly acts is detestable to God. It defiles the authority, power, and dignity of the position and the sphere of rulership to which the leader is governing.

> ***Proverbs 16:12*** *It is an abomination for kings to commit wicked acts, For a throne is established on righteousness.*
>
> ***The Amplified Bible*** *It is an abomination [to God and men] for kings to commit wickedness, for a throne is established and made secure by righteousness (moral and spiritual rectitude in every area and relation).*

The life leaders live in private should be the same life they live in public so that saints can get to know the truth of who they are – flaws and good qualities. This will help saints have a realistic perception of their leader and the life of salvation and holiness they are striving to live.

Leaders should not make saints feel shameful or condemned for having them on a pedestal of honor, as saints are expected to esteem and honor leaders for the work and sacrifice they do for the body of Christ. This is biblically founded and encouraged by God. So even in knowing that leaders are not perfect, saints should honor and regard their leaders. Leaders must accept responsibility for the honor and standards that come with their position. As they live a life of truth in God, they should know that there are people looking up to them – viewing them as a role model for Godly living.

> ***1Thessalonians 5:12-13 The Amplified Bible*** *Now also we beseech you, brethren, get to know those who labor among you [recognize them for what they are, acknowledge and appreciate and respect them all] – your leaders who are over you in the Lord and those who warn and kindly reprove and exhort you. And hold them in very high and most affectionate esteem in [intelligent and sympathetic] appreciation of their work. Be at peace among yourselves.*

The next scripture is actually about financially blessing those in ministry because of their work and dedication. The Bible is saying such leaders are deserving of double honor of financial gratitude. The leader therefore, must make sure they are receiving deliverance, healing, and being accountable to continuous transformation in the likeness of God, so their standard of living is in alignment with the financial and favored honor that is bestowed upon them.

> *1Timothy 5:17 The elders who rule well are to be considered worthy of double honor, especially those who work hard at preaching and teaching.*

When leaders fall, sometimes it causes others to transgress. Many saints leave the assembly, leave God, or feel justified to sin. Leaders are held accountable for leading others astray. It is better for a leader to drown in the sea than to sway a saint to sin.

> *Matthew 18:6 But whoever causes one of these little ones who believe in me to sin, it would be better for him to have a great millstone fastened around his neck and to be drowned in the depth of the sea.*

Saints are required to obey leaders and submit to them. It is indeed challenging to submit to a leader who is not effectively walking in the word they preach. Leaders are not being asked to be perfect. However, leaders should be striving to live a life of excellence in God. When they do fall, there should be quick repentance and a focus to change. When people see that leaders are pursuing the will of God consistently, they are able to honor, submit, and follow the leader with confidence. When leaders are upholding the standards of the Lord and being a positive example before the people, they are able to lead from a posture of fulfillment rather than dread and judgment. Truthfully, many leaders who live questionable or ungodly lives, lead through anguish and torment. They enjoy the position of a leader, but dread the accountability that comes with it, and live in constant tormenting fear of being exposed. Live holy as a leader so you reap the peace and delight of holy living.

> *Hebrews 13:7 Obey them that have the rule over you, and submit yourselves: for they watch for your souls, as they that must give account, that they may do it with joy, and not with grief: for that is unprofitable for you.*
>
> ***The Amplified Bible*** *Remember your leaders and superiors in authority [for it was they] who brought to you the Word of God. Observe attentively and consider their manner of living (the outcome of their well-spent lives) and imitate their faith (their conviction that God exists and is the Creator and Ruler of all things, the Provider and Bestower of eternal salvation through Christ, and their leaning of the entire human personality on God in absolute trust and confidence in His power, wisdom, and goodness).*

Even the world has standards for their leaders and consequences incur with certain transgressions. We are not to be like the world where they seek to justify and cover up their transgressions rather than accept responsibility for how their actions impact the companies they work for, the positions they are employed in, the people they oversee, their families and loved ones. Remember David attempted to cover up his sexual transgression with a married woman named Bathsheba (*2Samuel 11-12*). David got her pregnant while her husband was at war and operated in all kinds of wicked schemes that did not work. Instead of telling the truth, he had Bathsheba's husband Uriah killed. Prophet Nathan met with David and initially David was angry by the story of transgression Prophet Nathan told him about. When Prophet Nathan revealed that the story was about him, David was repentant. Yet, God still judged David by killing the baby that he and Bathsheba conceived. God also caused David's own children to defy him, bringing contention, reproach, and death to his own kingdom and generations.

> *2Samuel 12:10-14 Now therefore the sword shall never depart from thine house; because thou hast despised me, and hast taken the wife of Uriah the Hittite to be thy wife. Thus saith the Lord, Behold, I will raise up evil against thee out of thine own house, and I will take thy wives before thine eyes, and give them unto thy neighbour, and he shall lie with thy wives in the sight of this sun. For thou didst it secretly: but I will do this thing before all Israel, and before the sun. And David said unto Nathan, I have sinned against the Lord. And Nathan said unto David, The Lord also hath put away thy sin; thou shalt not die. Howbeit, because by this deed thou hast given great occasion to the enemies of the Lord to blaspheme, the child also that is born unto thee shall surely die.*

As leaders, we must understand that even in our repentance, there may be consequences to our actions. God spared David's life and allowed him to continue reigning as king, but took his precious seed, while causing division and derision between his other children and within the governmental throne of David. Often times, all some leaders care about is their lives and destinies not being killed, and them keeping their platforms and positions. However, other consequences still unfold. Many leaders who transgress may not lose a natural child, but plenty of spiritual children, mentees, sheep, and onlookers who want to believe in God have been sacrificed. They have fallen from grace, left destiny and the works they were to do under that leader, rejected God, or gave up on God and the church because of the transgressions of leaders.

DO NOT become a leader if you do not want the responsibility that comes with it. **YOU ARE HELD TO A HIGHTER STANDARD.** There is no way around that fact. And there is no way around the truth that people are looking up to you as you are a representation of God in the earth. You cause chaos in the body of Christ, and reproach upon God and his body when you do not keep his standards. You make matters worse when you make excuses for your actions, play the human card, or demand that those under you not question or judge you when you transgress. They would not have to judge if you took responsibility and committed to do better. And even in that, God gets the last word concerning the consequences of your actions. Lets' endeavor to be the change that the saints need by being better leaders that live the word in private and in public, that accept responsibility, while committing to transformation when we fall short of God's glory. **WE CAN DO IT! SHIFT!**

SPIRITUAL CLEANSING!
MAINTAINING DELIVERANCE!

Throughout this manual, I will share methods to bring cleansing, deliverance, and healing to areas of church hurt. This chapter will discuss what those methods are and how to utilize them in your prayer time to bring effective breakthrough.

> **Matthew 10:8** *Heal the sick, cleanse the lepers, raise the dead, cast out devils: freely ye have received, freely give.*

<u>Leprosy</u> in the Greek is *leora* and means:
1. scaliness, leprosy
2. the most offensive, annoying, dangerous, cutaneous disease
3. the virus of which generally pervades the whole body, common in Egypt and the East

<u>Cleanse</u> is *katharizo* in the Greek and means:
1. make clean, cleanse
    a) from physical stains and dirt
        - utensils, food
        - a leper, to cleanse by curing
        - to remove by cleansing
    b) in a moral sense
        - to free from defilement of sin and from faults
        - to purify from wickedness
        - to free from guilt of sin, to purify
        - to consecrate by cleansing or purifying
        - to consecrate, dedicate
2. to pronounce clean in a levitical sense

Leprosy is an infectious disease that causes disfiguring sores, nerve damage, and progressive debilitation. In the bible, lepers, or those infected with leprosy, were outcasts because of fear and necessity. Leprosy has the potential to spread from person to person. If lepers were not isolated, then they were a threat to society due to contaminating others with leprosy.

Lepers are also isolated due to how others react to them. The manner in which the disease physically alters a person, the fear others had regarding how lepers looked, and fear of contracting what they had were factors in them being in isolation.

> *Leviticus 13:45-46 And the leper in whom the plague is, his clothes shall be rent, and his head bare, and he shall put a covering upon his upper lip, and shall cry, Unclean, unclean. All the days wherein the plague shall be in him he shall be defiled; he is unclean: he shall dwell alone; without the camp shall his habitation be.*

> *Numbers 5:1-3 And the LORD spake unto Moses, saying, Command the children of Israel, that they put out of the camp every leper, and everyone that hath an issue, and whosoever is defiled by the dead: Both male and female shall ye put out, without the camp shall ye put them; that they defile not their camps, in the midst whereof I dwell.*

Though the bible does not exactly speak this truth, the revelation is clear that the people viewed leprosy as God's wrath and judgment on a person's life due to sin. God may not have caused people to have leprosy, yet, the manner to which leprosy would affect our lives is the same way sin affects our lives. Lets' take some time to explore the comparison:

- Sin causes us to be unclean, impure, unhealthy.
- Our sin contaminates and influences others; it pollutes society and the world at large.
- We think people cannot see our sins, but sins can be seen in our presentation, disposition, personality, clothing, conversation, perceptions, communication, interactions, relationships, how we handle situations, and how we live our lives (Out of our heart flows the issues of life *Proverbs 4:23*).
- Sin outcasts us from God's presence and his plan for our lives.
- Sin defames God and tarnishes his reputation, especially when we are living a life of sin, but contend we serve God.

When we consider the concept of cleansing the lepers or shall we say, cleansing sins, it is important to cleanse the infection and cleanse what is causing the infection.

> *Matthew 8:1-4 When he was come down from the mountain, great multitudes followed him. And, behold, there came a leper and worshipped him, saying, Lord, if thou wilt, thou canst make me clean. And Jesus put forth his hand, and*

touched him, saying, I will; be thou clean. And immediately his leprosy was cleansed. And Jesus saith unto him, See thou tell no man; but go thy way, shew thyself to the priest, and offer the gift that Moses commanded, for a testimony unto them.

A lot of times, we want to use will power to stop sinning or to cease from hurting. When using will power we are operating through a well of self-control. You are striving to control your impulses and choices. But if you could not keep yourself from engaging in the sin, how can you stop yourself from never doing it again? We need Holy Ghost power!

> ***Ephesians 3:16*** *He would grant you, according to the riches of His glory, to be strengthened with power through His Spirit in the inner man.*

God's Holy Ghost power empowers us to grow strong so we can withstand against sins and worldliness.

> ***The Amplified Bible*** *May He grant you out of the rich treasury of His glory to be strengthened and reinforced with mighty power in the inner man by the [Holy] Spirit [Himself indwelling your innermost being and personality].*

Even if you use your own will to stop sinning or to survive a wound, you are still unclean or broken if you do not allow God's Holy Ghost power to cleanse you from sin or to heal that wound.

In *Matthew 8:1-4*, Jesus laid hands on the lepers and they were made clean. This is miraculously awesome and is a form of deliverance and healing that many of us have experienced when encountering Jesus. Even with this miraculous cleansing, the leper still had to make a lifestyle change to remain clean.

- He could not return to the leper camp as he would risk being contaminated again.
- If his leprosy was a sin issue, then he had to reframe from that sin to maintain his deliverance and healing.
- Even as the leper's community had changed, his relationships and interactions had to be changed.

The leper's identity and lifestyle had to change to maintain his healing. Such a change requires a processing to wholeness. This requires a relationship with God beyond just the initial encounter of deliverance and healing. We have to journey with him in a lifestyle change, learn his plan for us in maintaining healing, and walk that plan out in our daily lifestyle.

This brings us to this scripture:

> **Isaiah 64:6** *But we are all as an unclean thing, and all our righteousnesses are as filthy rags; and we all do fade as a leaf; and our iniquities, like the wind, have taken us away.*

<u>*Unclean* is *tame* in the Hebrew and means:</u>
1. to be unclean, become unclean, become impure, regard as unclean
2. to be or become unclean, to defile oneself, be defiled
   - sexually
   - religiously
   - ceremonially
   - by idolatry
3. to profane (God's name)

<u>*Filth* is *ed* in the Hebrew and means:</u>
1. to set a period, the menstrual flux, soiling, filthy
2. menstruation
   - a filthy rag, stained garment
   - figuratively of best deeds of guilty people

> **The Amplified Bible** *For we have all become like one who is unclean [ceremonially, like a leper], and all our righteousness (our best deeds of rightness and justice) is like filthy rags or a polluted garment; we all fade like a leaf, and our iniquities, like the wind, take us away [far from God's favor, hurrying us toward destruction].*

Even our righteousness needs cleaning in God's eyes. Just like we cleanse our physical body, we must cleanse our hearts, minds, thoughts, emotions, loins, foundation, and the inner man of things lodged in our flesh. When we cleanse our physical bodies, we are detailed in making sure we clean every part of our bodies. We even purchase the correct hygienic products to assist us with cleaning our bodies, while making sure we remain clean. And if a product does not work, we do not keep using it. We will try different products until we find out what products work best in keeping our bodies clean, vibrant, and fresh.

We need this same standard for our spiritual lives. And because our righteousness is filthy, we should be cleaning our soul, hearts, minds, and our inner man daily just like we do our physical bodies. For even when we think we are clean, to God we have things that we need to be cleansed from.

Lets' explore the Holy Spirit equipping you with healing techniques you can use to bring cleansing to your life:

- *Infilling of the Holy Spirit (Acts 1-2, Acts 13:22 And the disciples were continually filled with joy and with the Holy Spirit).* All of us receive the Holy Spirit upon us when we accept Jesus as our personal savior. When I speak of infilling, I am referencing speaking in tongues where God's voice and power speaks through you and empowers you. When God's power flows through you, his voice equips you with greater heavenly sound and power to annihilate the enemy. There are somethings the enemy will not respond to in your voice, but he will if you speak in tongues. If you do not speak in tongues, begin to study the purpose of doing so, while asking the Holy Spirit to manifest his voice through you. If you do speak in tongues, practice praying in your prayer language for at least 30 to 60 minutes a day. I encourage people to speak in tongues the entire time they are in the shower or while they are driving to work. This is the perfect time because you are generally alone, and can focus on allowing the Holy Spirit to empower you. You do not have to know what you are saying or even have a prayer focus. The more you speak in tongues, the more you will know what you are saying, and the more the Holy Spirit will guide you in knowing what to pray for, against, and how to use your prayer language to cleanse yourself of the filth of the enemy.

- *Spirit of Lord* – Empowers you with the wisdom, revelation, knowledge, counsel, understanding, and guidance needed to handle your daily affairs and journey in a destiny lifestyle with the Lord. (*Isaiah 11:2 And the spirit of the LORD shall rest upon him, the spirit of wisdom and understanding, the spirit of counsel and might, the spirit of knowledge and of the fear of the LORD*). Declare continually that you are consumed in the spirit of wisdom, revelation, understanding, etc. Refuse to accept and cleanse all confusion, ignorance, foolery, witchcraft, bewitchment, mind control, mind blinding/binding, lack of knowing, lack of guidance, etc. Assert your right to have the spirit of the Lord teach you all things (*John 14:26 But the Comforter, which is the Holy Ghost, whom the Father will send in my name, he shall teach you all things, and bring all things to your remembrance, whatsoever I have said unto you).*

- ***Blood of Jesus*** – Purges, purifies, redeems, reconciles, sanctifies, sanitizes, forgives, heals, and frees you from death (***Ephesians 1:7*** *whom we have redemption through his blood, the forgiveness of sins, according to the riches of his grace*). We hear a lot about pleading the blood, but the blood is an application. Jesus applied his blood to our sins and sicknesses, and through his perfected blood, we were redeemed and made whole. You can apply the blood of Jesus to your soul, heart, mind, thoughts, personality, character, identity, righteousness, body, and command redemption, life, and wholeness to come. You can soak yourself in the blood until you see breakthrough in these areas, or as a daily application of being cleansed and free in God.

- ***Binding, Loosing & Casting Out Devils*** – Delivers you from demons, and strongholds (***Matthew 16:19*** *And I will give unto thee the keys of the kingdom of heaven: and whatsoever thou shalt bind on earth shall be bound in heaven: and whatsoever thou shalt loose on earth shall be loosed in heaven*). Bind means "*to knit, chain, tie, and to fasten, put under subjection, to forbid, prohibit, declare to be illicit.*" Loose means to "*loosen, cast off, break (up), destroy, dissolve, (un-)loose, melt, put off, to declare unlawful, to overthrow.*" You possess the power to bind up demons and demonic kingdoms, forbid them to remain in you and others. You can bind yourself, others, your ministry, your atmosphere, land and region to God and his kingdom. You can also loose yourself from demonic powers, and forbid and overthrow their workings in your life, lives of others, your ministry, your atmosphere, land, and region.

- ***Casting Out Devils*** – Deliverance ministry is a part of our right and health as believers of Jesus Christ. It is our daily manna and authority to be free of demons and their demonic stronghold. Jesus has given us power over all the power of the enemy. Cast out means to "*eject with violence, drive (out), expel, leave, pluck (pull, take, thrust) out, put forth (out), send away.*" We can cast the devil out of our lives and be free of his demonic fruit, filth, oppression, depression and possession.

    - ***Matthew 10:8*** *Heal the sick, cleanse the lepers, raise the dead, cast out devils: freely ye have received, freely give.*

- ○ ***Luke 10:19*** *Behold, I give unto you power to tread on serpents and scorpions, and over all the power of the enemy: and nothing shall by any means hurt you.*
- ○ ***Luke 11:20*** *But if I with the finger of God cast out devils, no doubt the kingdom of God is come upon you.*

It is important to assert power and authority over the enemy because he is always trying to claim rights to us and what belongs to us. The devil is not passive and is always seeking to possess, devour, and destroy what is ours. We must be offensive and aggressive in letting him know that he cannot have our lives, families, ministries, atmosphere, land, regions, nations.

- ***Fruit of God*** – Fills, restores, produces, reproduces (***Galatians 5:22-23*** *But the fruit of the Spirit is love, joy, peace, long suffering, gentleness, goodness, faith, Meekness, temperance: against such there is no law*). Cleanse yourself of all defiled, demonic, and unhealthy fruit that does not represent the character and nature of God, while filling yourself up in all the fruit that represents his character and nature.

- ***Breaking Curses*** – Provides personal, generational, regional, cultural freedom from negative words spoken over you, sent to you, or curses implemented due to personal and generational sins (***Galatians 3:13*** *Christ hath redeemed us from the curse of the law, being made a curse for us: for it is written, cursed is everyone that hangeth on a tree*).

  - ○ Repent for personal, generational, regional and cultural strongholds.
  - ○ Loose the blood of Jesus to cleanse the curse and all filth associated with it.
  - ○ Bind and cast out any spirits operating with the curse.
  - ○ Declare your freedom through Jesus Christ (***2Corinthians 3:17*** *Now the Lord is that Spirit: and where the Spirit of the Lord is, there is liberty*).
  - ○ Fill yourself back up with the fruit of God.

- ***Word of God*** – Discerns, divides what is of God and what is not of God, cuts out, does surgery, instills God's truth, will, and plan (***Hebrews 4:12*** *For the word of God is quick, and powerful, and sharper than any two-edged* *sword, piercing even to the dividing asunder of soul and spirit, and of the joints and marrow, and is a discerner of the thoughts and intents of the heart).*

- o Use the word of God to divide what is of God in your life from what is not of him.
- o Use the word of God to extract what is not of God from your soul, heart, mind, body, and spirit.
- o Use the word of God to overthrow every lie that the enemy uses to keep you bound to demons.
- o Use the word of God to cut out any word, character trait, hurt, pain, and flaw that keeps you bound to demons.
- o Spend time studying, meditating on, and soaking yourself in the word of God. Allow God's word to go inside of you (heart, mind, soul, identity), and cleanse everything that is contrary to the word of God for your life. Study and meditate on God's word and be refilled in his truth concerning your identity, purpose, destiny, and who he is as your daddy God.

- *Fire of God* – Burns out, fuses, refines, purges, purifies, consumes, and test (***Malachi 3:2-3*** *But who may abide the day of his coming? and who shall stand when he appeareth? for he is like a refiner's fire, and like fullers' soap: And he shall sit as a refiner and purifier of silver: and he shall purify the sons of Levi, and purge them as gold and silver, that they may offer unto the Lord an offering in righteousness*). Sometimes you will cast out demons, but their deposits and attributes are still lodged in you. Use the fire of God to purge and burn out these demonic deposits. You can also purify and refine yourself with the fire of God. Demons hate the fire of God and the blood of Jesus. Fire is judgment to demons. You can use the fire of God to torment demons and send them fleeing from your life, blood line, ministry, land, atmosphere, and region. (***Revelations 20:10*** *And the devil that deceived them was cast into the lake of fire and brimstone, where the beast and the false prophet are, and shall be tormented day and night for ever and ever*).

- *Fullers' Soap* – Is a washing by trampling, treading, stamping, scrubbing. It is likened to trampling or scrubbing something hard until it is clean. (***Malachi 3:2-3*** *But who may abide the day of his coming? and who shall stand when he appeareth? for he is like a refiner's fire, and like fullers' soap: And he shall sit as a refiner and purifier of silver: and he shall purify the sons of Levi, and purge them as gold and silver, that they may offer unto the Lord an offering* *in righteousness*). When there are things in you that require deep cleansing, use the fullers' soap of God to scrub and trample them out.

- *Power of God* – Delivers, overthrows demonic powers and governments, releases the virtue and government of God, releases miracles, signs, and wonders (***Acts 1:8*** *But ye shall receive power, after that the Holy Ghost comes upon you: and ye shall be witnesses unto me both in Jerusalem, and in all Judaea, and in Samaria, and unto the uttermost part of the earth*). Use the power of God to annihilate the powers of the enemy (***Luke 10:19*** *Behold, I give unto you power to tread on serpents and scorpions, and over all the power of the enemy: and nothing shall by any means hurt you*). Study the power of God as you will find that you have the ability to recreate and create body parts, birth forth things that you need, bring excellency to your heart, mind and soul, release virtue into your life, and annihilate the power of the enemy such that it brings deliverance and healing.

- *Glory of God* – Whatever we need and desire from God is inside his glory. The Glory refreshes, fills, refills, fulfills, creates, recreates, revives, renews, makes whole, establishes the presence of God, draws us into intimacy and relationship with God, while instilling God's character, nature, truth, knowledge, revelation, and pleasures forevermore (***Psalms 16:11*** *Thou wilt shew me the path of life: in thy presence is fulness of joy; at thy right hand there are pleasures for evermore*). You should be living inside the presence of God. This is where your direction of life is revealed. As you walk in alignment with God, continual fulness of joy and pleasures of God should be evident in your life. If you live in the glory of God, you should be living a fulfilled life no matter what trials and tribulations may occur. Ask God for revelation on how to build a relationship with him where you abide in his presence. Use his presence to refresh, fulfill, and fill you. Continually cultivate your life and atmosphere in his presence so you can be a true glory carrier (***John 15:4*** *Abide in me, and I in you. As the branch cannot bear fruit of itself, except it abide in the vine; no more can ye, except ye abide in me*).

- *Rivers of Living Water* – Stirs, replenishes, breeds life, vitality, beauty, youthfulness, creativity, strength, efficiency, and releases what is inside of you to whatever you are sending it to (***John. 7:38*** *He that believeth on me, as the scripture hath said, out of his belly shall flow rivers of living water*). It is important to spend time cleansing and stirring the rivers that are inside of you, such that the wells you flow out of are pure as whatever is in you will be released to those you minister too.

- *Pluck Out* – Roots out, pulls down, destroys, and throws down (*Jeremiah 1:10 See, I have this day set thee over the nations and over the kingdoms, to root out, and to pull down, and to destroy, and to throw down, to build, and to plant*). Some spirits and demonic attributes are imbedded in your foundation and need to be uprooted.

    o You can pluck out demons.
    o You can command demons and strongholds that are lodged deep within you to come up out of you by the root. Roots can even be generational so keep that in mind, or it can be a root in you that has been there for years.
    o You may have to cut the root in pieces then pull them out. You may have to pull down something such as pulling down strongholds, imaginations, and prideful spirits that have exalted themselves above God and may have even exalted themselves as idols in your life.

You cannot be nice to demons and with wickedness. Your mission has to be to destroy them just like they want to destroy you. The devil understands he is in a fight and will throw you around like you are a piece of paper. You must enter your fight with him and be willing to toss him and trample on him as if your life depended on it – because it does. Use the power and authority of God to uproot, pull down, destroy and throw down.

- *Hammer Down* – Walls, barricades, barriers, hindrances, and blockages must be hammered down (*Jeremiah 23:29 Is not my word like as a fire? saith the LORD; and like a hammer that breaketh the rock in pieces?*) Sometimes these fortifications are made by us, sometimes the words and ideologies of others cause these walls and barriers, and sometimes they are made by the devil. Either way they need to come down. Use the hammer of God to break down walls and barriers that have been erected to hinder your breakthrough.

- *Run Through Troops* – Blast through groups of troops that keep you bound or that may be blocking your breakthrough (*Psalm 18:30 For by thee I have run through a troop; and by my God have I leaped over a wall*). If you read **Psalm 18:30-51**, you will discern that it is the power of God that enables you to do this. When you find yourself in tough life situations, ganged up on by demons or you come up against a stronghold that does not want to budge in your life, ask God to empower you to run through troops. Then as you pray and deal with these situations in your natural life, use your faith, power and authority to blast through these bondages.

- *Resist the Devil* – Stand against, oppose, withstand, set against the devil and all that concerns him (*James 4:7 Submit yourselves therefore to God. Resist the devil, and he will flee from you*). Before demons and filth will leave you, you have to fall out of agreement with it. The devil and his filth cannot stay if there is nothing in you wanting him to remain. You must break every covenant with it, divorce it, hate it, dread it being in you, and resist it from being a part of your life. Spend time breaking covenants with the devil, sin, pleasures of sin, mindsets, errors, and anything that keeps you in relationship with the enemy and his filthiness.

- *Breaking Soulties* – Soulties can be Godly or ungodly in nature. Just how generational curses are passed down, soulties are transferred from you and the other person and vice versa. Soulties can be formed through close friendships and interactions, covenants, vows, commitments, promises, physical intimacy, and etc. You can also have a soultie by having an unhealthy attachment to something or someone that has taken the place of God in your life or that has become an addiction in your life. Your soul, heart, mind, and body can be intertwined, bound, knitted, or in covenant with that person, place or thing. In addition, you exchange parts of yourself with the person you are in a soultie with. Parts of their personality, soul, heart, thoughts, mindsets, character, nature, and other deposits infuse you and begin to influence and live in you and vice versa. Also, whomever they have had relationship with and have not cleansed themselves of, is being passed on to you and vice versa.

Godly Soultie – Soulties can be Godly and healthy. They possess the fruit and nature of God and empower your life, ministry, purpose and destiny. A healthy soultie has God's character, nature, fruit, will, and plan for our lives. As we can be tied to good things, but they may not necessarily be God's design.

> *1Samuel 18:1 And it came to pass, when he had made an end of speaking unto Saul, that the soul of Jonathan was knit with the soul of David, and Jonathan loved him as his own soul.*

> *Ecclesiastes 4:9-12 The Amplified Bible* Two are better than one, because they have a good [more satisfying] reward for their labor; For if they fall, the one will lift up his fellow. But woe to him who is alone when he falls and has not another to lift him up! Again, if two lie down together, then they have warmth; but how can one be warm alone? And though a man might prevail against him who is alone, two will withstand him. A threefold cord is not quickly broken.

> *Matthew 18:19* Again I say unto you, That if two of you shall agree on earth as touching anything that they shall ask, it shall be done for them of my Father which is in heaven.

Marriage Soultie – When we get married, our lives are knitted in covenant with our spouse and we become one with them. There is no longer I, or two people. The two become one when married. You are of your spouse and your spouse is of you.

> *Genesis 2:24* Therefore shall a man leave his father and his mother, and shall cleave unto his wife: and they shall be one flesh.

> *Matthew 19:5* And said, For this cause shall a man leave father and mother, and shall cleave to his wife: and they twain shall be one flesh?

Ungodly Soultie – An ungodly soultie is any knitting of ourselves with a person, place, or thing that is not of God or that is not God's will and plan for our lives. God will not have you bound to sin, idolatry, unhealthiness, unfruitfulness, or bondage. He will not have you engage or remain in a relationship that is a transgression against his word, will and plan for your life. God will not have you tie to something that is going to deplete you rather than build you in him and in your identity, purpose and destiny.

> *Corinthians 6:16* What? know ye not that he which is joined to an harlot is one body? For two, saith he, shall be one flesh.

> *Genesis 34:1-3* And Dinah the daughter of Leah, which she bare unto Jacob went out to seethe daughters of the land. And when Shechem the son of Hamor the Hivite, prince of the country, saw her, he took her, and lay with her, and defiled her. And his soul clave unto Dinah the daughter

of Jacob, and he loved the damsel, and spake kindly unto the damsel. Verse 8 And Hamor communed with them, saying the soul of my son Shechem longeth for your daughter: I pray you give her him to wife. Sexual involvement can form such entangling tentacles of soul ties that it is extremely hard to break off the relationship.

Proverbs 5:20-24 *And why wilt thou, my son, be ravished with a strange woman, and embrace the bosom of a stranger? For the ways of man are before the eyes of the Lord, and he pondereth all his goings. His own iniquities shall take the wicked himself, and he shall be holden with the cords of his sins. He shall die without instruction; and in the greatness of his folly he shall go astray.*

Psalms 1:1 *Blessed is the man that walketh not in the counsel of the ungodly, nor standeth in the way of sinners, nor sitteth in the seat of the scornful*

2Corinthians 6:14-18 *Be ye not unequally yoked together with unbelievers: for what fellowship hath righteousness with unrighteousness? and what communion hath light with darkness? And what concord hath Christ with Belial? or what part hath he that believeth with an infidel? And what agreement hath the temple of God with idols? for ye are the temple of the living God; as God hath said, I will dwell in them, and walk in them; and I will be their God, and they shall be my people. Wherefore come out from among them, and be ye separate, saith the Lord, and touch not the unclean thing; and I will receive you, and will be a Father unto you, and ye shall be my sons and daughters, saith the Lord Almighty.*

Soultie with a Place – You can be tied to a place and it can become a high place in your life, where you do not want to leave it or cannot leave it. You can be tied to a place where God has brought you out, but the tie keeps pulling you back in. Spiritually you are free, but your soul is bound to it. Lot's wife had a soultie with Sodom and Gomorrah. God was destroying the city because of the perversion, idolatry, lewdness, and lawlessness. God only allowed so many to live and allowed them time to get out of the city before he destroyed it. As they were walking out, Lot's wife looked back and turned into a pillar of salt.

Genesis 19:23-26 *Then the Lord rained upon Sodom and upon Gomorrah brimstone and fire from the Lord out of heaven; And he*

> *overthrew those cities, and all the plain, and all the inhabitants of the cities, and that which grew upon the ground. But his wife looked back from behind him, and she became a pillar of salt.*

Even though God had graced Lot's wife with deliverance, her eyes and heart had regard for what she was leaving behind. Because her soul was still knitted to Sodom and Gomorrah, God caused her to perish with it. Being tied to something that God is freeing you from will deplete your life and even bring destruction upon you.

Agreement with God's will for the relationship along with healthiness is important in a Godly Soultie.

> **Amos 3:3** *Can two walk together, except they be agreed?*

> **The Message Bible** *Do two people walk hand in hand if they aren't going to the same place?*

When the agreement is unhealthy, it makes for an ungodly soultie. Regardless of whether you agree or not, if a soultie is formed, it has to be broken in order for you to be free of whatever was knitted and transferred through that tie. This is vital, as rape, incest, abuse, mind control, religious sects, erred beliefs, etc. are ties that form without our agreement, out of ignorance, fear, or lack of knowledge, depending on the circumstance. When they are not broken, whatever the offender deposited lives in us. Some people result in manifesting traits of their offender, while others live in the false identity of what was deposited. Also, when you get divorced, it is best to break soulties with your ex-spouse. Many people have a difficult time moving forward because their souls are still tied to their ex-spouse. The covenant of marriage must be repented for and broken in the spirit realm, and soulties must be cleansed and broken so you can be free from all that was deposited and shared while married. It is important to break and cleanse soulties. This can be done by:

- Spending time before the Lord identifying every ungodly soultie you have in your life.
- Confessing and repenting for your role in the soultie, even if it was just giving into the lies and false identity of your offender.

- Forgiving the person you had a soultie with, and forgiving yourself for engaging in the soultie.
- Breaking and removing the soultie. Be sure to call out every person's name you have a soul tie with; go through these steps, and break and remove each tie.
- Using the blood of Jesus and the fire of God, cleanse yourself of all ungodly deposits, and command any parts of your soul, heart, mind and identity to be restored back to you.
- Occasionally spend time cleansing out any unhealthiness in your Godly soultie relationships, and any deposits that may have come from misunderstanding, miscommunication, taking one another for granted, being more to one another than God was saying, or becoming lax, fleshy or imbalanced in your interactions.

BIBLICALLY RESOLVING CONFLICT

Lets' explore how to biblically resolve conflict extensively, so we can understand the importance of taking care of one another's salvation, heart, and soul.

We Are Responsible If We Cause Others To Stumble

Malachi 2:8 But as for you, you have turned aside from the way; you have caused many to stumble by the instruction; you have corrupted the covenant of Levi," says the LORD of hosts.

Psalms 140:4 Keep me, O LORD, from the hands of the wicked; Preserve me from violent men Who have purposed to trip up my feet.

Matthew 5:29-30 And if thy right eye offend thee, pluck it out, and cast it from thee: for it is profitable for thee that one of thy members should perish, and not that thy whole body should be cast into hell. And if thy right hand offend thee, cut it off, and cast it from thee: for it is profitable for thee that one of thy members should perish, and not that thy whole body should be cast into hell.

English Standard Bible If your right eye makes you stumble, tear it out and throw it from you; for it is better for you to lose one of the parts of your body, than for your whole body to be thrown into hell. If your right hand makes you stumble, cut it off and throw it from you; for it is better for you to lose one of the parts of your body, than for your whole body to go into hell.

Matthew 18:7 Woe unto the world because of offences! for it must needs be that offences come; but woe to that man by whom the offence cometh!

New English Bible Woe to the world because of its stumbling blocks! For it is inevitable that stumbling blocks come; but woe to that man through whom the stumbling block comes!

New International Bible But whoever causes one of these little ones who believe in Me to stumble, it would be better for him to have a heavy millstone hung around his neck, and to be drowned in the depth of the sea.

Mathew 13:41 The Son of Man will send forth His angels, and they will gather out of His kingdom all things that offend (all stumbling blocks), and those who commit iniquity (lawlessness).

> ***Romans 14:13** Let us not therefore judge one another anymore: but judge this rather, that no man put a stumbling block or an occasion to fall in his brother's way.*
>
> ***Romans 14:21** It is good neither to eat flesh, nor to drink wine, nor any thing whereby thy brother stumbleth, or is offended, or is made weak.*

Sometimes the word offend in the Bible are the same as the word used for stumbling blocks. One of the Greek words for offenses is *skandalon* and means:

1. scandal; a trap-stick (bent sapling),
2. i.e. snare (figuratively, cause of displeasure or sin)
3. occasion to fall (of stumbling), offence, thing that offends, stumbling block

Another Greek word for offend is *skandalizō* and means:
1. to entrap, i.e. trip up (figuratively, stumble (transitively) or entice to sin
2. apostasy or displeasure)
3. to put a stumbling block or impediment in the way, upon which another may trip and fall
   A. to entice to sin
   B. to cause a person to begin to distrust and desert one whom he ought to trust and obey
   C. to cause to fall away
   D. to be offended in one, i.e. to see in another what I disapprove of and what hinders me from acknowledging his authority
   E. to cause one to judge

We are responsible for causing others to stumble even if it was unintentional. We are responsible for:
- ✓ How we treat one another
- ✓ What we place in one another's path
- ✓ How we effect or impact one another
- ✓ What we impart into one another

Therefore, if someone is offended by something we said or did, we are responsible for how they respond and must do everything we can to make sure they do not sin or backslide, and that they are restored in their fellowship with us and God. God holds us accountable if we do not attempt to restore that person back in alignment with him.

We Should Strive For Peace, Reconciliation, & Restoration.
Pursue Peace

> **Romans 12:18** *If it be possible, as much as lieth in you, live peaceably with all men.*

When we strive to live peaceably, we are to cultivate or keep peace and commit to live in unity and harmony. Therefore, we should desire to muzzle any conflict or storm that has caused a disruption of peace and unity.

Reconciliation

> **Matthew 5:23** *Therefore if thou bring thy gift to the altar, and there rememberest that thy brother hath ought against thee; Leave there thy gift before the altar, and go thy way; first be reconciled to thy brother, and then come and offer thy gift.*

How we handle one another's soul is just as important as the offering we give to God. In fact, it is an offering within itself. It reveals our heart posture, our character, and even our motive for presenting and offering to God. If we are not truly committed to living through the heart of God, he does not even want our gift. God deems reconciliation and restoration as an offering. He desires us to resolve any ought we have with our brother or sister before we give any other gift to him.

<u>Reconcile in this passage of scripture means:</u>
1. to change thoroughly
2. to change the mind of one another
3. to renew friendship with one another
4. to conciliate, which means to overcome the distrust or hostility of, to win or gain, to become agreeable

When we truly have reconciled, transformation has occurred where even if we agree to disagree, our mindset about one another is no longer one of anger, suspiciousness, distrust, etc. We are viewing and engaging the other person from a Godly perspective regardless of our differences of opinions or challenges. If this does not occur then we have not truly reconciled. We have simply dialogued about an issue and decided to drop it to move past it, or respected the other person's right not to change.

Even if that person is not willing to resolve the matter where you view them from a Godly perspective, your posture has to change regarding the situation, so you can release that issue unto the Lord and be reconciled unto him. Until you relinquish your anger, unforgiveness, etc., you are not pleasing before the eyes of God to give him an offering. You sacrifice your righteous justification, indignation, etc., by choosing not to remain offended by your brother or sister - changing your mind from offended to forgiving - so you can restore your sacrificial offering unto the Lord.

> *Ephesians 4:31-32* *Let all bitterness, and wrath, and anger, and clamour, and evil speaking, be put away from you, with all malice: And be ye kind one to another, tenderhearted, forgiving one another, even as God for Christ's sake hath forgiven you.*

Put away means to *"cleanse from it, release it, sacrifice it."* Choose to forgive and live through the heart of God. Sigh!!!! SHIFT!

Restoration
Reconciliation positions us to walk in fellowship and friendship, but only restoration breeds fellowship and friendship. We must pursue fellowship if we want to be restored in relationship one to another, where we demonstrate walking peaceably together and keeping one another's soul free of further offense.

> *Ephesians 4:1-3* *I therefore, the prisoner of the Lord, beseech you that ye walk worthy of the vocation wherewith ye are called, with all lowliness and meekness, with longsuffering, forbearing one another in love; endeavouring to keep the unity of the Spirit in the bond of peace.*

> *New International Bible* *As a prisoner for the Lord, then, I urge you to live a life worthy of the calling you have received. Be completely humble and gentle; be patient, bearing with one another in love. Make every effort to keep the unity of the Spirit through the bond of peace.*

We do not have to be the best of friends, but we should be committed to fellowshipping and interacting to a degree where we learn one another's personalities. And where we are able to endeavor to keep unity through the grace and love we develop for one another. Customarily, in the church, we only fellowship with our cliques. Many departments conduct ministry works together, but do not spend personal fellowship where respect, love, and grace are cultivated. Many attend church for worship and the word, so minimal camaraderie is cultivated where a spirit of unity, fellowship and friendship is cultivated. Without camaraderie the spirit of offense is residing in the pews, waiting to cause division and discord within the church.

We have to want more than just reconciliation and more than just to attend church. We have to endeavor to pursue restoration when offense occurs, and cultivate an atmosphere of fellowship, so we can have a mind to reconcile when challenges manifest.

Truth About Rebuke

>***Leviticus 19:17** Thou shalt not hate thy brother in thine heart: thou shalt in any wise rebuke thy neighbour, and not suffer sin upon him.*
>
>***English Standard Bible** You shall not hate your brother in your heart, but you shall reason frankly with your neighbor, lest you incur sin because of him.*
>
>***Luke 17:3** Take heed to yourselves: If thy brother trespass against thee, rebuke him; and if he repent, forgive him.*

Rebuke does not mean yell at, cuss out, belittle, degrade, give someone a piece of your mind, tell the person about themselves in a rough disrespectful manner.

>***Ephesians 4:29** Let no corrupt communication proceed out of your mouth, but that which is good to the use of edifying, that it may minister grace unto the hearers.*
>
>***New International Bible** Do not let any unwholesome talk come out of your mouths, but only what is helpful for building others up according to their needs, that it may benefit those who listen.*
>
>***New Living Bible** Don't use foul or abusive language. Let everything you say be good and helpful, so that your words will be an encouragement to those who hear them.*

<u>Rebuke is *epitimao* in the Greek and means:</u>
1. to tax upon, censure or admonish; by implication, forbid
2. (straitly) charge, rebuke, to show honor to, to honor, to raise the price of

3. to adjudge, award, in the sense of merited penalty, to tax with fault, rate, chide
4. reprove, censure severely, to admonish or charge sharply

Though you may be truthful, straightforward, open and honest with that person, you are not nasty, cynical, berating, degrading, disempowering, or demolishing.

You are not seeking to kill the person or their life. You are seeking to deal with the particular situation and make sure they have clarity that it is not God, and that it hurt you.

Rebuking correctly is about posture. Our posture should be to empower one another. When I am made aware of a wrong that is displeasing to God and my brothers and sisters, I should be empowered with conviction to change, not disempowered through conceit, vain glory, word curses, and abrasiveness which is ill will. There is a way to speak truth without further wounding and stripping people of their dignity and identity.

> ***Philippians 2:3*** *Let nothing be done through strife or vainglory; but in lowliness of mind let each esteem other better than themselves.*

If at all possible, peace, reconciliation and restoration should be our goal.

We Should Resist Retaliation and Revenge Tactics

> ***Romans 12:17-18*** *Recompense to no man evil for evil. Provide things honest in the sight of all men. If it be possible, as much as lieth in you, live peaceably with all men.*

> ***New Living Bible*** *Never pay back evil with more evil. Do things in such a way that everyone can see you are honorable.*

This is important because when we attempt to resolve conflict, it is to defend our truth and our honor, to tell the other person off, to retaliate and assert our justice or recompense for what has happened to us. It is not to promote or establish peace, reconciliation or restoration. Our posture is revenge and retaliation, which usually results in cursing and hurting people or ourselves; rather than blessing, empowering, and resolving the situation where we are blessed and empowered. We also present ourselves as dishonorable and contentious, in effort to reprove our name, yet we bring further reproach upon it.

> ***1Peter 3:8-12 The Amplified Bible*** *Finally, all [of you] should be of one and the same mind (united in spirit), sympathizing [with one another], loving [each other] as brethren [of one household], compassionate and courteous (tenderhearted and humble). Never return evil for evil or insult for insult (scolding, tongue-lashing, berating), but on the contrary blessing [praying for their welfare, happiness, and protection, and truly pitying and loving them]. For know that to this you have been called, that you may yourselves inherit a blessing [from God – that you may obtain a blessing as heirs, bringing welfare and happiness and protection].*
>
> *For let him who wants to enjoy life and see good days [good – whether apparent or not] keep his tongue free from evil and his lips from guile (treachery, deceit). Let him turn away from wickedness and shun it, and let him do right. Let him search for peace (harmony; undisturbedness from fears, agitating passions, and moral conflicts) and seek it eagerly. [Do not merely desire peaceful relations with God, with your fellowmen, and with yourself, but pursue, go after them!]*
>
> *For the eyes of the Lord are upon the righteous (those who are upright and in right standing with God), and His ears are attentive to their prayer. But the face of the Lord is against those who practice evil [to oppose them, to frustrate, and defeat them].*

Generally, when we experience church hurt, we are focused on the situation at hand instead of the full consequences our response could have on our lives, calling, or relationship with the Lord. We lack awareness of the inherited blessings we could be aborting by handling the situation inappropriately. Moreover, there may be minimal consideration for what the other person is going through, mercy for the growth and maturity they may need in God, respect or value for who they are in God and how our actions will impact them. When we lack this posture, we risk yielding to sinful behavior and making the situation worse. This is the reason it is important to go to God and ask him to give you his heart and plan for resolving the situation.

> ***1Thessalonians 5:15*** *Make sure that nobody pays back wrong for wrong, but always strive to do what is good for each other and for everyone else.*

God The Avenger

When church hurt occurs, it opens a door in us that wants to handle the situation like we would if we were in the world. We struggle between busting through that door and striving to operate through the word and character of God.

God does not handle conflict like the world does. Also, in most cases, both parties are children of God. We, therefore, are striving to understand how to acquire justice without hurting someone that God loves as much as he loves us.

I believe this is the reason the word says,
> **Deuteronomy 32:35** *It is mine to avenge; I will repay. In due time their foot will slip; their day of disaster is near and their doom rushes upon them.*
>
> **Hebrews 10:30** *For we know him who said, "It is mine to avenge; I will repay," and again, "The Lord will judge his people."*
>
> **Proverbs 20:22** *Do not say, "I'll pay you back for this wrong!" Wait for the LORD, and he will avenge you.*
>
> **Romans 12:19** *Do not take revenge, my dear friends, but leave room for God's wrath, for it is written: "It is mine to avenge; I will repay," says the Lord.*
>
> **Psalms 94:1-2** *The LORD is a God who avenges. O God who avenges, shine forth. Rise up, Judge of the earth; pay back to the proud what they deserve.*

We can ask God to release judgment and justice on our behalf, but we should not take it into our own hands unless God gives us specific instructions regarding how to do that. Much of the time, God will release instructions that position us for justice. We must trust what he tells us to do, and trust that he knows the most beneficial way to handle the situation. Church hurt will test your faith. Do not allow wounds to cause you to waver in who God is and what he can do.

Seven Times Seventy

Sometimes you may have to make several attempts to bring peace, reconciliation, and restoration.

> **Matthew 18:15-17 English Standard Bible** *If your brother sins against you, go and tell him his fault, between you and him alone. If he listens to you, you*

> *have gained your brother. But if he does not listen, take one or two others along with you, that every charge may be established by the evidence of two or three witnesses. If he refuses to listen to them, tell it to the church. And if he refuses to listen even to the church, let him be to you as a Gentile and a tax collector.*
>
> ***Matthew 18:21-22*** *Then came Peter to him, and said, Lord, how oft shall my brother sin against me, and I forgive him? till seven times? Jesus saith unto him, I say not unto thee, Until seven times: but, Until seventy times seven.*

You may have to endure several meetings before a conflict is resolved. You may need a mature mediator that can remain optimistic in helping to resolve a matter. Keep your focus on being peaceable with a pursuit to reconcile and restore so weariness will not zap your drive for resolution. If after several attempts resolution is not possible, seek to resolve the matter before God and to heal of your challenges, so you can be renewed in your mind concerning your brother or sister, and/or a ministry despite their choice not to reconcile.

Everyone Matters

You are important, and that person is important. All of us matter to God and should matter to one another. So, our hurts no matter how dramatic, realistic, misunderstood, etc., should matter one to the other.

> ***1Corinthians 12:27 The Amplified Bible*** *Now you [collectively] are Christ's body and [individually] you are members of it, each part severally and distinct [each with his own place and function].*
>
> ***Romans 12:5*** *The Amplified Bible So we, numerous as we are, are one body in Christ (the Messiah) and individually we are parts one of another [mutually dependent on one another].*
>
> ***Ephesians 4:25-27 The Amplified Bible*** *Therefore, rejecting all falsity and being done now with it, let everyone express the truth with his neighbor, for we are all parts of one body and members one of another. When angry, do not sin; do not ever let your wrath (your exasperation, your fury or indignation) last until the sun goes down. Leave no [such] room or foothold for the devil [give no opportunity to him].*

Be Wise

Use wisdom on what challenges are important to address.

Proverbs 19:11 *The discretion of a man deferreth his anger; and it is his glory to pass over a transgression.*

English Standard Bible *Good sense makes one slow to anger, and it is his glory to overlook an offense.*

Though your thoughts and feelings matter, it is important to have compassion for one to another and to give room for people to grow and mature. If you are challenged by every offense then there could be a root of bitterness, victimization, unforgiveness, strife, anger, and/or insecurity within you. We must use wisdom concerning what we can take before God and what is necessary to address with one another. Sometimes the enemy will use offenses as distractions. Devils will also use offenses to drain us and other people. We want to use wisdom regarding what is truly a challenge worth exploring, and what can be resolved with simple forgiveness and the releasing of that offense with prayer to God. If you are really desiring to please him, he will give you a plan that is in alignment with his character, purpose, and word.

CONFLICT RESOLUTION STRATEGIES & QUESTIONS

1. It is important not to avoid conflict. Doing so hinders your opportunity to grow, the opportunity for others to grow, and hinders the opportunity to give yourself a voice concerning a challenging matter.

2. When exploring a situation, examine what the conflict was about. Make sure you have clarity regarding the original situation that occurred. Commit to resolving the original experience. When resolving this, almost anything that occurred afterwards will be much easier to resolve.

3. Remain focused on the present situation. If you are harboring past unforgivenness, grudges and resentment, be conscious of your motive for bringing them up. Your motive should always be for resolution. It should not be to punish, retaliate, or win your case. Even if you are seeking to establish a pattern, it should not be from a place of disempowering the person, but enlightening them so they can be aware of the need for change. The well to which you operate will set the pattern for whether the conflict will be resolved, stifled, or further escalated.

4. Pray before and after your meeting. Be okay to stop and pray during the meeting if you feel a blockage or if emotions become uncontrollable.

5. Remain calm, peaceable, and resolution oriented. Commit in your heart and even with one another to be respectful in sharing your thoughts and feelings. It is important to practice expressing your thoughts and feelings in an appropriate manner as a lifestyle. If you do not learn to do this, then you will not be able to effectively resolve conflict. Practice being in tune with how you feel, what you think and journal your thoughts and feelings a few times a week. The more you are aware of how you feel and what you think, the better able you are to express them to others and to express them during conflicts.

6. As you are resolving a matter, recognize when you are becoming disconcerting. Take a moment when needed to settle yourself. Give yourself a moment to SHIFT your focus back to resolving the matter rather than defending yourself.

7. Listen to one another. Listen from a place of resolution. Trust that you will be provided your chance to speak. Resist the urge to interrupt, as doing so will cause walls to erect in your heart, and SHIFT you to responding out of defense. Be conscious to listen to what the other person is saying and to identify with their thoughts and feelings. Consciously listening helps you to respect the other person's perception, respect their viewpoint, and helps you to examine your own perspective.

8. It can be beneficial to write your thoughts and feelings down and bring them to the meeting with you. This will enable you to remain focused on the current situation, and to express all the thoughts and feelings you desire to discuss. This will also help you to remain calm and resolution oriented, as some people tend to become emotional when they are not able to express their thoughts and feelings effectively. They become defensive due to feeling insecure or fearful of not being heard, valued, and validated in their perception of the experience. Notes will help trigger your memory regarding what you feel is important to discuss. It also enables you to share your perspective in a detailed and productive manner.

9. Be okay with handling challenging questions and searching yourself regarding what will be spoken. Searching yourself does not make the question true, but it does give you an opportunity to consider if there is some validity, if you are presenting yourself in a way that would cause someone to make such assumptions about you, and helps you to answer appropriately if it is not true.

10. It is important to respect differences and to be okay if each party disagrees. Each party may have to accept the others perspective without holding a grudge regarding differences. Despite having a different perspective of the situation, you are choosing to view the person as your brother or sister and not your enemy. This is important because we have free will and are free to make choices. We must be conscious of not hindering one another's free will.

11. Even as you may choose to disagree, you can agree on how to SHIFT forward. Commit to at least two goals each of you are willing to work on so that the situation will not occur in the future, or that you handle it better in the future. Make sure these goals promote the opportunity to grow in fellowship and relationship where it breeds further compassion, conviction and dissolving of your initial disagreement. Sometimes as we work

together and learn one another, so we can discern and appreciate one another's perspective more clearly.

12. As you agree and resolve a matter, commit to at least two goals to work on to SHIFT forward. These goals could be as simple as not shutting down and refusing to communicate when you become upset. Or not gossiping and bringing others into the situation before talking to one another first. Sets goals that draw you into fellowship and caring for one another's heart and soul.

13. Be willing to forgive and let go of a situation whether you disagreed or agreed during your effort to resolve conflict. Forgiveness is not about who is right or wrong. It is about being willing to release one another of the transgression, and relinquishing the need to punish and hold one another captive to a transgression. Forgiveness is a choice and a supernatural act of love and compassion. You are choosing not to punish, harbor anger, resentment and retaliation in your heart that keeps both parties stuck in that moment of transgression. Doing this tends to deplete, drain and steal your progress. It also keeps you reliving the pain which causes your life to be filtered through the hurt of that situation. Even if you make a decision that the person is not be in your life anymore, and working on goals is not possible or the will of God, choose forgiveness so you can live through God's love and wellness. If you are not able to forgive on your own, seek God in prayer until you have dealt with your hurts and he has instilled his ability to forgive within you.

14. Some conflicts where abuse, infidelities, inordinate affections and cult like activities are present, may be more difficult to explore. Especially if a person is not willing to admit to their actions, is striving to hide their actions, and if public exposure or law enforcement are involved. In such cases, your safety is important and so is the resolution. It will be important to separate yourself from the situation. You may have to go to another church to heal and continue your walk with God. This will be difficult, as any loss even where there is contention and negativity can have a grieving component. Especially if you have ties with people within that ministry. However, your wellbeing is more important and if these relationships are of God's design, they will remain or be restored. Counseling is also beneficial in helping you to navigate through your transition, and to work a process of deprogramming from the webbing of the experience, forgiving, healing,

and restoring unto God, despite not being able to process the experience with the other party, and despite the challenges you endured.

Exploration Questions For Personally Resolving A Conflict:

1. Journal what specifically happened to you? Be specific about who hurt you and what occurred? This will help you weed out the generalizations of your experience as we tend to be challenged with all churches, all Christians, and all leaders when only one or a few people hurt us.

2. Journal what actions you took to resolve the situation? (e.g., Did you go to the parties and try to explore or resolve the situation, did you just leave the church and/or ministry, does the main leader of the ministry know what happened to you, how did they impact the situation).

3. Journal how you handled the situation (e.g., Did you seek God on how to resolve the conflict, did you seek wise counsel, did you cleanse your hurts where you could be objective and resolution focused, did you handle the situation in a Godly manner, did you handle it in an ungodly manner).

4. Journal whether the way you handled the alt impacted your experience. (e.g., Did it resolve the situation, escalate the situation, open the door for dialog, close the door of dialog, not have much impact on the person's perception or actions, not have much impact on your perception or impact, helped you or the other party consider one another's perception even if you agreed to disagree, negatively or positively impact the ministry or assignment at hand?)

5. Were other parties brought into the situation? Sometimes when other parties are brought into the situation, especially in effort to validate our truth, or if they are not mature, have a resolution mindset or in the proper ministry position to help rectify the situation, it ignites gossip that incites a bandwagon of naysayers and accusers who begin to induce slander, scandal and betrayal. It is important that if you are going to confide in someone they have the maturity, wisdom, mindset and heart for restoration and reconciliation. With instances of abuse, these assistants should desire to see you safe, protected, delivered and healed. Generally, people are made privy to a conflict that only makes the situation worse. They are messy, or they are so busy seeking justification and being the rescuer for us or the other person, that they escalate the situation.

6. Would God be pleased with how you handled the situation? Would God say daughter - son - I am well pleased? Be sure to ask him as even if you took your alt to your brother or sister, and resolved the matter. If you engaged in any behaviors that was not the character, nature, or heart of God, you need to be aware of that, so you can repent, be delivered and healed from those negative characteristics. You need to learn healthy communication and conflict resolution skills, so you can handle conflicts and challenges better in the future. Sometimes we think we are justified in our negative actions because we were the ones hurt. But how you handle and behave regarding the situation is just as important as attempting to rectify it in a biblical manner (e.g., you cannot be cussing, yelling, belittling, hitting, shutting down and refusing to dialog, throwing tantrums, engaging in gossip and slander, and think your actions are honorable to God). Seek his truth so you can grow in your ability to resolve conflict and please him.

7. If you did not make attempts to rectify the situation, is it possible to still do so? Journal your answer in detail. Search God to see if he desires you to make an effort to resolve the alt, or to repent unto him and move forward. Ask him to reveal what needs to be delivered and healed in you so you can handle the situations better in the future.

8. If you did not handle the situation in a Godly manner, is it possible to return to your brother or sister and rectify the situation? Journal your answer in detail. Search God to see if he desires you to make another effort, or to repent unto him and move forward. Ask him to reveal what needs to be delivered and healed in you so you can handle the situations better in the future.

9. After your attempts or non-attempts to rectify the situation, did you seek God regarding how to proceed? This is important as sometimes we make decisions in haste or anger and we claim it is God, but have not consulted God. Or we claim to have consulted God, but our wounds or the devil was really speaking to us. Or we heard God, but fear acting on what he said, or we act on it, while being malicious and messy.

   The plan God gives you will have his fruit, character, and nature. It will be rooted in his word and standards and geared towards you having a clear understanding of his purpose and will for you.

God will be seeking to restore you in the fundamental needs, foundational needs, and in his spiritual boundaries and covenants where you are established in being nurtured, loved, feel belong, safe, encouraged, empowered from a healthy well. This will enable you to heal, and restored in your boundaries and covenants, such that you can sustain and achieve life and ministry.

10. Did you seek wise counsel, counseling, and mature accountability partners that can help you remain accountable to the plan God gave you and to processing in healing with him? Accountability partners are not your friends you do not listen to or only listen to sometimes. Accountability partners are people who can hear God for you, see and understand God's vision for your life, have a heart to see you in the will and purpose of God, have a heart to see you healed; can help encourage, pray, support, empower, and walk with you as you process to wholeness with God.

11. Remember your focus should be peace, reconciliation and restoration. This includes having peace, reconciliation, and restoration within your soul, heart, mind, identity, in your relationship with God, and the entire body of Christ. That means we eventually must be restored unto the church. We must resist forsaking the assembly when we experience church hurt. We must be restored in God's total truth for our lives where we do not forsake his assembly or his bride.

> *Hebrews 10:25 Not forsaking the assembling of ourselves together, as the manner of some is; but exhorting one another: and so much the more, as ye see the day approaching.*
>
> *New International Bible Not giving up meeting together, as some are in the habit of doing, but encouraging one another--and all the more as you see the Day approaching.*
>
> *Ephesians 5:24-27 Therefore as the church is subject unto Christ, so let the wives be to their own husbands in everything. Husbands, love your wives, even as Christ also loved the church, and gave himself for it; That he might sanctify and cleanse it with the washing of water by the word, That he might present it to himself a glorious church, not having spot, or wrinkle, or any such thing; but that it should be holy and without blemish.*

As you seek God, journal the following inquiries:

- Ask God to give you revelation concerning the purpose of the church.
- Ask him to restore your faith within the church and give you a realistic perspective of what the church has to offer you and you have to offer the church.
- Ask God to give you revelation of the calling and destiny on your life and how your purpose impacts the body of Christ.
- Ask God to guide you as you seek a church that is in line with the calling and destiny upon your life. Take your time in examining churches. Make sure it is God leading you to join, and that you are realistic about the ministry vision and your expectations concerning leadership and the vision of the church.

CANNIBAL SPIRIT OPERATING IN CHURCHES

This chapter explores a revelation God spoke to me regarding church hurt as "*cannibalism.*"

Dictionary.com defines *cannibal* as:
1. a person who eats human flesh, especially for magical or religious purposes, as among certain tribal peoples
2. any animal that eats its own kind

This is such an interesting definition, as within the body of Christ, all of us are supposed to be for the good of God and his kingdom. Yet, there are instances where some people will literally devour others - eating on their own kind - for their own personal gain.

Bandwagon Cannibalism

One of the ways cannibalism occurs in the church is when something challenging happens, everyone jumps on the bandwagon and devours the person or ministry. The integrity or track record of that person or ministry is negated by one incident. Where you once were feasting on their anointing, you are now devouring it with your words, actions of slander, and malice based on one situation. There is only one perception being told with no regard that there may be other matters to consider.

Many partake in the events, teachings, trainings, and mentoring of their favorite minister, then an incident occurs and that favorite minister is now the devil and you are eating them alive. Many probably did not even think to pray and ask God for truth or for discernment to consider the entire matter aside from what was presented. Nor do they pursue God to see the reason for the situation and how the enemy may be using it to kill the person's ministry and destiny in God. When the slanderous news hits the church airways, social media, or even mainstream news, many jump on the bandwagon in helping to devour that leader's name and legacy. Such actions are cannibalism. You have gone from spiritually feasting from the person to physically eating them. You feast on them by:

- Helping to spread gossip and slanderous information by speaking about it, sharing information online; even sharing mocking information that is intended to be a joke, but really is a subtle and treacherous way to keep the gossip fueling.

- Adding your own opinions to the gossip and slander to confound the attack on the person; now all of a sudden, "*you always knew something was not right about the person.*"

- Engaging in malice acts to further devour with no mindset of trying to restore the person. The focus is to defame and dehumanize the person, stripping them of the right to minister the gospel or to be saved; while making sure that person is no longer a part of the church body, rather than hiding them in the cleft of God, and pursuing a plan to restore them.

In cannibalism, something is being devoured until there is no trace of it. Everything about that person is being gulped down - swallowed up.

> ***1Peter 5:8*** *Be sober, be vigilant; because your adversary the devil, as a roaring lion, walketh about, seeking whom he may devour.*

Those who are supposed to empower, support, pray, protect, correct, and restore the person are now an open door that the enemy uses to consume that person and their legacy. You are helping the devil to kill everything that person did for God, where they will only be known by that moment of reproach that you helped to unleash upon them.

Sheep Devouring Cannibalism
Another form of cannibalism is when people feed on the sheep for personal gain. They feed on the sheep to devour there:

- Giftings and talents
- Anointing and mantles
- Time and services
- Finances
- Blessings and rewards

They use the person's love for God and desire to be in the will of God to devour where what is in the person becomes their embodiment, spiritual and physical wealth, and inheritance, as they take advantage of and feast upon the person's:

- Relationship with God
- Uniqueness in God
- Submission to them because of God
- Gullible-ness
- Newness in God
- Hunger for more of God
- Drive to be who God has called them to be
- Religious mindset that has them believing they have to accept certain concepts and behaviors from leaders, people or the church.

***Ezekiel 34:1-6** The Amplified Bible AND THE word of the Lord came to me, saying, Son of man, prophesy against the shepherds of Israel; prophesy and say to them, even to the [spiritual] shepherds, Thus says the Lord God: Woe to the [spiritual] shepherds of Israel who feed themselves! Should not the shepherds feed the sheep? You eat the fat, you clothe yourselves with the wool, you kill the fatlings, but you do not feed the sheep.*

The diseased and weak you have not strengthened, the sick you have not healed, the hurt and crippled you have not bandaged, those gone astray you have not brought back, the lost you have not sought to find, but with force and hardhearted harshness you have ruled them. And they were scattered because there was no shepherd, and when they were scattered they became food for all the wild beasts

***The Message Bible** God's Message came to me: "Son of man, prophesy against the shepherd-leaders of Israel. Yes, prophesy! Tell those shepherds, 'God, the Master, says: Doom to you shepherds of Israel, feeding your own mouths! Aren't shepherds supposed to feed sheep? You drink the milk, you make clothes from the wool, you roast the lambs, but you don't feed the sheep. You don't build up the weak ones, don't heal the sick, don't doctor the injured, don't go after the strays, don't look for the lost. You bully and badger them. And now they're scattered every which way because there was no shepherd — scattered and easy pickings for wolves and coyotes. Scattered — my sheep! — exposed and vulnerable across mountains and hills. My sheep scattered all over the world, and no one out looking for them!*

Instead of taking care of the sheep, the sheep are the meal. They are never delivered and healed to the degree that they no longer need the devourer. The devourer's intent is to keep that person dependent on them, so they can continue feasting off who they are in God. Or they take the rewards of the people and present them as the blessings of God, while having the people desiring to be like them, but never providing enough truth, revelation, training, equipping, platform, or empowerment for the person to SHIFT into the fullness of what they identify with in that devourer.

If the person happens to outgrow the devourer or want to leave the devourer, manipulation, guilt, shaming, and shunning occurs to make the person think they will be out of the will of God if they leave the pasture. However, this is because of personal gain and not the true will of the Lord for that person's life. The person being preyed upon feels as if they are spiritually dying and being swallowed up, but they tend to stay because of the strongholds and soulties their devourer has webbed into their lives through demonic, false and half-truth teaching and preaching, and the depleting that comes through being eaten on over and over and over again.

Cannibalism In The Pews

Cannibalism occurs in the pews where new converts or unhealed converts are not being adequately watched, protected, and mentored. Sheep become victims to dominant sheep who are still working out their salvation, or they are just blatant witches, warlocks, and wolves scouring the pews for prey. This causes extreme church hurt because people have an innate need for fellowship, belonging, and love. These innate needs are being used to swindle them for sex, money, inordinate affectations, and acts of kindness. The sin the convert is working so diligently to be delivered from, often manifest in these relationships as each person begins to play roles in one another's lives that are not God. Or as the dominant sheep begins to lead, dictate, manipulate, seduce, and even abuse (verbally, emotionally, physically), the weaker sheep.

This is how some sheep marry the wrong person, lend to homosexual relationships and interactions, are abused, raped and molested within the church. Because no one is watching or discerning, these sheep are being devoured and taken advantage of. The victimized sheep feels someone should have heard from God and rescued them. They feel helpless and hopeless. Due to soulties and webbing of the bible and spiritual acts used to consume them where they believe there is no them without the devourer, they can remain in these cannibalistic relationship for years.

Most of these victimized sheep leave the church without telling what happened to them. They scatter in hopes of trying to separate themselves from the pain they endured. When they do surface to speak of it, many are largely angry at leaders, the church, and God. They are enraged and are in pursuit of revenge.

They feel someone should have discerned, but more importantly, someone should have protected them.

As leaders and saints, we cannot be so focused on our own walk or working the vision to advance ourselves and the ministry that we are:

- Not protecting the sheep
- Not recognizing when we are eating the sheep
- Not discerning and correcting those who are eating the sheep
- Not warning sheep that they are being eaten when leaders or other sheep are not trying to change

Matthew 17:15-20 Beware of false prophets, which come to you in sheep's clothing, but inwardly they are ravening wolves. Ye shall know them by their fruits. Do men gather grapes of thorns, or figs of thistles? Even so every good tree bringeth forth good fruit; but a corrupt tree bringeth forth evil fruit. A good tree cannot bring forth evil fruit, neither can a corrupt tree bring forth good fruit. Every tree that bringeth not forth good fruit is hewn down, and cast into the fire. Wherefore by their fruits ye shall know them.

A false prophet is a pretender or religious imposter that tells you what they think you want to hear so they can devour you. They are ravening wolves seeking to rob, extort, prey, seize, plunder, and voraciously engulf the sheep. They are not just in the pulpit, they are in the pews, bathroom, parking lots, and on social media. It is amazing how we leave sheep unprotected, we watch people being eaten, or we know we are being eaten, but we will still partake, give and serve that person or ministry. We are so focused in our idolization of a leader or ministry, that we sacrifice sheep and the existence of our destiny and calling to cannibalism.

Social Media Cannibalism

Social media is the capitalist of idolatrous cannibalism within the church body at this moment. Most churches have no protocols in place for how saints should conduct themselves on social media, and if they put some in place, many people would rebel because they deem it *"my page and my life."* Many are devouring every word others post without any personal study or discernment as for whether the word is biblically correct or from God. As they devour the word of imposters, erred or immature ministers, they themselves are being sacrificed through the fire.

Many are so busy following their favorite preacher until they have lost their own identity. Many even contend that this pursuit is their destiny, but there is minimal to no growth in what they claim is being imparted into them. Their favorite preacher keeps getting richer and more popular, while they continue to cycle in their personal lives. Many of them brag and repeat their favorite preacher's revelation, while having no true depth, study, insight, or revealing of the word for themselves or manifested in their lives. The fruit they brag about is their ability to attend their favorite preacher's conferences, trainings, webinars, online schools, etc., while the cultivation of their true identity is not adequately formed. This is because there is no true relationship and mentoring with many of the preachers and teachers people are following. And many are not submitted under an adequate leader or mentor who can make them accountable to the teachings and impartations they are receiving, or help them decipher if this information is from God and for their lives.

True shepherding is hands on. A sheep cannot be shepherded through an atmospheric relationship. Even God is tangible despite being a spirit. It is an atmospheric relationship when you are just receiving information but no personal time, attention and equipping from the person you are receiving the impartation from. It can border on fantasy as people can make it whatever they want it to be since it is suspended within spiritual realms rather than reality. The seed ends up being stolen if it is not adequately nurtured, cultivated, and protected. Get under a covering that can help decipher, develop, empower, and release you in what you are receiving from social media ministers. Otherwise, you are just operating in idolatry and being passed through the fire.
Churches **NEED TO SHIFT** into this century and put some protocols in place to help govern the sheep on social media such that their souls are protected.

> *Matthew 13:18-23 Hear ye therefore the parable of the sower. When any one heareth the word of the kingdom, and understandeth it not, then cometh the wicked one, and catcheth away that which was sown in his heart. This is he which received seed by the way side. But he that received the seed into stony places, the same is he that heareth the word, and anon with joy receiveth it; Yet hath he not root in himself, but dureth for a while: for when tribulation or persecution ariseth because of the word, by and by he is offended. He also that received seed among the thorns is he that heareth the word; and the care of this world, and the deceitfulness of riches, choke the word, and he becometh unfruitful. But he that received seed into the good ground is he that heareth the word, and understandeth it; which also beareth fruit, and bringeth forth, some an hundredfold, some sixty, some thirty.*

Strategies For Protecting Yourself From Internet Cannibalism

1. Stop just liking and sharing posts and live teachings; study what is being released so you can receive further impartation or insight to cleanse yourself of error if it ends up not being of God.
2. Be clear regarding God's will and vision for your life so you will not be tossed to and fro by every word and doctrine.
3. Resist yielding to flattery where you accept every word because of who the person is, it tickles your ears, keeps you bound to your favorite sin or character flaw, or because it is positive or sounds good. Everything good is not God or his timing. Be discerning to avoid being misaligned or tainted by a word that is not God's vision for your life.
4. Be submitted to a tangible church, leader, and/or mentor who can hold you accountable to Godly internet etiquette, to the teachings and events you partake of, and to seeing Godly healthy growth in your CHARACTER, life, giftings, and ministry. Character growth is essential as some people are growing in gifts and callings but are poor in character.
5. Submit to the protocols of your church concerning internet etiquette. If they do not have a protocol, implement some regulations for yourself and commit to them.
6. Take fast days from the internet and from your favorite preacher, and commit to hearing God and growing in God through your own personal well.
7. Commit to daily communing with God and hearing a word from him before you engage social media such that you rely on him first, and everything else is an additional blessing to what you receive from him.
8. Commit to making your page a ministry page that glorifies God, so that you are not sharing what is popular, but are sharing what you are sensing those that follow you need in that moment.
9. Every couple of weeks, spend time cleansing yourself of negativity, depression, fear, dread, terror, anxiety, criticalness, a lack of love and compassion, lukewarmness, fantasy, false identity, idolatry, need for fame and attention, covetousness, and demonic spirits that run rampant on social media.

IDOLATROUS CANNIBALISM!
THE SACRIFICE OF PREACHERS
KIDS & CHURCH KIDS

Some people willingly submit to cannibalism due to idolizing a person or ministry.

> ***Leviticus 18:21*** *And thou shalt not let any of thy seed pass through the fire to Molech, neither shalt thou profane the name of thy God: I am the LORD.*
>
> ***2Kings 21:6*** *And he made his son pass through the fire, and observed times, and used enchantments, and dealt with familiar spirits and wizards: he wrought much wickedness in the sight of the LORD, to provoke him to anger.*

"*Passing through the fire*" is a form of sacrifice through the consumption of fire. The person willingly sacrifices their lives, children, families, mantles, callings, regions and sphere of influences to be connected to a person or ministry. All of who they are is devoured by the witchcraft fire of that ministry. It burns and illuminates like it is God, but it is really idolatry.

As people are sacrificed, they succumb to church hurt. They realize they were not engaging in God's true church, but witchcraft, cultism, and idolatry.

Idolatrous cannibalism is how preacher kids and church kids resort to rebelling, hating God, hating the church; and when they grow up they get as far away from the church and God as possible.

- ✓ Their needs, desires and childhood have been consumed by the responsibilities of the church.

- ✓ Their time with their parents has been devoured by the responsibilities of the church.

- ✓ The guidance and support they need has been eaten up by the responsibilities and duties of the church.

- ✓ They are demanded to love God rather than taught how to have a personal relationship with God and his church.

- ✓ They are demanded to love and serve the church just because they are preachers' kids or saints' kids, and their parents must be at church. There is no cultivating of a love for God, his word or ministry, just demands and sacrifices.

- ✓ They have an overwhelming false reality of who God is as a father, because of the lack of presence from their own father and even their mother. Sometimes their mother is doing just as much sacrificing as they are, so she is more focused on soothing her own wounds, than recognizing and healing the wounds of her children.

- ✓ They are witnesses of and carry some of the warfare that their parents endure, even though they are kids and may not be ready for that level of warfare and ministry. They are carrying the warfare and helping with the ministry, but are not being personally cultivated in who they are in the Lord where they could be fortified and protected to some degree against the warfare. Essentially, they are thrown into battles that are not even theirs, and then they are devoured by the fiery darts and bombs of those battles.

- ✓ They must deal with hardship and stressful situations that come with how their parents may have to deal with unruly church members. They may experience their parents being treated badly and hear them being talked about. Since they are kids, and no one is explaining these challenges to them or helping them to navigate through them, they internalize them and begin to hate the church and its people.

- ✓ They lack a true identity, because they are required to present themselves a certain way in order to portray a "Godly" lifestyle that they may not have revelation about. They may have to present a portrait of family togetherness that is not the reality of their home life - their real life. They tend to live out and act out from a false persona because the true them has NEVER been cultivated.

- ✓ They are cultivated in their gifts and talents, and demanded to use them for the church without any revelation of how their gifts and mantles impact God and the world. How they are used within the ministry is more through works than their calling, or an understanding of their destiny. They usually do not learn this until adulthood when they have sacrificed their own gifts and mantles to the world in an effort to find themselves and find a realness with God. They are usually cultivated with a mindset to take over the ministry one day, but many do not want it because of what they have endured.

- ✓ They have an unhealthy perspective of relationship and many view relationships as works and sacrifice rather than time, pleasure, support, cultivation, and empowerment.

- ✓ They have resentment towards the church and the people in it because nothing belongs to them. They fear enjoying things because someone in the church may want it or they may have to give it to them. I have known preachers' kids who have said they get gifts and hate opening them because it is just going end up at the church or at some saints' house. It makes them feel devalued and as if the saints are more important than they are. Due to the constant sacrificing, they live this as their truth. It is the truth no matter how much their parents tell them otherwise, or try to make up for this by blessing them or spending time with them every now and again.

- ✓ They have a need and desire to be accepted but do not know how to effectively communicate that without manipulating and devouring others because that is what they have been taught through their interactions with their parents, saints, and the church.

- ✓ They believe the church is fake and God is a facade. They assume that because their parents and church is like this, all leaders and churches are like this. They cultivate and formulate their own doctrine from their hurt and submit to its' teachings, while developing their life from their new found painstaking doctrine.

Many preachers' kids and church kids are told that this is the cost of living for Christ, but really this is the neglect of sacrificing the child in the fire of misperceived and unrealistic works, religious sacrifices, and unhealthy drives for success that eat up the family with the lie that it is for God's kingdom.

The children suffer in silence as cannibalism strips them of their voice and right to have an opinion - to feel, think, and express themselves. All of that is sacrificed through the fire. They are bound in trauma and rebellion that keeps them stuck in a place of memory recall - recalling the hardships of church life as a preacher/church kid. Whether we realize it or not, this is abusive witchcraft -

cannibalism of our own seed, children, marriages, and families. It is also cannibalism of the inheritance and wealth of families serving God all down through the generations.

> ***Psalms 145:4*** *One generation shall commend your works to another, and shall declare your mighty acts.*
>
> ***Psalms 71:18*** *So even to old age and gray hairs, O God, do not forsake me, until I proclaim your might to another generation, your power to all those to come.*
>
> ***Luke 1:50*** *And his mercy is for those who fear him from generation to generation.*

LEADERSHIP & PARENTAL STRATEGIES FOR HEALING PREACHER & CHURCH KIDS & FAMILIES

This strategy is to help leaders and parents bring healing and restoration to broken relationships with their children because of cannibalized church hurt.

1. Explore with God what ways you have sacrificed your marriage, family, and children through the fire. Repent to God for what he reveals to you.

2. Break the strongholds of cannibalism off you, your children and family line. Break generational curses of witchcraft, idolatry and break the powers of religion and tradition off your family line.

3. Take your time with God and journal as he reveals every way you and your family engaged in these idolatrous acts. Be specific regarding what they are. Denounce them and break every webbing they have around you and your family. Be open to revisiting this with God multiple times until you have a clear unraveling of the religious system of cannibalism and its snaring.

4. If you are married, talk to your mate first regarding the revelation of cannibalism and what God shared with you. You all can complete the first three steps together, and even spend time repenting to one another and to God for wounds within your marriage. If they are not willing to do this, continue forward. God will honor your willingness to accept the truth and your pursuit for you and your family to be transformed.

5. Cleanse all shame, guilt, condemnation, confusion, shock and trauma you may be experiencing from receiving the cannibalism revelation and examining yourself before God. Cleanse all bitterness, anger, resentment, rebellion, etc., you have concerning yourself, your spouse, children, saints, the ministry, and God. Do not allow these negative attributes to overtake you. God is not about condemning you. He is focused on reconciling and restoring you and your family. Keep that focus, while casting all the devil's condemnation back upon his own head.

6. Cleanse all unforgiveness you have concerning yourself, your spouse, children, saints, the ministry, and God.

7. Ask God to reveal to you when it is time to have a sit down with your children. Make sure you have dealt with your own hurts and feelings and even forgiven them for rebelling against the system of your home and church. Make sure you are certain you are ready. Your children may have pent up rage, pain, trauma, and hate that you are not cognizant of. If you are not ready to allow them to express themselves and to HEAR THEIR TRUTH where you will not be trying to put the rod to them, or justify your actions, THEN WAIT until you have had ample time to really accept the fullness of all that has occurred with you and your family, and you are ready to deal with it in a humble - resolution focused - manner. Remember you are not the pastor, minister or the religious parent in this moment. You are a person trying to reconcile with another person that is your child. You are also striving to annihilate cannibalism. This requires accepting and remaining in the truth that though your heart for ministry may have been pure, your child was still negatively impacted by some choices you made.

8. If you have more than one child, have a sit down with each of them. After you have reconciled with them individually, bring them together so they can reconcile with one another, and you all can reconcile as a family. Then set some goals to work on restoring the relationships personally and as a family.

9. As you are having these sit downs with your children, no matter how old they are, apologize to them for the things God revealed to you that hurt them and hurt the family. Be specific and allow them to share their heart concerning what you shared.

10. Allow your children to share freely and present an open environment where you desire and welcome truth. Let them know you are not there to be a parent in the sense of chastisement, but this is a meeting focused on reconciliation and restoration. Let them know that their truth is necessary for that to occur. Encourage them to share anything that you may have overlooked that hurt them. Do not be quick to interject or correct them. Hear what they are saying through their eyes and the compassion of God. Remember even their false perceptions have become a part of their identity, therefore, do not negate these thoughts and feelings and cast them off as untrue.

11. Repent to them for things they may reveal that you were not aware you did or aware happened to them. Share with them ways you should have been there for them. Do not make flighty promises in this moment. Just listen,

repent, acknowledge what you could or should have done, and love on them.

12. Let them know that they can come to you as they remember things and need to talk, so that you can repent, love on them, and heal.

13. If they do not apologize in this moment, let it go. In time they will. They need to see that your changes are genuine. This is not about them admitting their rebellion as you probably have already corrected that plenty of times.

14. Do not criticize any ungodly lifestyle your child is currently in. Allow the healing process to take its course and trust God to work with them. You work on engaging them from a healthy place and demonstrating balance and wellness in God, and allow them to be drawn to you regarding the revelations and insights they need concerning being restored unto God.

15. End the meeting by setting two goals you all promise to work on to restore the relationship. Revisit these goals in a month. As you are consistent with previous goals, add more goals until sufficient healing and restoration is evident. Keep open communication so you can revisit challenges that may arise in your present interactions. Sometimes old wounds resurface with children so be mindful of this. Seek God regarding how to bring complete healing if your children are having challenges forgiving and SHIFTING forward.

16. In your private time, pray for your children and further break the webbing of rebellion, trauma and cannibalism that is causing them to engage in the generational cycle of cannibalism by sacrificing themselves to the world, or things that are not in alignment with their destiny.

17. Ask God to show you who your children are spiritually. Journal God's destiny plan for their giftings, mantles, lives, for the inheritance they are to have through the ministry you have or what you have imparted into the kingdom. From time to time, declare out the plan on their behalf. As they begin to demonstrate that they are being restored to God, share it with them and ask them to take it before the Lord in prayer so he can speak to them for themselves.

18. Ask God your role in your child's destiny plan and fulfill whatever he shares. Be conscious of what is God and anything you may try to implement

out of guilt, shame of past actions, or out of religious works. Implementing

things through guilt, shame, and works will cause contention. You will be trying to make the child be something God has not said, which opens the door to cannibalism. Allow God to guide you. Trust him for full restoration as he heals and renews the destiny plan of your children, family, and lineage.

19. This strategy may take some time to reap restoration and fruit. It is also possible that your child may even get worse and more rebellious before they fold and return to the Lord. The prodigal son lost all he had before he returned to his father. Study that parable in *Luke 15:11-32*. It will encourage you to keep praying and trusting God for restoration.

20. Depending on how long the cannibalism occurred, it may take some time to revive and restore trust, and to redevelop and cultivate a relationship, where healing is evident in your interactions towards one another. Be patient and allow your family to work the healing process with God.

STRATEGIES FOR HEALING PREACHERS' KIDS & CHURCH KIDS

This strategy is to help preachers' kids and church kids be healed due to cannibalism church hurt.

1. It is essential to have a desire to forgive and to be healed. This is very important because part of the hurt and cycle tends to be going back and forth with trying to let go, wanting to forget it ever happened, and seeking to kill your past by getting as far away from it as possible; yet, battling the constant tugging of being called of God and the inherited blessings that are your portion. You may have the challenging testimony of many people trying to make you forgive and be healed. Or you have tried over and over, to SHIFT into wellness and realign with God. But in your pursuit, it may have been difficult to really forgive and heal, especially if the underlying issues have not been dealt with, therefore, your efforts have been short lived. You cannot adequately serve God, walk in destiny and be bound by church and family trauma at the same time. There will always be a measure of God you will not journey in until complete healing occurs.

2. Once you decide you want to forgive and heal, commit to it. Do not allow your pain to dictate your ability to SHIFT into a process of deliverance and healing. Stay consistent with pressing into healing and acquire mature accountability partners that can keep you focused and committed to your healing process. You cannot live a productive life and be bound by church hurt, so whether in or out of the church, pursue healing.

3. Explore with God what you are hurt about regarding your family, church people, ministry, and the body of Christ. Be clear in journaling your thoughts and feelings in each area.

4. Spend time allowing God to separate truth from false or misperceived perceptions in each area. You may experience some shock, trauma, and a plethora of emotions as you recognize truth from falsehood because these perceptions are weeded into your identity and has been the truth of you.

5. Break the powers of shock, awe and trauma. Gut out anyway it is imbedded in your soul, heart, emotions, mind, perceptions, body, personality, and behaviors.

6. Break the powers of the false perceptions and anyway they have become the truth of you. Fall out of agreement with these truths and break their ability to govern your life, destiny, and relationships with your family, church, and God.

7. You could have so many challenging or traumatic experiences, thoughts, and emotions that you may need to spend a season processing with the Lord and that is okay. Stay in the process and focus on your own healing.

8. Ask God to show you the religious system of cannibalism that has been operating in your family and within the church to devour you; journal the revelation that God reveals to you. Pray against what God shows you.

9. If there is discord and division between you and your family, unless God says otherwise, wait until you are sufficiently healed before you attempt to mend relationships. You want to make sure you are not operating from a need for approval and belonging. You want to make sure you are ready to deal with your experiences with others.

10. Ask God to restore your love for your personal family and his church body. As God does this, ask him to give you a plan of how to reconcile and restore with your family. Also, ask God to give you a plan for how you are to reconcile and be restored unto his church body. Not the church you left, but the body of Christ in general.

11. Ask God to let you know when it is time to meet with family. Ask God to lead you in what to share and discuss with them. Be open and trusting of what he says. Your family may not have the revelation you received from this manual. They may still be stuck in the religious cannibalistic system and view you as a rebellious child. Do not try to prove that you are not. Allow your healing process to speak for itself. Remember you are focused on forgiveness and moving forward, so regardless of their responses and actions, you are committed to SHIFTING forward. Your healing process is not dependent on them, it is dependent on God, and the process of healing you are working with him.

12. If you do feel led to share the revelation in this manual, be prepared to express the reason you believe it applies to your experience and your family. It may be best to share this revelation before the meeting, so your family will have time to process it themselves. Journal your thoughts and feelings so

you can be clear and defined in your purpose for sharing this revelation, and wanting to discuss your church hurt experiences.

13. Many leaders and church parents have their identity interwoven in ministry and so the success of ministry validates them. You are one challenge that they have put in the Lord's hands or you are the one thing they felt they could not save. They definitely have their own hurt where you are concerned, especially, if there has been discord over the years. They may see the situation differently than you, and it will take time and compassion to break down their walls and receive truth. Maybe the initial meeting is just talking about the church hurts and then there are meetings thereafter to fellowship and breakdown walls to help bring truth and healing. Ask your family members to keep an open mind, and to search God in prayer regarding the challenges discussed. Be praying that the strongholds of cannibalism break in and around them where truth can invade. Do not take them on as a project that you are focused on your own personal transformation. Remain in your own healing process. Your process is already breaking many generational curses that will impact them and the family line.

14. Know that exploring these hurtful issues with your family may be a process in and of itself. Be willing to do the work and to remain in the process until reconciliation and restoration manifest. Utilize the strategies in the conflict resolution chapter of this manual to navigate through this season of healing with your family.

15. It will be important to visit multiple churches before considering whether God is leading you to join. Unless God says otherwise, visit for a season before joining. Be clear in what you need and desire from a church body, and be honest with yourself in whether that church can give that to you. There may be certain things you will have to receive from outside the church or maybe that church is not for you. It is okay if a church does not have everything you need. The body of Christ can make up the slack of what a personal ministry cannot provide for you. Allow God to lead you to other ministries who can empower and equip you as necessary. Be clear that the things that are important to you and that help to further deliver and heal you are available at your home church. This is essential to further cleanse and heal the wounds of church hurt.

16. Seek God for when or whether you are to return to the church that hurt you, especially if they are operating in the same system as when you were a member. Only God can tell you if this is your ground to plow and if reconciliation and restoration is possible. You will receive your inheritance regardless, because you are now realigned with God. Do not go there with a mind to reclaim your portion or setting order. That is a subtle vengeful focus. If God sends you back, he will give you healthy strategy. If he does not send you back, he will bless and restore where he sends you.

17. You may need to pursue counseling to help you in your healing process as sometimes we need assistance processing to wellness. Do whatever is beneficial to you SHIFTING out of church hurt into wholeness.

Work this strategy and anything else God gives you until you see personal healing and breakthrough for yourself. Know that you are worth the process. It will impact your destiny and your generations. SHIFT!

HEALING PREACHERS' KIDS OF FALSE IDENTITIES & LABELS

By: Minister Mercedes Carr
Kingdom Shifters Ministries, Muncie Indiana

We are all assigned names when we come into the earth. Our name is the first label that sets us apart from others. Names are the very identification that is used to describe, specify, and designate us in a particular family. The assigning of a name is never to be taken lightly. *Ecclesiastes 7:1 ESV* states that *"A good name is better than precious ointment, and the day of death than the day of birth."* When the children of preachers, ministers, leaders, deacons, etc., are birthed into the earth, not only are they assigned names from their natural families, but also the people in the parsonage who have been waiting on their arrival. To their families they may be considered individuals who are unique, loved, and chosen by God. Unfortunately, by the time many of them have grown and been cultivated in the church, they are merely labeled and revealed as the *"preacher's kid."* The term *preacher's kid* (abbreviated as PK), refers to a child of a preacher, pastor, deacon, lay leader, priest, minister or other similar church leader. Regardless of their desires, needs, individuality, giftings, callings, and identity, they are still identified as a "PK." "PK" becomes their identity rather than the true identity God ordained for them.

The title "PK" can also be attached to many negative or misperceived stereotypes. In addition, it can be unintentionally used as a label to strip a child of their own personal identity and purpose in the earth. The term "PK" is associated with many assumptions that can be true, but do not describe the entirety of all ministers' children. Oftentimes, the media portrays the "PK" as the rebellious, disobedient, lack of purpose seeking, runaway child, who wants nothing to do with the church. Although this has been the detriment of some preacher's children, this does not sum up the entirety of their identities. Nor does it help them receive the healing, deliverance, and breakthrough that is needed to break free from the stigmas that have been placed upon them. Instead of bashing and judging the preacher's kid, we as a church and parents of these children must get to a place where we are seeking to get to the root of these issues.

- Why is it that some "PKS" have rejected purpose and destiny?
- Why is it that many of them want nothing to do with the church?

> What are the reasons many "PKS" live a rebellious lifestyle, while secretly wanting God, yet hating the church and church people?

These are all questions that we should ask ourselves especially as we consider church hurt that "PKS" endure. The weight and responsibility of the "PK" can be very heavy. Many "PKS" come into the world with a standard that they never asked for.

- ✓ Many did not have the opportunity to choose God for themselves.
- ✓ Many have been living their lives according to the laws and regulations of the church. The children have been the churches accountability, their sound board, the very ones who have taken on responsibilities and duties that are sometimes, not a child's burden to bear.
- ✓ Many have been placed under the magnifying glass of the church at all times.

According to the church and society, "PKS" are not supposed to make the same mistakes and decisions as other believers in the body of Christ. Therefore, the scrutiny of their decisions and the reflections of their choices on their parents can be devastating. Many preachers' children are constantly warring between their need to experience life in their own lane, and their desire to please and protect their parents by keeping their reputations clean. This can cause an identity crisis within them, because they sometimes desire to walk in purpose and destiny, but are afraid of what the repercussions may be if they step up and voice that their destiny and purpose may not look like their parents.

God has chosen a specific path and plan for the preachers' children just as he did their parents. It is detrimental to the preachers' child and the entire body of Christ, to assume that God would want to put them in a box by stripping them of their own blueprint and strategy for destiny and purpose, and simply placing them in the mold of religion. *Jeremiah 29:11 says "For I know the plans I have for you," declares the LORD, "plans to prosper you and not to harm you, plans to give you hope and a future.* If the purpose and plan that we are releasing and imparting into these children is harming rather than helping and void of bringing hope, or the expectation for their future destiny to be fulfilled, then we need to reconsider what we are aligning them with. True destiny will bring hope and fulfillment not dread and misery. We must seek the blueprint for every child that is birthed into the earth by seeking God for his original plan for their lives. The fact that their parents are ministers does not change this truth or its necessity in the body of Christ.

As a church, we must be more responsible and mindful of the labels we place on preachers' children. Referring to the child as a "PK" alone can diminish their own personal abilities, gifts, and self-discovery to walk in their own truth and personal identities, as it pertains to what God is saying for them. Even the label and name itself has the ability, to strip the child of their identity where they are not even valued as individuals but just the Preachers kid. The perceptions of their existence tend to flow through the filters and identities of their parents, while they are being suffocated and stifled from really coming forth in their personal destinies. The gifts, mantles, visions, and the rest of the spiritual inheritance of leaders and ministers are passed down to the children. However, many of them hate the church before they can even embrace destiny or their inheritance, because the church and more importantly their parents, refuse to see them for who they truly are as individuals. Many neglect to ask them what they want to do with their lives or what is God saying to them personally. They are told they are powerful and will be mighty preachers, evangelist, teachers, prophets and other types of leaders, but many of these children just want time, love, and to be cultivated and accepted as individuals first, without the titles and weight of their parents' ministries. Where are the parents and the churches who will not only walk these children to the deliverance line, but will walk with them in their everyday activities and lives? Where is the church family who will say *"Not only do I care about your soul, destiny, and purpose, but I care about your heart and who God says you are outside of the pulpit and outside of who your parents are?"* We have to have the heart of God for the preacher's kid.

The ability to value the preacher's child as an individual, must be realized in the church. We must first see the children of leaders as children of God like we would see any other believer. Preachers' children are not their parents, nor do they necessarily have to walk in the same mantle and calling that their parents have been chosen for. If those who were closest to Jesus only recognized him as Mary's son or the carpenter's child and refused to see him as Jesus, the son of God, they would have missed the entire purpose of his life here on the earth. Unfortunately, many did not grasp the revelation of Jesus' full identity until it was too late. We do not want to make the same mistake with these children of God!

It is so essential to begin cultivating a personal identity in Christ with the preacher's child at a very young age so that they may train their ears to hear from God personally concerning their own destiny and purpose. ***Proverbs 22:6 (KJV)*** *"Train up a child in the way he should go: and when he is old, he will not depart from it."* This scripture does not say train a child up in the way that their parents went, nor does it denote that the child has to follow the footsteps of their parents to be in the will of God. This is a mindset that must be broken in the church. Too many children are walking in the footsteps of their parents, while their identities and purposes have never been fully matured, trained up, or fulfilled. Then we are confused when they depart from the church because they have been trained up in religion and not in the true ways of God. They have merely stepped in the shadow of the ones who have gone forth before them.

The term *train* means to *"initiate, to dedicate or to discipline."* Frequently, there has not been a dedication of time or discipline to the preacher's child, because the preacher's responsibility and time has been eaten up by the church. If the proper time and discipline is not allotted to the preacher's child, they will become a casualty of the "PK" stereotypes, and walk in rebellion, brokenness, lack of identity, while never experiencing true salvation in Christ. The preacher's child cannot go forth living a life through the revelation of their parents and grandparents. They know church, they know how to pray, they even know the language of God, but without relationship they will be lost in the casualty of war that comes with being a child of a pastor, preacher, or minister.

It is time to unveil the true purpose of the preacher's child in the earth. It is time that we stop sacrificing the preacher's child as a casualty of the responsibilities of church and start building them up in their personal calling, identity, and destiny at home, so when they go into the church they are not devoured and weighed down by the labels, stereotypes, expectations and experiences projected onto them by the church. It is time we take the preacher's kid off the altar as a sacrifice and bring them into a sacred place where they can truly grow, develop, receive deliverance and healing, and be cultivated into who they are called to be.

Many preachers' children will need counseling, mentorship, and a safe place to grow where they do not feel condemned or judged when it is time for them to be delivered. Pastors can pray for a blueprint for their children as well and pray a cleansing of anyway that offense, wounds, and other hits have come through labels or their lifestyle alone has impacted the child. It is the parents place to implement boundaries and standards in the home that make it a safe place for their children to grow into who God says they are. It is essential that boundaries are set in the church as well, so that the children are not always exposed and put on display for the church to criticize and condemn. It is time we start being more responsible with the preacher's child, their callings, their hearts, and their lives as a whole. It is time we start calling them forth by name, and allowing them to experience God for themselves, while cultivating them into who he desires them to be. SHIFT!

HEALING PRAYER FOR PREACHER'S KIDS

By: Minister Amanda Barnhill
Kingdom Shifters Ministries, Muncie, Indiana

Lord God release your healing presence to completely soak and saturate the hearts and souls of preachers' children that have swallowed how they felt, endured secretly in pain, hated your church (both secretly and blatantly), rejected your call, and rejected relationship with you because of church hurt. Cleanse the trauma and pain that has consumed their behaviors, actions, and habits. We command cleansing to every way they were sacrificed for the "cost of Christ," and every way that mindset embedded behaviors into their lives that would not allow them to come into their true identity. We uproot the places where these mindsets and behaviors have made them feel unworthy or misaligned in their destiny and calling. We cleanse these webbings and strongholds out of them right now with the blood of Jesus and command the healing power of God to consume them in Jesus name. We suffocate anything the enemy has used as a weapon to erect a mindset in the preachers' kids that would push them away from true healing and wholeness.

We call forth a healing and cleansing to the little girl and little boy that has been wounded by the words, the attacks, the abuse, the offenses, and anything else that has caused anger and bitterness towards God, his church, and their destiny. We cleanse the memory recall that has been lodged in their behaviors, actions, and emotions. We speak wholeness to those places right now in the name of Jesus.

We repent as the body of Christ for every way we made preachers' children feel like they had to put on a mask and portray a false identity. And every way we stifled who God designed them to be because it did not fit how we thought a preacher's child should present themselves. We cleanse out all rejection that has come through these open doors. Even now we close, seal, and lock those doors from operating in their lives. We cancel the distortion that has come to their identity through these wells. We cleanse every place where they picked up behaviors, actions, habits, and even the identity of others just to please the saints.

We cleanse and uproot all rebellion that has entered while the preacher's child has battled with trying to find who they authentically are. We set God's hammer of judgement to all masks and false identities and perceptions. We ask that true transforming, confirming, and affirming healing come to the very core of their identities. Cleanse, heal and restore the very places where their true voices have been silenced or even distorted by operating in a false identity. We activate their God given and personally designed blueprints to become clear and evident to them. We speak healing to their self-esteem, self-worth, and value. We speak directly to their hearts and souls, and command them to receive the truth that God intricately created them with a purpose and destiny that is needed. Even now Lord, allow truth to pierce their very being and become solidified in them as you process them to wholeness.

Lord God fill the preacher's child with your peace and love. Cause your love to smother the chaos and the tug of war within them. Restore the clarity and the joy of who they are and what you have called them to do. We call forth healing and restoration to their perceptions and how they see your church and body of Christ. Lord God give them clarity and truth concerning the body of Christ that will release the fullness of your transformation to their very core.

We SHIFT the preacher's child now into your secret place to fortify them in the safety of your wings, as they become vulnerable in you, and allow you to pour in your healing oil. Immerse them now and forever in your continuous love, healing, and restoration. Let it be an eternal work that cannot and will not be sifted. We seal this prayer decreeing it is so in Jesus name, Amen!

HURTS LEADERS ENDURE

There is much leadership bashing from the world and from the saints. Though there are some concerns the body of Christ need to address and change regarding the character, integrity and Godly standards of leaders, bashing only breeds reproach, hardship, and division. The word tells us to esteem leaders and to pray for leaders.

> *1Timothy 2.1-3 I urge, then, first of all, that petitions, prayers, intercession and thanksgiving be made for all people – for kings and all those in authority, that we may live peaceful and quiet lives in all godliness and holiness. For this is good and acceptable in the sight of God our Saviour;*

Many folks have hurtful things to say, but many of these people are not praying for leaders. There is minimal compassion where leaders can be strengthened by the petitions, prayers, intercession, and honor of the saints, such that they endure less burnout and hardship. Some leaders are hesitant to ask for prayer for fear of being viewed as incompetent, flawed, or experiencing public exposure. Many leaders are left uncovered and exposed to the wiles of the enemy. We must acknowledge that leaders experience church hurt as well. Chiefly, leaders have to press through despite the pain they endure. This is probably the reason many do not acknowledge, or address church hurt. They have been conditioned to believe it comes with the territory, and for them, this is indeed a truth. Leaders tend to be taken for granted so there is minimal to no regard for their church hurt pains. We want to dismantle this injustice by exposing the hurts leaders endure. As leaders are delivered and healed, the oil of healing with flow to the sheep.

Hurts leaders endure are as follows:

- Being misunderstood by members.
- Being misunderstood and judged by family members, loved ones and even peers.
- Judged harshly based on opinion and not through a Godly well.
- Having to deal with the fickleness and flakiness of people.
- People feeling entitled to judge and assassinate God, ministries, the body of Christ.
- Members leaving without attempting to resolve conflicts or without a willingness to work through conflicts.

- Members and people in general, aborting relationships or ministry endeavors with the leaders.
- Members hurt and take advantage of one another and leaders must intervene; leaders are blamed for these transgressions even though they had nothing to do with the situation.
- People lacking responsibility and accountability for their part in growing the ministry and advancing the vision.
- Enduring warfare from the demonic realms for being the ultimate vision carrier.
- Enduring word curses and witchcraft spells from saints, witches, warlocks, ignorant people, and wicked people.
- Having to constantly sacrifice for the good of the ministry and people with minimal to no appreciation.
- Enduring ridicule of having to choose between family and ministry responsibilities.
- Unrealistic expectations where the leaders feel pressured or are pressured to be perfect; or where their position somehow translates to perfection.
- Being dishonored, unaccepted, or made to feel less important depending on their platform or ministry calling.
- Not being supported personally or ministerially by members, other ministries, or the body of Christ.
- Enduring division and church splits.
- Being usurped by people who covet the vision or feel they can do a better job than the leader.
- Experiencing betrayal from members and peers.
- Being made to bear the mistakes of other unhealthy and/or fallen leaders.
- Being blamed for the peoples' lack of growth then they are being given everything they need to align and advance with destiny.
- Not being sufficiently restored when they fall due to a transgression.
- Being ridiculed and persecuted by the world for the gospels' sake.

HEALING PRAYER FOR LEADERS

By: Minister Amanda Barnhill
Kingdom Shifters Ministries, Muncie, Indiana

We call for a double portion of the healing power of God to consume and saturate the very atmosphere and core of every kingdom leader right now in the name of Jesus. We shift them now under your wings, Lord, to receive cleansing, deliverance, healing, and refreshing in every place that has been subjected to church hurt. Cleanse every area of pain, hurt, and trauma that has been lodged in the leader's heart, mind, body, will, and emotions. We command a dislodging of every root, memory, word, rejection, judgement, and assassination of character or vision right now in the name of Jesus. We close every door and gateway the enemy would try to utilize to fortify the leaders' and the body of Christ, in unhealthy, unhealed, and imbalanced mindsets.

Lord God let your refreshing reign and rain upon your leaders. We call forth your waves of healing to rush over them and soak them like drenching rain. Heal and refresh their hearts Lord, in the deep places where they have been misunderstood by members and loved ones as they have plowed, persevered, and aligned with you. Every way the enemy has tried to steal their love for what you have granted their hands to do through warfare of being the vision carrier, or any way he would try to make them give up, we cancel that right now in the name of Jesus, and we release a new love and a new level of joy and enlightenment as you shift them deeper and deeper into your healing. Heal and refresh the places where your leaders have been judged by the body of Christ due to personal opinions and not from a Godly well of revelation of who they are in you. We cleanse every word that is lodged in the memory, emotions, and behaviors right now in the name of Jesus. We command full healing to manifest in their interactions with those that they lead, shepherd, and govern. Restore a new love and compassion for your people in your leaders Holy Spirit and let the strength of your presence shine through them.

We speak a healing and refreshing to every manner to which your leaders have felt unappreciated, disregarded, dishonored, and unsupported. We cleanse all hurt that came through sacrificing for others but never really receiving appreciation. We cleanse the pain and heal the wounds resulting from betrayal, unrealistic expectations, and not being supported personally or ministerially. We cleanse hurt that came through members leaving and aborting relationships. We cleanse challenges and wounds in which they have been blamed for the lack of growth in others when it was truly that person's choice. We command the fire of God to burn up any way these hurts have caused shame, guilt, or false burdens within your leaders. Heal, refresh, and restore your leaders Lord. We declare liberation to their inward parts, to their behaviors, habits, emotions, will, and body right now in the name of Jesus.

We declare even as you are bringing complete and full healing to your leaders that they would recognize the places where church hurt is operating within the body of Christ and begin to stand against it and annihilate it within their sphere of influence. We decree a mounting up of your standard of healthiness and wholeness within every leader and declare that it will flow from the head down. Penetrate the hearts of your leaders in this hour to govern and protect your vision, and your people with your love and compassion oh God. Cause your leaders' bowels to be moved with compassion for your people Lord, where there is an urgency within them to not brush over church hurt, but to address that church hurt is real. As they acknowledge and heal your people of church hurt, let revival of healthy leaders arise in the body of Christ where your kingdom is established and advanced in purity, truth, righteousness, healing, and wholeness. We seal your leaders in the fullness of your healing, and cleansing power, expecting limitless fruit to manifest not only in them but all those connected to them. We decree it and establish it as so. In Jesus name, Amen!

DISMANTLING THE PAIN OF BETRAYAL

People are appalled and stifled when they experience betrayal within the church. This is understandable as betrayal is an excruciating experience. I do not know many leaders or mature saints who have not experienced betrayal. Jesus experienced betrayal. In ***John 6:20***, Jesus states the following to the disciples:

Jesus answered them, have not I chosen you twelve, and one of you is a devil?

He knew that a betrayer was among him. Jesus knew the church was not perfect, but he also knew that the team that "HE CHOSE" was not perfect. If we knew that a team member would betray us, there would be no way we would allow them to walk in ministry with us. Even though Judas had a devil, he was given the same opportunity as the other apostles to learn from Jesus, be equipped by Jesus, and be transformed by Jesus. Jesus was more concerned about Judas having an opportunity to be delivered and with doing the will of the Lord, than protecting his heart from wounds. Usually, we are more concerned with people not getting over on us than we are about their soul being saved and healed.

One key Jesus had is that he discerned Judas' spirit so he knew what he was dealing with. Even though they were conducting ministry together and Judas was the treasurer, Jesus was well aware of Judas' demonic oppressions, sin issues, and propensities for betrayal. Jesus did not allow relationship, the fact that they walked in ministry together, or the fact that they were a part of the kingdom of God, sway him from the truth of who was around him. This is so important because **1Thessalonians 5:12** tells us, "*And we beseech you, brethren, to know them which labour among you, and are over you in the Lord, and admonish you.* *Beseech* in the Strong's Concordance means to "*earnestly plea, to beg and to pray.*" *Admonish* means to "*warn, seek counsel, exhort.*" So basically, it is essential to clearly know those who labor among us and who are over us. We tend to know peoples' gifts, callings, and good qualities. But we fail to consider, prayer about, and keep in mind their propensities to sin and be open doors to demonic activity. Though betrayal will hurt whether we are aware of our betrayer or not, being ignorant to truth regarding a person's potential to be used of the enemy can compound betrayal, and complicate deliverance and healing.

Jesus let Judas know that he had a devil. Jesus was providing an opportunity for Judas and even the other disciples to search themselves and to be delivered. In many ministries, there is not a safe place where truth is spoken for self-exploration, deliverance, and where people are empowered despite having issues. Many who have issues are disempowered and shamed. It is taboo to acknowledge that as Christians we have issues, devils, need Jesus, but are still mighty men and women of God. Judas having a devil did not change the fact that he was a team member, a disciple, an apostle, the treasurer, chosen by Jesus himself, and was equipped and empowered in his destiny and calling. Within many ministries, these positions and training opportunities would have been determined by whether a person was already delivered and healed. But to Jesus, having the opportunity to be utilized and to be empowered in one's destiny and calling, positions people for deliverance and healing.

In *John 13:25-28*, Jesus again openly exposes Judas as one who would betray him to the disciples. But none of them discerned what he was speaking about.

> ***The Amplified Bible*** *Then leaning back against Jesus' breast, he asked Him, Lord, who is it? Jesus answered, It is the one to whom I am going to give this morsel (bit) of food after I have dipped it. So when He had dipped the morsel of bread [into the dish], He gave it to Judas, Simon Iscariot's son. Then after [he had taken] the bit of food, Satan entered into and took possession of [Judas]. Jesus said to him, what you are going to do, do more swiftly than you seem to intend and make quick work of it. But nobody reclining at the table knew why He spoke to him or what He meant by telling him this.*

How the disciples responded is how saints respond in the church when someone reveals a potential betrayer in our midst. We either fail to discern it altogether or ignore it. Even though it was evident as to what Jesus was speaking, the disciples chose to believe what they wanted to believe concerning that which Jesus was stating and did not probe further regarding the matter.

Despite knowing Judas was a devil, Jesus esteemed Judas and the disciples higher than he did himself.

> ***1Thessalonians 5:13*** *And to esteem them very highly in love for their work's sake. And be at peace among yourselves.*

Before exposing Judas again, Jesus washed Judas feet just as he did the other disciples (*John 13:12*). Jesus did not punish Judas for being the betrayer. He did not quit ministry because he knew Judas would betray him. He did not even try to stop Judas from his purpose as the betrayer. Jesus did not abort his own purpose and destiny. Jesus told Judas not to tarry in his quest. Jesus knew that Judas was vital to his next SHIFT in his purpose and destiny. We like to think that when these SHIFTS come, they entail blessings, joy, favor, and celebration. But some destiny SHIFTS come with trial and tribulation. Sometimes that hardship manifests through the friendly fire of the ones that are closest to us or that are in our camp. I am not expressing this to make light of betrayal within the church. However, I do want to speak truth that it is most likely an experience that many of us will endure and will have to overcome. You cannot allow betrayal to keep you stagnant in destiny. You must assert your authority to pursue the next SHIFT you were to achieve before betrayal entered your life. I would have to admit that I have not experienced pain so treacherous than when being betrayed. It was like an exposed, bleeding, painful wound that I thought would never stop hurting, throbbing, and revealing itself, while spilling all over me. The pain consumed my heart, my soul, my thoughts, and my body. Though I clearly knew who I was, whose I was, my calling and destiny, the betrayal sought to consume my perception of myself, my perception of others, my perception of God, and what he had called me to do. The betrayal tried to define and redefine me. It was after my identity and after my next dimension in destiny.

See betrayal comes for your existence, worth, position, and purpose. Betrayal tries to get you to prove who you are, even though it clearly knows who you are, and wants you dead. This is the reason Jesus would not save himself from being crucified - he had nothing to prove.

> *John 10:17-18 Therefore doth my Father love me, because I lay down my life, that I might take it again. No man taketh it from me, but I lay it down of myself. I have power to lay it down, and I have power to take it again. This commandment have I received of my Father.*

Betrayal usually occurs with someone who has partaken of who you are. They are aware of your identity, your value, your ability, and your purpose, but they are willing to sacrifice who you are for their personal gain.

Though not always the case, oftentimes betrayers do not realize they are betrayers or that they are going to betray you. Most betrayers think they are doing a good deed by sacrificing you for what they perceive to be the greater good. If they gain from their good deed then, "*all is well in love and war.*" Their payment - their advancement - is simply a reward for a job well done. Though betrayal is meant to ignite death, the betrayer may not consider this when they are sacrificing you. Many of them do not realize they have opened a portal to your demise. Many do not realize this until it is too late, as whether done ignorantly or unintentionally, there is no undoing of betrayal. Though not always the case, there are instances where relationships of betrayal cannot be mended because the betrayer either cannot forgive themselves, or cannot SHIFT pass what they did to you. Your very presence is a constant reminder of their actions, and so in order to have relationship with you, they have to see you from a new place. Not from what they can gain from you being sacrificed, but what they gain from you being a valuable part of their life and the world at large. They must be delivered and healed to acquire a new enlightenment about you. Many are so bound by shame and guilt, that even if they obtain a measure of healing, it rarely lends itself to restoration of the relationship, because the spirit of condemnation kills it. This is the reason Judas killed himself. He could not bear the affliction of his folly.

> ***Matthew 27:3-5 The Amplified Bible*** *When Judas, His betrayer, saw that [Jesus] was condemned, [Judas was afflicted in mind and troubled for his former folly; and] with remorse [with little more than a selfish dread of the consequences] he brought back the thirty pieces of silver to the chief priests and the elders, Saying, I have sinned in betraying innocent blood. They replied, What is that to us? See to that yourself. And casting the pieces of silver [forward] into the [Holy Place of the sanctuary of the] temple, he departed; and he went off and hanged himself.*

Many betrayers will not physically take their life, but they will kill the relationship with you, because they cannot stomach the responsibility of their actions toward you.

When betrayal spirals, it causes others to betray you. Even if they do not agree or have no clue why you are being betrayed, they just jump on the bandwagon, "*crucify him,*" simply because the others around them are doing it.

> ***Luke 23:20-24*** *Once more Pilate called to them, wishing to release Jesus; But they kept shouting out, Crucify, crucify Him! A third time he said to them, Why? What wrong has He done? I have found [no offense or crime or guilt] in Him nothing deserving of death; I will therefore chastise Him [in order to teach Him better] and release Him. But they were insistent and urgent, demanding with loud cries that He should be crucified. And their voices prevailed (accomplished their purpose). And Pilate gave sentence, that what they asked should be done.*

This is the reason Jesus said: "*Forgive them for they know not what they do*" (**Luke 23:34**).

Though not always the case, often when leaders are betrayed, the only thing you have done wrong is be you. Most times the only transgression that occurred was that you were about your father's business. You were walking in destiny and the enemy wanted to thwart it. He rattled a few haters and had them whisper in an insecure person's ear that had access to you; or maybe he had haters show their indignation towards you, and that insecure person became the catalyst for the spirit of betrayal to operate. This happened to Jesus. Jesus was just "*doing him*" and in came the vile of betrayal. Fact is, you are who you are and there is nothing betrayers or devils can do about it.

> ***Matthew 26:60-65*** *But they found none, though many witnesses came forward [to testify]. At last two men came forward and testified, This Fellow said, I am able to tear down the sanctuary of the temple of God and to build it up again in three days. And the high priest stood up and said, Have You no answer to make? What about this that these men testify against You? But Jesus kept silent. And the high priest said to Him, I call upon you to swear by the living God, and tell us whether you are the Christ, the Son of God. Jesus said to him, you have stated [the fact]. More than that, I tell you: You will in the future see the Son of Man seated at the right hand of the Almighty and coming on the clouds of the sky. Then the high priest tore his clothes and exclaimed, He has uttered blasphemy! What need have we of further evidence? You have now heard His blasphemy.*

Many of the people who you did not expect to get on the bandwagon, those you ministered to and poured into, well - they are insecure too. Many of them do not know their identity and are broken in their identity. While jumping on the bandwagon, they now feel betrayed by you for doing God's will, and being an example of how they need to grow up, mature in the Lord, and stop using you to identify and bring worth to them. They are not ready to grow up even though you have been equipping them. Since betrayal is nobody's friend and has exposed them, they will be forced to mature or reap the consequences of their actions. But let me leave that alone. You get the point right???? If not, my point is:

- Do not leave God because you were betrayed
- Do not blame and make all saints pay because you were betrayed
- Do not leave the church because you were betrayed
- Do not leave destiny because you were betrayed

LEAVE THE DEVIL WISHING HE NEVER BROUGHT BETRAYAL TO YOUR DOORSTEP.

Leave the devil wishing he was not lurking around the church seeking whom he could use to betray you. Regain your authority over your experience by processing to wellness and realigning in the dimensional SHIFT that is about to release resurrection power into your life. Below are some wisdom keys to help you dismantle and heal from betrayal.

Wisdom Keys For Dismantling Betrayal:
Know your Identity - Know who you are and whose you are, so when you experience betrayal, no matter how confusing or baffling, you will not be shaken in your identity.

Do Not Defend Yourself - Do not defend who you are to jealous, covetous, and hating people. Even those in authority will come for you and try to shake you in your identity, make you feel like what has occurred is your fault and you should rectify it. They will try to use their platform and position to get you to agree with lies that have been spoken about you and untruths regarding your identity. Speak the facts - the truth in love and meekness. Do not argue and do not defend. Respect whatever they believe is their truth, while peacefully not wavering in yours. Just be who you are, and let the God in you speak for itself.

Choose Your Battles - Even as God will redeem you, you will have to pick and choose when to stay silent as the process of betrayal unfolds, and when to speak truth. Jesus said that all would know the truth after the betrayal was over, and he was sitting at the right hand of God, and floating in the clouds. The power, miracles, signs and wonders after the betrayal is where your life really speaks and defends you. This may not come for days, months, or years later. Be okay with allowing it to be your voice rather than you defending yourself from an experience that has already unfolded and cannot be stopped. Yes! Once betrayal begins, it fulfills its agenda whether we like it or not. The pain, reproach, and death is inevitable. I would have to say you die a spiritual death then you are raised to life in resurrected power. The challenge is that once the betrayal unfolds, many people try to stop it. This just makes matters worse and makes you look guilty. You are fighting against a transaction that has taken on a spiritual assault within the minds and ideologies of the people, and within the spirit realm. The best way to combat this is to walk it out, and let God and your destiny avenge you.

Forgive - Forgive and release those who persecute you no matter how hard it is to let the pain go. When considering my experience with betrayal, since I had done everything as God had required, I was not expecting to be betrayed. I mean I should have expected it as all the signs were there. But I was still hoping to be celebrated and supported by those who knew me, knew my character, who was close to me, and who I had spent years pouring my life into. I had to diligently pray until real forgiveness was birthed in my heart. I spent countless days and hours in prayer releasing those who betrayed me, begging God to stop the bleeding, and take away the pain. Sometimes my mind would be tormented with thoughts of those who betrayed me. I also have a gift of being able to hear what is going on in the enemy's camp, and the thoughts of others. I was plagued by the continual betraying that was occurring. I could confront people with literal words they had spoken about me, and they would stand awed, unable to deny what I shared. Sometimes I spent days rebuking thoughts and releasing forgiveness, all while working a fulltime job and doing ministry. I share this because forgiveness is not a choice. It is a commandment. It poses a contingency where you are only forgiven if you forgive.

> *Matthew 6:14-15* For if ye forgive men their trespasses, your heavenly Father will also forgive you: But if you do not forgive others their sins, your Father will not forgive your sins.

> *Matthew 18: 21-22* Then Peter came to Jesus and asked, "Lord, how many times shall I forgive my brother when he sins against me? Up to seven times? "Jesus answered, "I tell you, not seven times, but seventy-seven times."

> *Colossians 3:13* Forbearing one another, and forgiving one another, if any man have a quarrel against any: even as Christ forgave you.

I wanted to forgive because I wanted to heal and be healthy. I also wanted God to be pleased with me and how I handled the situation. Others were watching me, so I knew it was important for me to handle my experience in a healthy manner. In addition, I never want to put myself in a position to wound others. Wounded people wound others. For that reason alone, it was worth doing whatever necessary to forgive. You must figure out what is more important to you, retaliating, begrudging, or forgiving and healing? It may be difficult to process through it, but it is so worth it. You are worth it! Your destiny is worth it!

Release The Pain - You are going to be bitter, angry, enraged, appalled, baffled, confused, tormented, feel rejected, and etc. You are going to want to fight, retaliate, defend yourself, prove yourself, slander those who slandered you, tell your side of the story to whoever will listen. You are going to feel shame, guilt, reproach; wonder why you did not discern it, condemned that it is happening to you, and reproached by being in the negative spotlight. You are going to cry and cry and be grieved by what happened. Even grieve the relationships you lost due to the betrayal. You are going to grieve the loss of the betrayer, especially if they were close to you. You are going to want to quit ministry and never help people again. You are going to want to distrust everyone, even those who support you. Every part of you may hurt, and you will just want it to stop. I felt like I was being stabbed over and over and over, in my heart and soul. Sometimes I would be bowed over in agony, while asking God to heal me. Though I wanted to get a knife and get to cutting some folks up, I did not lash out at anyone. I took my pains and tortured feelings to God, and I kept taking them and kept taking them and kept taking them, until he healed me.

> **Ephesians 4:31-32** *Get rid of all bitterness, rage and anger, brawling and slander, along with every form of malice. Be kind and compassionate to one another, forgiving each other, just as in Christ God forgave you.*
>
> **The Amplified Bible** *Let all bitterness and indignation and wrath (passion, rage, bad temper) and resentment (anger, animosity) and quarreling (brawling, clamor, contention) and slander (evil-speaking, abusive or blasphemous language) be banished from you, with all malice (spite, ill will, or baseness of any kind). And become useful and helpful and kind to one another, tenderhearted (compassionate, understanding, loving-hearted), forgiving one another [readily and freely], as God in Christ forgave you.*

This may not be what you want to hear, but I am revealing a process to you that will save you a lot of extended heartache. You already in pain, why add to it?

Conquer the Shock & Trauma - Do not get stuck inside the shock, trauma, and pain of betrayal. Do not bury the trauma and woundedness of betrayal. Jesus could have died and refused to raise up as savior. But Jesus had work to do. He had purpose beyond the betrayal. You will want to quit, you will want to hide, you will be trying to figure out how to get the pain to stop so you can deal with what you are experiencing. You will have to be wise in not quitting, hiding, stuffing, and blowing a gasket as you walk through the betrayal and deal with the aftermath.

Your body, heart, and soul, will start to go numb in effort to deal with the shock and trauma of the ordeal. Do not see this as a good thing, as it will feel like the pain has lessened. But please do not mistake this as healing, because it is not healing. You are actually absorbing the feelings and pain, and it is becoming a part of you. It is becoming a part of your soul, heart, spirit, body, personality, and identity. If you do not get true healing, it will overtake your ministry and destiny. Remember these are bleeding wounds that are spilling on everything. Purpose to "*get rid*" of them. That means you are not agreeing with them. You are opposing them, rejecting them, and refusing to allow them to become your truth.

Just as you did with forgiveness, you will have to spend time before God being honest about your feelings, releasing your pain to him, receiving his healing, while rebuking and casting out any demonic spirits, thoughts, and feelings that are trying to become a part of you. Deal with trauma and shock as demonic spirits as they are like weapons that lodge inside of you that create knife like wounds. You may literally feel these spirits lodged in your heart, back, spine, etc. Deal with the spirit of betrayal as a death spirit as it did come to kill your identity and destiny.

Break Powers Of Fiery Darts - Break the powers of shame, guilt, public reproach and accuser of the brethren. Declare favor and blessings over yourself with man and God. Cleanse yourself of all fiery darts, daggers, and word curses that will be sent by those who jumped on the bandwagon.

Stand In Your Godly Truth - Confusion and bewitchment will come for your truth. They will come for your truth concerning the situation, your identity, who God is, your purpose, authority, and destiny. God is not the author of confusion (***1Corinthians 14:33***). This is the work of the enemy trying to further entangle you in the bondage of betrayal. Spend consistent time declaring out your truth in every area, and be quick in rebuking thoughts of confusion and bewitchment that come for your truth.

Annihilate Depression & Loneliness - Depression and loneliness will also come for you. Study the story of Jesus in the garden of Gethsemane (***Matthew 26:36-56***). He had disciples not too far from him, and they meant well, but there was only so much support they could give him in this time of betrayal and preparing for the cross. Jesus felt depressed, grieved, and lonely. He rebuked the disciples for not staying awake and praying with him. He even asked God to take the cup of destiny away from him. Jesus could have just sat in the garden and drowned in his sorrow. Instead he chose to commune with God. In these instances, know that you are not down trodden or alone. God is with you and journeying with you. Resist yielding to depression and loneliness, while drawing nigh to God for strength and rejuvenation to press forward in the battle.

Give Up The Need To Avenge - Please know that you have to give up your drive and burning lust for revenge and to be avenged, in order to really forgive and heal. With the experiencing of betrayal, God does the judging and avenging. God is going to bring justice to you, redeem you, and bless you right in the midst of your enemies. But it is by his design and timing. Trust him with this part of the experience. As I pondered on revenge in my prayer times, it became scary to think about the fact that people had to be judged and chastened by God, rather than to be avenged by me. I actually began to have pity and mercy for them. Truth is we should want people to be delivered and saved over being destroyed. When I gained this revelation, I was excited; it revealed maturity in my healing process, and that I had fully released this situation to God.

> ***2Chronicles 20:15*** *And he said, Hearken ye, all Judah, and ye inhabitants of Jerusalem, and thou king Jehoshaphat, Thus saith the LORD unto you, Be not afraid nor dismayed by reason of this great multitude; for the battle [is] not yours, but God's.*

> ***Romans 12:19*** *Dearly beloved, avenge not yourselves, but rather give place unto wrath: for it is written, Vengeance is mine; I will repay, saith the Lord.*

Possess God's Eyes - Ask God to give you a love and compassion for those who betrayed you, and to help you discern and engage them as he sees them. This will help you as you continue to deal with the betrayal, the aftermath, and process forward in complete healing. This will also help you in times where you may have to interact with those who betrayed you. Operating through the love and compassion of God will give you a desire to want to see them delivered rather than destroyed. In my ordeal, God had placed such a love in me that I was praying for him to take the judgment he had released against my betrayers away. I was standing in the gap asking God to forgive them for what they did to me, repenting on their behalf, and to spare them of hardship. Even to this day, I have, and I will be given the opportunity to minister deliverance and healing to them. The very persons that betrayed me, will one day need me to save their life. You may be chosen to save those that betrayed you. Leave the justice to God, and ask him for the ability to love the unworthy and the unlovable.

Be Watchful, Meek & Temperate - Ask God for a meek and temperate spirit to deal with conflicts and challenges that will arise during the aftermath of the betrayal. Also, be slow to speak and slow to become offended. Rest in the truth of God and search God for what to say and how to speak it.

> ***James 1:19*** *Understand this, my dear brothers and sisters: You must all be quick to listen, slow to speak, and slow to get angry.*

Be okay when you do not have an answer right away for what is being asked of you. Let the person/people know that you need time to pray and consider what is being spoken, and you will yield and answer when God has released you to speak. This is important because you will be enthralled with debates and gossip regarding the betrayal. People may testify wrongly against you to further strengthen what has been spoken. People you do not know or barely know may make you feel obligated to defend gossip. They will come to you as middle men claiming that God sent them as mediators to bring restoration with those that betrayed you. Be careful not to end up in a lion's den situation that God has delivered you from. A lion's den situation is when someone is trying to get you to reenter a situation that God has already delivered you from. They claim that they want to reunify and bring healing between you and your betrayers, and this may very well be their heart. But if it is not God's will, then it is a set up to devour you through a false unification that God has not designed. If Judas wants to apologize and restore relationship, he will come on his own accord. He will not send a mediator to do his work for him.

People are going to come to you in private appearing to have your best interest at heart, but they will just be seeking to obtain more information to further slander you. Be watchful and diligent so you will not be tricked into speaking and doing something that will incite drama or grieve God.

Avoid Re-Wounding - Those who support you will want to discuss the situation over and over, as they are trying to process their pain and challenges too. Guard your heart in making sure you do not continuously relive the betrayal over and over through those who are players in the experience. You are before God and he is healing you, but your healing is stolen by those who still mean bad for you, or those who are trying to understand the situation. Jesus never relived the situation with the disciples. Not even those who denied him, or those who did not believe that he was savior. And he never relived it with those who witnessed him being betrayed or raised from the dead. Nor did Jesus return to those who betrayed him, and try to get them to acknowledge what they had did to him. I had to learn that these actions, even if well intended, reopened my wounds, and restarted my healing process. To stop the reopening of wounds, the re-bleeding, I began to guard my heart.

> *Proverbs 4:20-23 My son, attend to my words; incline thine ear unto my sayings. Let them not depart from thine eyes; keep them in the midst of thine heart. For they are life unto those that find them, and health to all their flesh. Keep thy heart with all diligence; for out of it are the issues of life.*

Have Accountability Partners - I only had a few people that I would discuss the betrayal with. They were mature leaders committed to making sure I had healthy dialog that kept me focused on God healing me. They did not feed into my pain. They acknowledged my pain, provided wisdom as God led, and prayed for me in that moment so that I could be strengthened in my process to complete healing.

Resist Gossip - If people came to me discussing the betrayal, even if they had my best interest at heart, I would tell them I do not care to discuss the matter. I respected their hurt and shared how I was taking my pain and challenges to the Lord. I encouraged them to do the same. I also would share keys I was receiving to deal with the betrayal in a healthy way. If gossipers came to me, I would immediately stop them from being messy. I would bless my betrayer and speak well of them. That often silenced the slanders, or they would try to change what they were speaking of. If they were trying to get me to share my story, I would tell them I do not care to discuss the matter. Gossipers cannot defend you, as they are not able to carry truth. By the time they repeat whatever is stated, a lie has already intertwined with it. Save yourself some heartache by not entertaining their slanderous character.

When I did share my story, it was at God's leading. Sometimes I knew the purpose and sometimes I did not know the reason God led me to share. This was few and far between, and was for God's glory. In those moments, I did not see God redeeming me. I saw the supernatural strength and character he had given me to endure the situation.

Be A Godly Example - Be cognizant of the people watching you. Even if they are waiting for you to fall, they are learning from your experience. You are teaching them how to overcome betrayal. The more we have people dealing with betrayal in a healthy manner, the less hurt and drama we will have in the body of Christ.

Consistently Check Yourself - Conduct healing checks with the Lord. Ask him if you are healed yet and allow him to show you areas where you are still wounded. This is important because the more you process towards healing, the better you will feel, and the more confident you will be. But you want to make sure nothing is hiding, nothing has been stuffed, and that there is no residue of betrayal on you. You want to be fully resurrected in the new place and identity that you are to journey into.

Wisdom Keys for Reconciling - Some of those that betrayed you, particularly the bandwagon betrayers, will want to restore relationship with you. Though not always the case, the most you may achieve is the initial part of reconciliation, yet full reconciliation where the relationship can be restored takes work.

> ***2Corinthians 5:18-21*** *And all things are of God, who hath reconciled us to himself by Jesus Christ, and hath given to us the ministry of reconciliation; To wit, that God was in Christ, reconciling the world unto himself, not imputing their trespasses unto them; and hath committed unto us the word of reconciliation. Now then we are ambassadors for Christ, as though God did beseech you by us: we pray you in Christ's stead, be ye reconciled to God. For he hath made him to be sin for us, who knew no sin; that we might be made the righteousness of God in him.*

If we consider this scripture, reconciliation is a twostep process. Initial reconciliation says we have acknowledged our faults and forgiven one another. Now we have SHIFTED to a place where we favor one another enough to consider relationship again. But the latter end of reconciliation means that I am accepting all that comes with being forgiven, and want to be restored with the intent to rebuild, revive, and reestablish our covenant relationship. This means we are committed to learning one another from this new restored place; learning our potential in this new restored place, and practicing engaging one another from this place until a new unimpaired relationship forms between us. The challenge with this is that the original relationship was killed by betrayal. Paul told the people to be reconciled as ambassadors of Christ. Christ as they knew him had changed, and their position as resurrected believers had changed. You are now a different resurrected person because of betrayal, so you cannot go back to that person even if you wanted to. You are not sure if the other person is just sorry or has really changed. You cannot know that just from the initial exchange of reconciliation. You can only know that by relationship.

Let me say it another way: Initial reconciliation is the resolving of an alt, a breech, or transgression. The relationship part of reconciliation is the mending of that alt, breech, or transgression, where division no longer exists. That is the reason many believe in God and acknowledge him as their savior, but they are not fully reconciled back to him. They are sorry and want a savior, but not truly converted into salvation. They believe he is the savior and want the fruit of that. Though God has forgiven them of their sins, they are not fully converted into salvation, such that they receive all it entails, as that only comes with journeying in relationship with him.

It takes a strong person, to really accept forgiveness of their sin, especially betrayal, and then commit to walking in a renewed covenant relationship from a new place, trust that you have forgiven them, forgiven themselves, have received deliverance and healing, and are willing to live out that deliverance and healing in a relationship with you. Many say that is what they want, but do not do the work to see that come to pass. Therefore, do not be surprised if you reconcile with Judas, but do not restore covenant with them.

Those that betrayed you may assume that because you all have initially reconciled that there is restoration of relationship. Let me say it another way: Relationship means we are actively working on building healthy interactions with one another beyond toleration. If we are just tolerating one another, then we are being cordial and respectful, while sharing a common space. God does this all the time with people. They contend they are walking in relationship with him, but he does not have covenant with them.

Rest In Your Healing Process - It is important to receive peace concerning those who you have cordial reconciliation with, and even those who have betrayed you and never tried to reconcile. It may feel awkward to be around them, but do not succumb to being fearful. No, you are not going to give them a chance to betray you again, but you are not going to engage them from an unhealthy place either. Remain loving, compassionate and discerning, while guarding your heart through the truth of who you are in God. If something is not right then God will let you know, and he will direct you in how to deal with it. I know you are probably saying "*God didn't guard me the first time.*" Well he did not leave you either. He was right there with you, helping you to overcome. And if you are really towering in your resurrected place, then you will know the real reason the enemy wanted to kill you. He did not want you to walk in that power that would save masses and set captives free. He could not thwart your destiny then, and he cannot thwart it now. Stand strong in your identity and conquer in destiny, as betrayal SHIFTS you to operating in resurrection power. You are re-birthed in Jesus' resurrection power! SHIFT!

GUARDING YOUR HEART

An essential key I learned early into my experience of church hurt is the importance of guarding my heart. As I guarded my heart, I was able to maintain my healing and operate through the integrity and character of a healed well.

> ***Proverbs 4:23*** *Keep thy heart with all diligence; for out of it are the issues of life.*

<u>Keep</u> is *nâsar* in the Hebrew and means:
1. to guard, in a good sense (to protect, maintain, obey, etc.) or a bad one (to conceal, etc.)
2. besieged, hidden thing, keep, monument, observe, preserve, keep watch over
3. to watch, guard, keep, to preserve, guard from dangers, observe, guard with fidelity
4. keep secret, to be kept close, be blockaded, watchman

<u>Dictionary.com defines *issues* as:</u>
1. the act of sending out or putting forth; distribution (*when your issues are not being dealt with, you are distributing your issues every time you talk*)
2. something that is printed or published and distribute (*you are literally publishing what is inside of you on the airwaves, in the atmosphere, inside of those listening to you. Your issues are being printed like a vision plan or a written script concerning you and whatever you are discussing*)
3. a personal or emotional problem (*revealing matters you need to work on or be delivered and healed from*)
4. any problem or difficulty (*revealing the challenges you are having in your inner man*)

The Amplified Bible uses the word "*springs*" rather than "*issues.*" Basically, when your heart is not guarded, what is inside of you is suddenly spewing up out of you like water, blood or sparks of fire (like when you turn on a faucet and water immediate flows out of it or you have a cut and blood immediately gushes out of it). Your issues start to rule you and become the identity of you, because your heart is not guarded.

When I experienced church hurt it felt like someone had stabbed me in the heart with a sharp knife and continuously twisted and pierced that knife into my heart. This was not just a pain I felt for a couple of days or weeks. I experienced it for months. During my initial experience of church hurt, I would have people coming to me with different questions.

- ❖ Some were nosey
- ❖ Some had concern for me
- ❖ Some wanted me not to leave
- ❖ Some thought I was aborting destiny because I transitioned out of the church
- ❖ Some were hurt themselves and wanted to share and compare stories or have confirmation that their hurt was legit
- ❖ Some thought they had the word of the Lord or warning for me
- ❖ Some wanted to be a mediator between me and those who hurt me
- ❖ Some just like to hear themselves talk and was not saying anything beneficial or relevant to the situation

What I learned quickly was, as people would approach me, though I would simply say, "*I have challenges with no one - I bless my old church and leadership and am only leaving to do the will of God,*" if I allowed them to speak anything good or bad, the time I spent with God letting him soothe me, stop the piercing knife stabs, etc., would be undone. Their words would re-wound and re-injure me, and would make the twisting - piercing - knife pains worse.

- ❖ I had to tell people that I did not want to hear their gossip - what people had to say about me, the situation or leadership.
- ❖ I had to tell people that I did not want to hear what was going on at the church I left.
- ❖ I had to tell people who were experiencing church hurt that their focus had to be on being healed not wallowing in their pain, offense, need to defend themselves or seek revenge and that I was not the support for them.
- ❖ I had to tell people that would try to word curse me with fear and threats, or coerce me to return to the lion's den that I reject their word curses.
- ❖ I had to tell friends that I could not rehearse my pain with them, so they were not my accountability partners. I did not need sympathy, I did not need my homies to get in the car with me, so we can go throw rocks at the church. I needed healing.

I asked the Holy Spirit every day for keen discernment, so that I would be discerning beforehand what people were going to say to me, and I would shut them down before they got started.

- ❖ I did not do this disrespectfully.
- ❖ I did not do this because I did not love them.
- ❖ I did not do this because I did not want to support their pain, hear and calm their concerns, or help them process their challenges with my situation and transition.

I did this to guard my own heart, and at the time, I was no good to anyone if I was bleeding all over the place from the constant re-wounding of reliving my situation with everyone that had contact with me.

I will admit that this cut off a lot of relationships and interactions. People could not handle being around me without trying to process an experience that they:

- ❖ Had little to no knowledge about
- ❖ Had mostly gossip, half-truths, twisted truths and lies
- ❖ Lacked the trusting of my heart or my integral track record
- ❖ Was not discerning or seeking God for truth
- ❖ Was not supposed to be privy to in the first place and was not a true part of my life anyway
- ❖ Could not handle that ultimately, I just wanted to be in the purpose of God and operate through his likeness

Some people had already chosen sides and it was not mine. They were only coming to me to stir up more gossip. I refused to be a part of my own demise. Yes, that is what you are doing when you speak through your issues - you become a part of your own destruction. The enemy uses your hurt against you to further discredit, disgrace, betray, and destroy you.

Because of the hurts, anger, offense, resentment, vengeance, hatred, that is spewing out of your heart rather than healing when you pray and process your experience, you SHIFT deeper and deeper into the dimensions of your pain. This is the reason I recommend getting wise accountability partners and even a counselor who can allow you to share your issues, while effectively processing you to wholeness. No matter how much you rehearse your pain - and you will rehearse it because of the baffling you are experiencing with church hurt - wise accountability partners and a counselor will be able to validate your truth. They will also SHIFT you onward in your healing process.

One of the biggest challenges with guarding your heart is when you have people who follow or sit under your ministry, and you have had to share your experience with them. This is especially a challenge in this world of social media where we have built platforms and followings. We tend to feel obligated to not just share but to also be the spokesperson, counselor, protector, and healer for others who have endured church hurt. If your heart is bleeding where you feel like you are dying, how can you revive someone else? Though it is your passion to help them as you understand their pain, the greatest blessing you can give them and yourself, is to refer them to a counselor or seasoned leader who can process them to wholeness. This is a time to be guarding your heart, not exposing it. The more you relive your pain through the hurts of other people, the more you prolong your own healing, and take away from time you really should be processing with the Lord. Doing this also SHIFTS you into being an advocate and a poster child for an experience that you have not conquered yet. Because you are not healed, you may bless others with your presence, knowledge, and ability to relate; however, you do not possess the authority to bring true healing others. An abundance of hurt people result to gravitating to you and sucking on your bleeding wounds. And though you are bleeding all over the place and being validated in your hurt, you are not properly positioned to be healed. You are actually exposed, and opening yourself up for more experiences of betrayal and hardship.

Another challenge with social media is that if the person or church that hurt you is on your media site, and you have not disconnected from their pages or from those who are a part of the ministry that remind you of the hurt, then you just relive your pain every time you see their posts, videos, comments, pictures, etc. Guard your heart by deleting and unfollowing some folks. Resist going on their pages, viewing their videos, reading their post. Want your healing more than you want to be nosey and to see if God is dealing with them, or if they have changed, or if God has avenged you by wreaking havoc on their life.

- ✓ I wanted healing more than I wanted information to fuel my rage and pain.
- ✓ I wanted healing more than I wanted to be nosey and to further validate my truth about them.
- ✓ I wanted healing more than I wanted the relationships and connections that tied me to them.

Be willing to sacrifice all to get into that place of really abiding in God, such that deep healing begins to overtake you.
Most people who experience church hurt tend to put other people above themselves. This is their nature. However, in this season of healing, it will be

important to make your heart a priority and guard it diligently. One of the Hebrew definitions for *diligence* is *prison*. You literally want to put your heart in prison. You want to make sure it does not escape where it is reoffended where you become the offender. You must take this time for yourself and know that you will be a better person, Christian, leader, minister, friend, because of it.

Exploration Questions:
1. Ask God for a simple respectful sentence you can state to silence those who inquire about your experience (e.g. I bless my leaders and my old church, and I am focusing on SHIFTING forward with God).
2. Ask the Holy Spirit for discernment so you can shut down conversations immediately when people approach you.
3. List three wise accountability partners who are not connected to the situation and can be optimistic, realistic, honest, and future focused in helping you process to wholeness. Ask these people to be your accountability partners and talk to them ONLY when you need to vent to process your thoughts and feelings, be validated, encouragement, support, truth, counsel or prayer.
4. Pursue a professional Christian counselor or one strong leader who can counsel you at least twice a month for no less than six months.
5. Delete, unfollow, and disconnect yourself from social media platforms to avoid interactions with those that hurt you and those who will remind you of your experience. Do not frequent their pages or watch their videos. Once you COMPLETELY heal, you can seek God regarding who to follow and reconnect with on social media.
6. Only share your story on social media if it directly impacts your followers. DO NOT post or do anymore videos after you have shared your initial information.
7. DO NOT defend yourself, chase gossip or get into social media brawls with your offenders. Remember you represent God and he will avenge you in his timing.
8. Refer all your church hurt followers to someone who can bring them healing. DO NOT try to counsel them yourself. DO NOT succumb to being validated in your identity by helping others and rehearsing your pain with hurting people. After you are COMPLETELY healed you can help people in this area, but until then DO NOT become a rescuer or a bleeding poster child. Trust the process you need to take to be healed, and trust God with those who are hurting.
9. You can post and conduct videos on various topics, but DO NOT post or do videos regarding your church hurt. Wait until you heal COMPLETELY and until God releases you to share your story.

WHEN THE GLORY HAS DEPARTED

There are people who have experienced and are experiencing church hurt because they are a part of Ichabod houses. They are not able to discern that it is an Ichabod house. This is because these people equate a thriving ministry to be that with lots of members, liberated and exuberant worship, wealth and material flourishment, personal advancement and the utilization of giftings, and when miracles, signs, and wonders are prevalent. These should be signs of a healthy flourishing church, but some of the times, the glory of God has left these churches. Though the gifts are operable and producing fruit, they are not of God and God is not in it.

> ***1Samuel 4:19-22*** *Now his daughter-in-law, Phinehas' wife, was with child, about to be delivered. And when she heard that the ark of God was captured and that her father-in-law and her husband were dead, she bowed herself and gave birth, for her pains came upon her. And about the time of her death the women attending her said to her, Fear not, for you have borne a son. But she did not answer or notice. And she named the child Ichabod, saying, The glory is departed from Israel! – because the ark of God had been captured and because of her father-in-law and her husband. She said, The glory is gone from Israel, for the ark of God has been taken.*

In this passage of scripture, the Philistines were in a war battle with Israel. The Philistines won and took the ark of the covenant. Eli's sons both died in the slaughter. When Eli, the Jewish priest, who served God in the tabernacle, heard that the ark was captured, he fell off his seat backwards, his neck broke, and he died. His sons did not follow the ways of God. They did wickedness in the Lord's house (*1Samuel 2:22-25*). Eli rebuked his sons for their wickedness, but did not stop them from profaning the tabernacle of God. He lacked the zeal, fervency, and fear of the Lord, to stifle their behaviors. Thus judgment came upon Israel and Eli's generations. Eli knew the importance of the ark of the Lord. He knew that there was no life without the presence of God. Hearing that the ark of the Lord was stolen brought such shock that it incited the judgment of death that was upon him.

Phinehas, Eli's daughter in law, was pregnant at the time of war and judgment. She died while giving birth to a son whom she called Ichabod, which means, *"the glory has departed."* In multiple Ichabod churches today, people tend to see and focus on the birthing that is occurring, but they fail to discern the death and judgment that is occurring. They fail to recognize that God's presence has left the house and what they are equating as his glory, is really the unrepentance of gifts in operation. You see, God lets us know in **Romans 11:29** that our gifts are without repentance. That means God will not take our gifts from us. He freely gives them to us, and no matter what we do, he does not regret equipping us with his gifts. God's gifts are a part of his identity and kingdom. He desires them to be operable in the earth. The gifts within us will flourish whether we use them for God or the devil. This is the reason various ministries appear to have the power, favor and blessing of God, but operate in a form and fashion of God (**2Timothy 3:5**). Form in the Strong's Concordance means *"semblance or a concrete formula."*

Dictionary.com defines *semblance* as:
1. outward aspect or appearance
2. an assumed or unreal appearance; show
3. the slightest appearance or trace
4. a likeness, image, or copy
5. a spectral appearance; apparition

Anyone else scared at the fact that semblance means "unreal, a show, a copy?" It is an assumption but not truth. It is the outward appearance of God, but does not have his inner nature, character, truth or substance. HELP US GOD!

Dictionary.com defines *apparition* as:
1. supernatural appearance of a person or thing, especially a ghost
2. a specter or phantom; wraith: a ghostly; manifestation
3. anything that appears, especially something remarkable or startling

This means that when the glory has departed, the church and people are engaging an apparition of God, a ghost, something that is remarkable and awe striking, but is not the Holy Ghost. It is not the Spirit of God or the presence of God. Yet because people are being enticed and even impacted by these experiences and encounters, they think it is God.

Unlike Eli, some leaders may not know the glory has left the house. They are so enthralled in the signs and wonders, that they ignore the transgressions and even the judgment that is occurring. Like Phinehas who was pregnant, things are growing even as they are dying, they think they are ok.

Some leaders like Phinehas, know the glory has departed, but they do not want to sacrifice the hard work they put into the ministry; or sacrifice the times they were walking right before God, so they just hope grace is covering them. They accept the judgment of personal death, while embracing the life that is birth from what they are doing. Phinehas died, but her seed still lived. Some leaders are spiritually dead but their ministries – there seed – gives the appearance of life and the appearance of God. The seed makes them look alive even though they are dead to God. The seed itself does not possess God and is even named in the likeness of truth of what it really is, "Ichabod," void of glory.

Some leaders like Eli, know that God is not pleased with them, and know that judgment is their portion, but they are sullen and lukewarm to God's challenges with them. They lack zeal to fear him and his judgment. They preach and even rebuke people for their transgressions. They may even apologize for their own transgressions, but there are no plans or actions that demonstrate change. These leaders may give public apologizes, preach about their transgressions, their humanness and need for change, have emotional altar calls full of people crying out about their transgressions and need for change, but there are no applicable tools implemented to change the character, nature, and behavior of the leader, the people, and the ministry. True repentance is demonstrated. This is the reason God held Eli accountable for his sons' actions. Eli did not implement anything where his sons' behaviors no longer affected God's house or swayed God's people. It is not enough to be in a ministry where there are lots of members, wealth, flowing gifts, signs and wonders. The leader and the ministry must also have the character, nature, and truth of God. When these are not present or there is no action oriented indication that these attributes are essential and being worked on, it is an Ichabod house. It has the semblance of God, but God is not in it.

> *Mark 7:21-23 Not everyone that saith unto me, Lord, Lord, shall enter into the kingdom of heaven; but he that doeth the will of my Father which is in heaven. Many will say to me in that day, Lord, Lord, have we not prophesied in thy name? and in thy name have cast out devils? and in thy name done many wonderful works? And then will I profess unto them, I never knew you: depart from me, ye that work iniquity.*

> *Luke 13:24-27 The Amplified Bible Strive to enter through the narrow door [force aside unbelief and the attractions of sin]; for many, I tell you, will try to enter [by their own works] and will not be able. Once the head of the house gets up and closes the door, and you begin to stand outside and knock on the door [again and again], saying, 'Lord, open to us!' then He will answer you, 'I do not know where you are from [for you are not of My household].' Then you will*

begin to say, 'We ate and drank in Your presence, and You taught in our streets;' but He will say to you, 'I do not know where you are from; depart from Me, all you evildoers!'

Ichabod churches are full of drama, contention, covetousness, jealousy, competition, pride, haughtiness, idolatry, witchcraft, control, manipulation, hierarchy, effeminacy, worldliness, perversion, culture dynamics that may not necessarily be sin, but for some, if they are not delivered from them, yield to sin. Ichabod churches appeal to the desires of man more than the standards and purposes of God. They justify these desires, while making them God. They do this by manipulating scriptures and giftings, where people believe what they are doing is okay and is the will of God.

In *1Samuel 2:22*, Eli's sons were sleeping with women at the door of the tabernacle of the congregation. Because they were Eli's sons, they were giving the impression that this behavior was acceptable to God even though it was a reproach against God and his tabernacle. Ichabod churches make people think it is okay to defy God and his temple. They make people think they can walk in sin, live through the standards and cultures of the world, and still do the work of the Lord. This is all an apparition – a ghostly delusion. It looks like it is God because no one is recognizing the judgment that they are all spiritually dying even though, they culturally and emotionally appear as if like they are living a Godly life.

I could go on and on about Ichabod churches, but I am going to digress and SHIFT to the next chapter, where I will discuss true glory of God versus witchcraft. This will help people discern Ichabod churches from God's true church. We must know the difference if we are going to dismantle the powers of darkness within our assemblies that cause reproach upon God, his church, and us as his people.

GLORY VERSUS WITCHRAFT

Dictionary.com states that *witchcraft* is *"the practice of magic, especially black magic; the use of spells and the invocation of spirits."* Some of the synonyms for witchcraft are *"sorcery, black magic, white magic, magic, witching, witchery, wizardry; spells, incantations; Wicca."*

Witchcraft also rebellion, stubbornness, pride, sin, idolatry, and can be anything that exalts itself about God, attempts to be God or to take the place of God.

> ***Exodus 30:7-9*** *And Aaron shall burn thereon sweet incense every morning: when he dresseth the lamps, he shall burn incense upon it. And when Aaron lighteth the lamps at even, he shall burn incense upon it, a perpetual incense before the Lord throughout your generations. Ye shall offer no strange incense thereon, nor burnt sacrifice, nor meat offering; neither shall ye pour drink offering thereon.*

The incense was a symbol of the prayers and intercession of the people going up to God as a sweet fragrance. God wanted His dwelling to be a place where people could approach Him and pray to Him. *"…for my house will be called a house of prayer for all nations"* (***Isaiah 56:7***).

> ***Psalms 141:2*** also confirm this as it declares: *May my prayer be set before you like incense; may the lifting up of my hands be like the evening sacrifice.*

> ***Roman 8:34*** contends that,*"Christ Jesus, who died — more than that, who was raised to life — is at the right hand of God and is also interceding for us."*

<u>Strange</u> is *zur* in the Hebrew and means:
1. to turn aside (especially for lodging); hence to be a foreigner, strange, profane
2. specifically (active participle) to commit adultery -- (come from) another (man, place), fanner, go away, estrange, strange, stranger

<u>Dictionary.com defines</u> *profane* <u>as:</u>
1. characterized by irreverence or contempt for God or sacred principles or things; irreligious
2. not devoted to holy or religious purposes; unconsecrated; secular (opposed to sacred)
3. unholy; heathen; pagan

4. not initiated into religious rites or mysteries, as persons
5. common or vulgar
6. to misuse (anything that should be held in reverence or respect); defile; debase; employ basely or unworthily.
7. to treat (anything sacred) with irreverence or contempt; violate the sanctity of

<u>Dictionary.com defines *fanner* as:</u>
1. to move, stir, or agitate (the air) with or as if with a fan
2. to cause air to blow upon, as from a fan; cool or refresh with or as if with a fan: He fanned his face with a newspaper
3. to stir to activity with or as if with a fan: to fan a flame; to fan emotions
4. (of a breeze, current of air, etc.) to blow upon, as if driven by a fan

This is interesting because whatever we offer unto God is released into the atmosphere. We agitate and stir the atmosphere with it. We agitate and stir God with it. If it is strange, we are contaminating the atmosphere. We could also be stirring God to anger.

We must realize is that anytime we do anything strange in our worship, to God we are committing adultery, being profane, turning away from him and have become a foreigner in his sight.

- Being in the sanctuary that we built for him does not make it holy
- Being in his presence does not make it holy
- Sacrificing it as an offering does not make it holy
- Being chosen as a priest or glory carrier does not make it holy

It is only acceptable if he has approved it as a reasonable sacrifice unto him.

> **Romans 12:1** *I beseech you therefore, brethren, by the mercies of God, that ye present your bodies a living sacrifice, holy, acceptable unto God, which is your reasonable service.*

We are quick to say that we do not engage in witchcraft, we do not serve idol Gods, we would never bow down to any other God. Yet to God, offering up strange incense is adultery, which to him is the serving of another God. When we yield to another God, even in error or ignorance, to God, it is idolatry. To serve idols is witchcraft.

> ***Romans 6:13*** *Neither yield ye your members as instruments of unrighteousness unto sin: but yield yourselves unto God, as those that are alive from the dead, and your members as instruments of righteousness unto God.*

- ❖ Members actually mean criminal intercourse
- ❖ Unrighteousness means violating law and justice, or committing a wrongful act
- ❖ Sin means to err, to make a mistake or miss the mark

Whether we mean to be inappropriate in our worship or not does not matter. If God deems it a violation of his law or what he deems just - righteous. To him it is a criminal act that violates intimacy. It is criminal intercourse.

Let's explore a couple of instances in the bible where people committed strange acts and the consequences of their actions.

> ***Numbers 3:3-4*** *These are the names of the sons of Aaron, the priests which were anointed, whom he consecrated to minister in the priest's office. And Nadab and Abihu died before the Lord, when they offered strange fire before the Lord, in the wilderness of Sinai, and they had no children: and Eleazar and Ithamar ministered in the priest's office in the sight of Aaron their father.*

The New English Bible says, "Nadab and Abihu offered unauthorized fire before God." Now these two were anointed (called) and consecrated (chosen and set apart) to minister in the office (a governmental position) as priests - as officers that governed the glory-the present of the Lord. Their position nor favor did not change God's mind about what he would receive as an offering. God did not look down and say *"oh that is Nadab, that is Abihu - they announced and set a part for this so even though they are considered dedicated for this purpose, equipped and even purified to worship and praise me – to govern my glory, I will receive whatever they present to me."*

God did not say, *"they smell strange today, but I receive it."* No, God took no thought to any of that. Nor did he take thought to the fact that they did not have kids, and no one to carry on their lineage. God judged their actions as strange, took their lives, and cut off lineage. He killed them, while making sure strange fire was cut off in this generation line.

> ***2Samuel 6:1-7*** *Again, David gathered together all the chosen men of Israel, thirty thousand. And David arose, and went with all the people that were with*

him from Baale of Judah, to bring up from thence the ark of God, whose name is called by the name of the Lord of hosts that dwelleth between the cherubims. And they set the ark of God upon a new cart, and brought it out of the house of Abinadab that was in Gibeah: and Uzzah and Ahio, the sons of Abinadab, drave the new cart. And they brought it out of the house of Abinadab which was at Gibeah, accompanying the ark of God: and Ahio went before the ark.

And David and all the house of Israel played before the Lord on all manner of instruments made of fir wood, even on harps, and on psalteries, and on timbrels, and on cornets, and on cymbals. And when they came to Nachon's threshingfloor, Uzzah put forth his hand to the ark of God, and took hold of it; for the oxen shook it. And the anger of the Lord was kindled against Uzzah; and God smote him there for his error; and there he died by the ark of God

We find David and 30,000 chosen men – acceptable men. Those seen as excellent bringing the ark of God from Judah to the house of Israel. They were in full out praise and worship that included singing, instruments, dancing, rejoicing, praise and worship. But as you read the story, the ark was being carried on a new cart. The new cart represented something fresh, something cutting edge, different and unique.

It was a chariot – a new one – fashioned for the glory and honor of God. What reasons would God not receive it? We know God love chariots, right? And we know God loves new things and new movement and witty ideas, right?

The oxen shook the ark and Uzzah reached out to stop it from falling. He was preventing the ark of the covenant from hitting the dirty ground. God became angry and struck Uzzah for his irreverence and he died in the presence of God. He died by the ark of God.

Two violations were made in this passage of scripture. The Old Testament law had rules about how the ark should be transported, which did not include the ark being carried by an ox cart. This was a violation of the Old Testament requirement that the Ark was to be carried by staves and placed upon the shoulders of the men of Levi, of the family of Kohath (***Num. 3:30-31; 4:15; 7:9; Exod. 25:14-15***). Uzzah touched the Ark. This violated ***Numbers 4:15***, which states that if the holy things are touched, the penalty is death.

When you read *Numbers 4:15*, God says that the carrying of the ark is to be a burden upon the sons of Kohath. These were the children of the Levi priest who were responsible for handling the sacred things of God.

> *Numbers 4:15 And when Aaron and his sons have made an end of covering the sanctuary, and all the vessels of the sanctuary, as the camp is to set forward; after that, the sons of Kohath shall come to bear it: but they shall not touch any holy thing, lest they die. These things are the burden of the sons of Kohath in the tabernacle of the congregation.*

The word *bear* insinuates a burden. A burden insinuates that there is a great obligation, oppression, responsibility and accountability in making sure that task is done with precision, excellence, integrity, and righteousness. It is as if that calling or task is weighing down upon you and you are humbled up under the pressure of it. Literally because the glory of God is called *Kabad* which means *weight* in the Hebrew, there should be a great burden upon us to handle the glory of God with great care.

We should be approaching the presence of God with a complete sensitivity and deep reverence. And the heavier the *Kabod* weighty glory gets, the more cautious, attentive and honoring we should become. We should also be seeking God for how to carry the glory instead of dressing the glory up and presenting it to God how we deem appropriate. To God this is not reverence, this is flesh and we know what the word says about flesh and God's glory.

> *1Corinthians 1:30 That no flesh should glory (boast) in his presence.*

> *Psalms 34:2 My soul shall make her boast in the LORD: the humble shall hear thereof, and be glad.*

<u>Boast is *halal* in the Hebrew and means:</u>
1. to be clear (orig. Of sound, but usually of color); to shine
2. to make a show, to boast; and thus to be (clamorously) foolish
3. to rave; causatively, to celebrate, to commend, (deal, make)
4. glory, give (light), be (make, feign self) mad (against), give in marriage, (sing, be worthy of) praise, rage, renowned

Even if we act like a mad man or woman in God's presence, all glory should go to him. Nothing about us should be seen or take center stage of his glory. This is the reason those who offered up strange fire died. There desires, will, and actions took precedence over God's standard. They end up being magnified as an idol god rather than serving and exalting the only true and living God.

I believe Uzzah died as an example to David and Israel that you cannot do whatever you want with the presence of God. His actions to stop the cart from hitting the ground was genuine, and David may have had good intentions when he had a new cart made for the ark, but the new cart took away from the pureness of worshipping and praising God in spirit and in truth. It made it a performance – a show. In all the excitement, the show of bringing the ark of the covenant to God's house magnified, above the reverence of God.

We think because we are not dropping dead, God is pleased with what we present to him or pleased with how we officiate his glory. It scared me when people contend a service or event was so awesome, but their lives were not transformed, and they cannot remember anything that was taught. They were emotionally impacted by the high praises, glowing lights, high pitched proclamations that provoked them to worship and praise. Yet, many have encounters with the experience, but do not have true encounters with God. We must consider the fact that if we are attending services every week and we are boasting that the glory is being poured out, if we are not changing, are we experiencing some form of spiritual death? What we consider a mighty move, God may consider strange. Strange equals no change. No change equals stagnation. Stagnation equals death.

What Is Acceptable In Worship:
- Flesh should not glory in God's presence
- We should not offer up anything to God that is new, cutting edge without asking him if it is acceptable
- We should not present anything to God that would risk us getting glory over him, or that would risk us falling into adultery, idolatry
- We should make sure what we are offering aligns with God's word and how we should bear his presence, and how we should praise and worship him
- We should not commit any vulgar or profane acts before God
- We should not commit any acts that violate his temple or that are not righteous, just, holy
- We should not offer up anything to God that would agitate God due to stirring up mixture, stickiness, confusion, grief, anger
- If it is going to dishonor God, we should not engage in it

- If God has given us direction on how to worship him, we should follow those standards, and not waver from his desires without his permissions

John 4:23-24 contends that *"Now is, when the true worshipers shall worship the Father in spirit and truth; for such people the Father seeks to be His worshipers. God is spirit, and those who worship Him must worship in spirit and truth.*

Acceptable worship, praise, and servitude, is birthed and operated through the spirit and truth of God. Anything else we experience or do is secondary. Truth and the Holy Spirit are the primary manifestations of whether we are encountering God and offering him acceptable worship. Lets' explore how to discern the presence of God.

The Glory Of God:
Has the character and identity of God. It will be important to study the word and to study God in your prayer time and interactions, so you will know his character. Having a covenant relationship with God helps us to know, value, reverence, and discern his identity and character. The glory of God can incite his:

Revelation	Correction	Deliverance
Truth	Grace	Generational Mindset
Knowledge	Mercy	His Purpose
Wisdom	Salvation	Liberty
Purity	SHIFTER	Transformation
Holiness	Transcendence	Eternal Presence & Workings
Righteousness	Weightiness	Omnipotence
Virtue	His Mind	Omniscience
Love	His Thoughts	Immanence
Goodness	His Heart	Immutability
Joy	His Emotion	Self-Existence
Peace	His Tangible Touch	Sovereignty
Kind	His Will	His Purpose
Gentle	His Tangible Touch	Anger
Conviction	His Will	Covenant Relationship

Exodus 3:14 *And God said to Moses, "I AM WHO I AM."*

Exodus 33:19 *And he said, I will make all my goodness pass before you and will proclaim before you my name 'The Lord.' And I will be gracious to whom I will be gracious, and will show mercy on whom I will show mercy.*

Psalm 37:28 *For the Lord loves justice; he will not forsake his saints. They are preserved forever, but the children of the wicked shall be cut off.*

Psalm 102:12 *But You, O Lord, shall endure forever, and the remembrance of Your name to all generations.*

Isaiah 6:3 *And one called to another and said: "Holy, holy, holy is the Lord of hosts; the whole earth is full of his glory!"*

Ephesians 2:4-5 *But God, being rich in mercy, because of the great love with which he loved us, even when we were dead in our trespasses, made us alive together with Christ – by grace you have been saved.*

Ephesians 2:8-9 *For by grace you have been saved through faith. And this is not your own doing; it is the gift of God, not a result of works, so that no one may boast.*

Hebrews 13:8 *Jesus Christ is the same yesterday and today and forever.*

Possesses his fruit of his spirit. We see people perform all kinds and wonders but their character is horrible, their ability to rightly divide the word is suspect, and their behaviors resemble the world or the devil. God's fruit is not contaminated. It will not just produce his goodness but be void of his character, nature, truth, or standard. It will have his goodness inside and out. It will produce his miracles, signs, and wonders, and have the character and substance of his identity accompanied with it. We have to stop acting like bad fruit is God or overlooking it, because we want the signs and wonders. We keep thinking we can eat the good and throw away the bad, but some people's issues are so engrossed in their ministry works, until there is no way to partake of their ministry without being contaminated and even poisoned by their issues. We are not that hard up for a word or manifestation of God that need to keep settling for a fruitless and tainted gospel. We have to start rejecting this gospel and making one another accountable to pursuing, living, manifesting, and producing the pure fruit of God.

Matthew 12:33 Either make the tree good and its fruit good, or make the tree bad and its fruit bad; for the tree is known by its fruit.

Luke 8:14-15 The seed which fell among the thorns, these are the ones who have heard, and as they go on their way they are choked with worries and riches and pleasures of this life, and bring no fruit to maturity. "But the seed in the good soil, these are the ones who have heard the word in an honest and good heart, and hold it fast, and bear fruit with perseverance.

Ephesians 5:8-11 For you were formerly darkness, but now you are Light in the Lord; walk as children of Light (for the fruit of the Light consists in all goodness and righteousness and truth), trying to learn what is pleasing to the Lord.

Galatians 5:22-23 But the fruit of the Spirit is love, joy, peace, longsuffering, gentleness, goodness, faith, meekness, temperance: against such there is no law.

Philippians 1:8-11 For God is my record, how greatly I long after you all in the bowels of Jesus Christ. And this I pray, that your love may abound yet more and more in knowledge and in all judgment; That ye may approve things that are excellent; that ye may be sincere and without offence till the day of Christ. Being filled with the fruits of righteousness, which are by Jesus Christ, unto the glory and praise of God.

Provokes a holy fear, reverence, awe, wonder, and amazement for God and who he is. We should have a holy reverence for God. We should want his presence but have a holy honor for him when his presence manifests. This holy honor should be so consuming that we are conscious and even cautious of what we do as his presence is among us, and how we respond to his presence.

1Chronicles 5:13-14 It came even to pass, as the trumpeters and singers were as one, to make one sound to be heard in praising and thanking the Lord; and when they lifted up their voice with the trumpets and cymbals and instruments of musick, and praised the Lord, saying, For he is good; for his mercy endureth for ever: that then the house was filled with a cloud, even the house of the Lord.

Psalms 22:23 You who fear the LORD, praise Him; All you descendants of Jacob, glorify Him, And stand in awe of Him, all you descendants of Israel.

Acts 2:43 Then fear came upon every soul.

Acts 3:10 They were filled with wonder and amazement at what had happened to him.

Acts 9:31 So the church throughout all Judea and Galilee and Samaria enjoyed peace, being built up; and going on in the fear of the Lord and in the comfort of the Holy Spirit, it continued to increase.

Convicts and provokes conviction. Was there a crying out for forgiveness of sins? Did it provoke a contrite and broken spirit in the people?

2Chronicles 7:14 If my people, which are called by my name, shall humble themselves, and pray, and seek my face, and turn from their wicked ways; then will I hear from heaven, and will forgive their sin, and will heal their land.

Psalms 51:17 The sacrifices of God are a broken spirit: a broken (torn, humbled, surrendered, given into birth, wrecked, broken hearted) and a contrite (crushed, collapsed, crushed to pieces) heart, O God, thou wilt not despise.

Provokes a desire for holiness and purity. Did you want to be holy like God? Holy is the founding identity of God. He desires us to be holy as he is holy. We should want our sins cleansed and to be delivered from anything that contaminates our existence.

Ephesians 5:27 That He might present her to Himself a glorious church, not having spot or wrinkle or any such thing, but that she should be holy and without blemish.

1Peter 1:15-16 But as he which hath called you is holy, so be ye holy in all manner of conversation; Because it is written, Be ye holy; for I am holy.

Titus 1:15-16 Unto the pure all things are pure: but unto them that are defiled, and unbelieving is nothing pure; but even their mind and conscience is defiled. They profess that they know God; but in works they deny him, being abominable, and disobedient, and unto every good work reprobate.

God's truth is present and received. Did truth manifest, where people desired and were literally set free.

> ***John 8:32*** *The truth will set you free.*
>
> ***John 16:13*** *Howbeit when he, the Spirit of truth, is come, he will guide you into all truth: for he shall not speak of himself; but whatsoever he shall hear, that shall he speak: and he will shew you things to come.*
>
> ***2Timothy 3:16*** *All scripture is given by inspiration of God, and is profitable for doctrine, for reproof, for correction, for instruction in righteousness.*

Provokes a desire to change and transformation. If it just felt good, but you have no desire to be different, go higher in God, or was not changed in some fashion, then you were at the glory party, but did not encounter God in the glory.

> ***2Corinthians 3:18*** *And we all, who with unveiled faces contemplate the Lord's glory, are being transformed into his image with ever-increasing glory, which comes from the Lord, who is the Spirit*
>
> ***Delight in God is evident and the focal point.*** Are you delighting in God, who he is, and what you are experiencing with God, rather than what you are feeling or wanting to feel or experience? Is your delight creating a hunger in you for more of God or for more of what you are feeling? If it is for more of God, there should be changes in you and an increase seek for him in your personal prayer, worship, and study time. If it is just a feeling, then your flesh and emotions have just become addicted to the experience of his presence. You are having an intimate exchange with the worship experience, but not with God.
>
> ***Job 22:26*** *For then you shall delight in the Almighty and will lift up your face to God.*
>
> ***Psalms 37:4*** *Delight thyself also in the LORD; and he shall give thee the desires of thine heart.*

> *Matthew 7:7 Ask and it will be given to you; seek and you will find; knock and the door will be opened to you.*

God delights in the people. Did God delight in you? God will respond to praise and worship, but that does not mean he is delighting in us. When God delights in us, an exchange occurs. Even if it is just him resting with us or upon us, we sacrifice something about ourselves, for an impartation of him.

> *Psalms 149:9 For the LORD takes pleasure in His people; He will beautify the afflicted ones with salvation.*

> *Psalms 145:19 He fulfills the desires of those who fear him; he hears their cry and saves them.*

Signs may be unique, unusual, but are pure. Were the signs strange or pure? Even if you cannot describe your encounter, can you describe something miraculous or supernatural that occurred around you? Did God's power explode and overtake the people and the service? Did someone get healed, miracles occur, signs, and wonders manifest? Did these signs appear strange, lack God's character, identity, fruit, standards of his word?

> *Acts 2:19-20 I will show wonders in heaven above and signs in the earth beneath.*

> *Acts 2:43 And many wonders and signs were done through the apostles.*

> *Acts 4:31, 33 They were all filled with the Holy Spirit and they spoke the word of God with boldness. And with great power the apostles gave witness to the resurrection of the Lord Jesus."*

> *Acts 19:11-12 Now God worked unusual miracles by the hands of Paul.*

Leaders and ministry workers possess the likeness of God. Did those conducting the ministry live, possess, and manifest the character, nature, truth, and standard of God?

> ***Genesis 1:26-27*** *And God said, Let us make man in our image, after our likeness: and let them have dominion over the fish of the sea, and over the fowl of the air, and over the cattle, and over all the earth, and over every creeping thing that creepeth upon the earth. So God created man in his own image, in the image of God created he him; male and female created he them.*
>
> ***Proverbs 8:15*** *By me (wisdom) kings reign and rulers make laws that are just.*
>
> ***Proverbs 11:14*** *For lack of guidance a nation falls, but many advisers make victory sure.*
>
> ***Proverbs 25:4,5*** *Remove the dross from silver and out comes material for the silversmith; remove the wicked from the king's presence, and his throne will be established through righteousness.*
>
> ***Proverbs 16:5 says,*** *Everyone who is arrogant in heart is an abomination to the Lord; be assured, he will not go unpunished.*
>
> ***Proverbs 16:12*** *Kings detest wrongdoing, for a throne is established through righteousness.*
>
> ***Proverbs 16:13*** *Righteous lips are the delight of a king, and he loves him who speaks what is right.*
>
> ***Proverbs 16:18*** *Pride goes before destruction, and a haughty spirit before a fall.*
>
> ***Proverbs 16:22-23*** *Good sense is a fountain of life to him who has it, but the instruction of fools is folly. The heart of the wise makes his speech judicious and adds persuasiveness to his lips.*
>
> ***Proverbs 20:8*** *When a king sits on his throne to judge, he winnows out all evil with his eyes.*
>
> ***Proverbs 20:28*** *Love and faithfulness keep a king safe; through love his throne is made secure.*

Proverbs 21:1 *A king's heart is in the hand of the Lord; he directs it like a water course wherever he pleases.*

Proverbs 29:2 *When the righteous thrive, people rejoice; when the wicked rule, people groan.*

Proverbs 29:4 *By justice a king gives a country stability, but one who is greedy for bribes tears it down.*

Proverbs 29:25 *Fear of man will prove to be a snare, but whoever trusts in the Lord is kept safe.*

Proverbs 31:4-5 *It is not for kings to drink wine; not for rules to crave beer; lest they drink and forget what the law decrees and deprive all the oppressed of their rights.*

Psalm 40:10 *I have not hidden your deliverance within my heart; I have spoken of your faithfulness and your salvation; I have not concealed your steadfast love and your faithfulness from the great congregation.*

Mathew 7:15-20 *Beware of false prophets, who come to you in sheep's clothing, but inwardly they are ravenous wolves. 16 You will know them by their fruits. Do men gather grapes from thornbushes or figs from thistles? 17 Even so, every good tree bears good fruit, but a bad tree bears bad fruit. 18 A good tree cannot bear bad fruit, nor can a bad tree bear good fruit. 19 Every tree that does not bear good fruit is cut down and thrown into the fire. 20 Therefore by their fruits you will know them.*

James 1:19 The Amplified Bible *Understand [this], my beloved brethren. Let every man be quick to hear [a ready listener], slow to speak, slow to take offense and to get angry.*

Deliverance power overthrows darkness. Did deliverance breakout? Did demons flee, or did they hang out in the service and go home with people? Did strongholds break? Did liberty come to the bound?

Mark 16:17-18 *And these signs shall follow them that believe; In my name shall they cast out devils; they shall speak with new tongues; They shall take up* serpents; and if they drink any deadly thing, it shall not hurt them; they shall lay hands on the sick, and they shall recover.

2Corinthians 3:17 *Now the Lord is that Spirit: and where the Spirit of the Lord is, there is liberty.*

Isaiah 61:1 *The Spirit of the Sovereign LORD is on me, because the LORD has anointed me to proclaim good news to the poor. He has sent me to bind up the brokenhearted, to proclaim freedom for the captives and release from darkness for the prisoners.*

The lost are saved. YAY! Was salvation available? Did people get saved, baptized, filled with the holy spirit? We should all be seeking to evangelize and bring people to church, so they can be saved.

Matthew 3:11 *As for me, I baptize you with water for repentance, but He who is coming after me is mightier than I, and I am not fit to remove His sandals; He will baptize you with the Holy Spirit and fire.*

Acts 2:47 *Praising God, and having favour with all the people. And the Lord added to the church daily such as should be saved.*

Proverbs 11:30 *The fruit of righteous is a tree of life, And he who is wise wins souls.*

Acts 2:21, 41 *"That whoever calls on the name of the Lord shall be saved."*

Prayers are answered. Were the prayers that had been continually before the Lord answered?

Matthew 7:8 *For everyone who asks receives; the one who seeks finds; and to the one who knocks, the door will be opened.*

John 15:7 *If ye abide in me, and my words abide in you, ye shall ask what ye will, and it shall be done unto you.*

Prophesy is present and confirming. Did prophecy come forth to give empowerment, direction, correction, strategy to God's people?

> ***Proverbs 3:12*** *For whom the LORD loves He reproves, even as a father corrects the son in whom he delights.*
>
> ***Hebrews 12:6*** *For whom the Lord loveth he chasteneth, and scourgeth every son whom he receiveth.* ***Sidebar:*** *Chasteneth means to train up, instruct, educate, discipline, teach, learn, punish, judge, mold the character of*
>
> ***Daniel 12:3*** *"Those who have insight will shine brightly like the brightness of the expanse of heaven, and those who lead the many to righteousness, like the stars forever and ever.*
>
> ***Acts 2:1-4*** *And when the day of Pentecost was fully come, they were all with one accord in one place. And suddenly there came a sound from heaven as of a rushing mighty wind, and it filled all the house where they were sitting. And there appeared unto them cloven tongues like as of fire, and it sat upon each of them. And they were all filled with the Holy Ghost, and began to speak with other tongues, as the Spirit gave them utterance.*

Vision enlightenment manifests. Did visions manifest that further produced revelation, deliverance and healing? Was the service vision and ministry vision further enlightened, empowered or advanced?

> ***Acts 2:17*** *And it shall come to pass in the last days, saith God, I will pour out of my Spirit upon all flesh: and your sons and your daughters shall prophesy, and your young men shall see visions, and your old men shall dream dreams.*
>
> ***Ephesians 1:18*** *The eyes of your understanding being enlightened; that ye may know what is the hope of his calling, and what the riches of the glory of his inheritance in the saints.*
>
> ***Exuberance overrides depression and sullenness.*** Did praise, favor, an unexplainable joy or gladness manifest? Did great celebration overtake the people, ministry, and even the region?

Isaiah 61:1-3 *The Spirit of the Lord God is upon me; because the Lord hath anointed me to preach good tidings unto the meek; he hath sent me to bind up the brokenhearted, to proclaim liberty to the captives, and the opening of the prison to them that are bound; To proclaim the acceptable year of the Lord, and the day of vengeance of our God; to comfort all that mourn; To appoint unto them that mourn in Zion, to give unto them beauty for ashes, the oil of joy for mourning, the garment of praise for the spirit of heaviness; that they might be called trees of righteousness, the planting of the Lord, that he might be glorified.*

Acts 2:47 *Praising God and having favor with all the people.*

Acts 8:4-8 New International Bible *Those who had been scattered preached the word wherever they went. 5 Philip went down to a city in Samaria and proclaimed the Messiah there. 6 When the crowds heard Philip and saw the signs he performed, they all paid close attention to what he said. 7 For with shrieks, impure spirits came out of many, and many who were paralyzed or lame were healed. 8 So there was great joy in that city.*

The supernatural becomes natural. Did people have encounters inside the supernatural realms? The supernatural though unique, is not spooky. It does not incite confusion or fear, but draws people to God and his spirit.

Amos 3:7 *Surely the Lord GOD will do nothing, but he revealeth his secret unto his servants the prophets.*

Acts 8:37-39 *Then Philip said, "If you believe with all your heart, you may." And he answered and said, "I believe that Jesus Christ is the Son of God." So he commanded the chariot to stand still. And both Philip and the eunuch went down into the water, and he baptized him. Now when they came up out of the water, the Spirit of the Lord caught Philip away, so that the eunuch saw him no more; and he went on his way rejoicing. But Philip was found at Azotus. And passing through, he preached in all the cities till he came to Caesarea.*

Ephesians 6:12 *For we wrestle not against flesh and blood, but against principalities, against powers, against the rulers of the darkness of this world, against spiritual wickedness in high [places].*

Hebrews 1:14 *Are they not all ministering spirits, sent forth to minister for them who shall be heirs of salvation?*

> *1Corinthians 14:23 For God is not the author of confusion, but of peace, as in all churches of the saints.*

Provision is prevalent. Did supernatural provision or generous giving manifest? Did people give cheerfully rather than being manipulated and seduced to give? Sometimes offerings multiply when the glory of God is present. God will also provide strategy to get wealth or resolve matters while the glory is present.

> *Acts 2:45-47 And sold their possessions and goods, and parted them to all men, as every man had need. And they, continuing daily with one accord in the temple, and breaking bread from house to house, did eat their meat with gladness and singleness of heart. Praising God, and having favour with all the people. And the Lord added to the church daily such as should be saved.*

> *1Corinthians 9:7 Every man according as he purposeth in his heart, so let him give; not grudgingly, or of necessity: for God loveth a cheerful giver.*

> *Philippians 4:9 And my God will supply all your needs according to His riches in glory in Christ Jesus.*

Angels are drawn into the midst. Sometimes angels manifest and aide in the work of God, minister with the saints unto God, or just enjoy the presence of God.

> *Psalms 34:7 The angel of the LORD encampeth round about them that fear him, and delivereth them.*

> *Acts 5:17-19 But at night an angel of the Lord opened the prison doors and brought them out.*

Resurrection power occurs. Was the dead raise? Were dead visions and destinies raised? Where spiritually dead people raised? Was physically dead people raised?

Matthew 8:10 Heal the sick, cleanse the lepers, raise the dead, cast out devils: freely ye have received, freely give.

John 14:12 Verily, verily, I say unto you, He that believeth on me, the works that I do shall he do also; and greater works than these shall he do; because I go unto my Father.

Acts 9:36-37, 40 And she opened her eyes, and when she saw Peter she sat up.

Godly truth and biblical teaching and preaching will provoke God's presence. Was the presence provoked out of God's word, divine exhortation, or cleaver enticing words, witchcraft words, or words that appeal more to your desires or needs than God's will and purposes for your life and the lives of those in the services?

Acts 10:44-46 The Holy Spirit fell upon all those who heard the word.

Mark 16:20 And they went forth, and preached every where, the Lord working with them, and confirming the word with signs following. Amen.

1Corinthians 2:4 And my speech and my preaching was not with enticing words of man's wisdom, but in demonstration of the Spirit and of power.

God's glory continually increases. There are no high places in the presence and experiences of God. God operates in a constant upward momentum and elevation. He is always outdoing himself. His presence and fruit of the glory becomes stronger and stronger and more powerful, as he is worshipped, praised, proclaimed, provoked, empowered, imparted, and established.

Haggai 2:9 The glory of this latter temple shall be greater than the former.

2Corinthians 3:18 And we all, who with unveiled faces contemplate the Lord's glory, are being transformed into his image with ever-increasing glory, which comes from the Lord, who is the Spirit.

God's presence draws people to the ministry. As the ministry grows and matures, are people joining and helping to carry the vision of the ministry? Is this growth because of the presence, teachings, conviction, exaltation, and wellness of God, rather than the idolatry of man or emotional camaraderie due to similar experiences of woundedness or mantles and callings?

> ***Isaiah 60:2*** *For behold, the darkness shall cover the earth, and deep darkness the people; but the Lord will arise over you. And His glory will be seen upon you.*

> ***John 12:32*** *And I, if I be lifted up from the earth, will draw all men unto me.*

Community and fellowship in love is present. Is there a desire to continually attend church and fellowship among the saints while growing in God evident?

> ***Acts 2:42*** *And they continued steadfastly in the apostles' doctrine and fellowship, in the breaking of bread, and in prayers.*

> ***Acts 2:46*** *So continuing daily with one accord in the temple, and breaking bread from house to house.*

> ***Acts 6:4*** *But we will give ourselves continually to prayer and to the ministry of the word.*

Above all, the character, identity, nature, truth, and standards of God is everything. If you are continually questioning leadership, the experiences of the ministry, and have a constant check in your spirit regarding what is occurring, trust your Holy Ghost radar and seek God as to whether you should leave or stop associating with that leader or ministry. It is better to be in a ministry where you have peace, rest, and safety in your spirit, than to be in one where you are constantly on guard regarding what you should and should not partake of in that ministry. Ichabod wants you to remain in its void. Doing so prevents you from journeying in the truth, destiny, wellness, and sustaining success of God. Reject Ichabod and pursue God's true leaders and ministries. SHIFT!

CULT LIKE BEHAVIORS IN MINISTRIES

I entitled this chapter "cult like behaviors" so that people and ministries would consider this revelation as a caution and avoid such tactics. The concept of cult like behaviors occur within ministries and are perceived as God. Yet, they have no real biblical truth, they are measured truth, or they are biblical principles used incorrectly. Commonly, the concepts we will discuss in this chapter are used because of the needs and mandates of the ministry, the drive for success and advancement, familiarity of erred doctrines being passed from ministry to ministry or if it was God's will in one instance, we build a high place out of it and make it a doctrine that people must become obedient to. I say this because most leaders and ministries do not desire to be a cult or to become a cult. Many may be unaware they are operating in occult behaviors. And then there are some leaders and ministries that have become their own God, and though they may deny it as most cults do, their doctrines and behaviors radiate the evidence of a cult.

Kingdom Shifters Ministries Team Definition
Cult is defined as a group of people knowingly or unknowingly locked into a set of self-made ideologies, rules, regulations, or submitting to certain people or persons for the sake of an idolatrous doctrine, system, or set vision. This doctrine, system or vision appears to be sacred, God designed, or God led, but is rooted, grounded, and guided by erred philosophies, misperceptions regarding God, or idolatrous gods.

The concepts of cult like behaviors are as followed:

- Leaders are idolized, worshiped, exalted above God or in the place of God. There is no balance between honor for the leader and God being supreme in the person's life.
- Members do not have their own identities aside from that of the leader and/or ministry.
- Disempowering and degrading preaching, teaching, and counsel utilized within the ministry, strips people of their identity, while rebuilding them as clones.
- Gimmicks are used to entice people to the ministry. These gimmicks are usually connected to an emotional need, void, desire, hopes, or brokenness within a person, yet there is no true power and liberty of the Holy Spirit to sustainably deliver and heal people. People are healed just enough to feel

obligated and grateful to the ministry, but not enough where their lives are completely transformed to live without the leader or ministry.
- Flattery, mesmerism, and seduction are used to draw people then once they connect, rebuke and chastisement is used to keep people bound to the leader and ministry.
- Members are controlled or manipulated by leadership and ruled by intimidation, religious fear tactics, threats, and condemnation.
- The leader and departmental heads program and groom people by constantly dictating to them how they should think, feel, or act. People in turn do these things out of obligation and duty rather than relationship with God.
- Members are bound to secret oaths, covenants, false loyalties that may have a measure of biblical truth, but are erred and rooted in control and manipulation.
- Strict doctrines and religious policies solidify the control and manipulation of the people where they feel it is God's will to follow these principles.
- Members are seduced into giving their money and time to the ministry. If they give money and time to other endeavors, they are sinning or out of the will of God.
- Offerings are tied to religious hustling tactics rooted in the misguided biblical principles regarding giving. People are made to feel like they must give to get from God, and their generosity is a determinate to their own salvation, protection, blessing, wealth, and advancement.
- Sacrificing one's last is placed above being a responsible steward of one's finances, family, and household (*1Corinthians 4:2*). It is one thing if God leads you to give your last, it is a whole other thing if this is a religious doctrine consistently used to swindle you out your money. In the bible, when saints gave their all to the church, the material goods and finances were distributed where each person and household was cared for. No one lacked. If the ministry is hustling you for your last where you lack, and they cannot help you, that is not a Godly principle, that is cult like behavior. Whether intentional or unintentional you are being used for the personal gain of the ministry or leader with no regard to your own personal needs and responsibilities (Study *Acts 2-4*). Giving should be done cheerfully and can also be done through the leading of the Lord. If you are helping to advance the vision of a ministry, God may instill within you a responsibility to give. However, you should never give out of obligation or manipulation. God may unction you to give, but he will not seduce you to give. Study the

principles of tithes and offering in the Old and New Testament. Ask God to give you his revelation regarding giving and how to give.
- Unreasonable and ungodly demands are placed upon people that advance a manmade agenda rather than advancing the kingdom of God.
- People are made to feel like they cannot hear or experience God outside of the leader or ministries' guidance.
- Spooky spiritual and flighty experiences and revelation are regarded above practical biblical principles and standards. People are given the impression they are not saved or spiritually mature if they are not having super spiritual encounters with God. These encounters feed the flesh and emotions and have minimal spiritual relevance or transformation power.
- Members feel like or are given the impression that the ministry is the only true God ordained ministry. All others are not of God's design or do not compare to this ministry.
- Members endure sexual, emotional, and physical abuse that is linked to the twisting of scripture, so it is perceived as God's will, and/or a form of purification, rectitude, or judgment.
- Sex with the leader is viewed as a spiritual honor, and a Godly duty or sacrifice.
- Generational abuse and the brain washing of children is utilized to control the lineages of families.
- Questioning leadership and the vision of the church is prohibited and viewed as ungodly.
- The leader does not apologize or correct erred behavior and may even justify his/her actions through the misuse of scripture. The leader may justify their actions with no regard that they are held to a higher standard than the average saint. They will continuously use this concept to excuse discrepancies, and the fact that they are not dedicated, mature and responsible enough to lead God's people (See ***James 3:1, John 3:30, Hebrews 13:7, 1Timothy 3:2-12, 1Peter 5:1-4***).
- Pride is just as potent in the leader as their spiritual gifts and anointing.
- People are more seduced by the anointing on the leader's life than they are transformed by it. The anointing is awe striking and appears to be life changing, but is witchcraft and magic as the gifts and anointing is void of God's complete transformation power. People are wowed, feel a sense of empowerment and measured deliverance, but are not fully transformed. People measure fruit by the gifts and anointing. God measures fruit by the person's ability to be productive, to produce, and reproduce what was imparted into them. This fruit should not only have the resemblance of God

and his kingdom, it should possess the DNA of God and his kingdom – his essence. You shall know them by their fruits (See *Matthew 7:14-24*).
- Promotion and utilization within the ministry is dependent on your loyalty to leadership and the religious doctrines than being empowered, equipped, and released in who you are in God.
- Respect of persons and favoritism is evident as people who are inordinately submissive are provided more opportunities for growth and advancement.
- Members are promised and preached elevation, equipping, and release, but are really pew members and ministry numbers used as false measuring rods of religious growth and God's hand being upon the ministry.
- The ministry provides goods and services to members then makes them feel indebted to God, the leader, and the ministry.
- A person's growth is attributed to the leader and the ministry with no regard to that person's personal relationship with God, their personal study or pursuit for growth, and the destiny and calling that is upon their life.
- People are given the impression they cannot reach destiny without the leader and the ministry.
- Male dominant hierarchy is prevalent. Men are empowered and provided ministry opportunities, while women are disempowered or only provided measured opportunities or no opportunities at all. Women tend to be shunned and put in their place quickly when demonstrating that they have gifts and anointing comparable or even greater than men.
- Women are made to feel like or told they are not to have their own ministries, operate in leadership roles, or that their role is behind the man or behind the scenes.
- Certain apparel dictates salvation and holiness. People are shunned, shamed, rebuked and chastised if they do not comply to certain rules and regulations that are more religious control than adhering to Godly modesty.
- People feel like or are given the impression that they cannot leave a ministry and if they do leave are shamed, defamed, ostracized and/or physically harmed.
- People feel hopeless or out of the will of God if they leave, and feel that they should stay to please God and to reach destiny.
- People feel like or are given the impression that if they leave a ministry they have backslid, betrayed the people and that ministry, and/or disobeyed God.
- People feel like or are given the impression that if they exposed challenges they had regarding a leader or a ministry, then they are cursing or

dishonoring that leader or ministry, and will be judged for "*touching the anointed*" of God.
- Members feel like or are told they cannot socialize with people outside the ministry.
- People feel like or are given the impression that if they partake of training outside of the ministry they are defiant, a renegade, disloyal, a sinner.
- Members are isolated from their family, friends, and even society.
- Family and friends are given the impression or told they cannot communicate with those who leave the ministry.
- There is a constant impression and fear that the end times are near and supreme loyalty is essential to going with Jesus when he returns.

As churches and ministries, it is important that we cleanse these concepts and behaviors out of our ministries and interactions with one another. We must remain aware of these cult like behaviors so we can annihilate them when they begin to manifest in our midst. We do not want to give any room to the enemy in misrepresenting our fellowship and ministries as cults. Though we must honor God's standards for holiness, excellence, and divine order, we must also respect people's Godly right to free will and choice. SHIFT!

THE DIFFERENCE BETWEEN OFFENSE VERSUS CHURCH ABUSE

Oftentimes, people will experience offense within a church and contend they were abused. Though abuse causes offense, not all offensive experiences constitute abuse. Both are transgressions against a person, and if unrepentant, a transgression against themselves and against God. Yet, the Bible lets us know that offenses will occur. We are subject to offense because of our emotional and soulish nature, unique identities, and tendency to have different perceptions regarding matters. We may become offended, but we are not to remain offended. How we handle offense determines whether we have yielded to sin or not and even whether we subject ourselves and others to behaviors of abuse. Abuse should never occur. Abuse is idolatrous in nature. Whether intentional or unintentional, it is a self-absorbed act that seeks to please self. Abuse lets us know that something foreign has entered our emotions and souls, and has sought to reign through us where it becomes our nature.

Offense is a transgression. Offense means *"to step over the line, knowingly or unknowingly violate a law or moral standard, breech or break a covenant, vow, or boundary."* Offense causes anger, resentment, aggression, vexation, bitterness, contempt, hatred, mistrust, hurt and pain. Offenses can trap, ensnare, and be a stumbling block, where one yields to sin, fall into sin, or backslide.

> ***Luke 17:1-4*** *Then He said to the disciples, "It is impossible that no offenses should come, but woe to him through whom they do come! It would be better for him if a millstone were hung around his neck, and he were thrown into the sea, than that he should offend one of these little ones. Take heed to yourselves. If your brother sins against you, rebuke him; and if he repents, forgive him. And if he sins against you seven times in a day, and seven times in a day returns to you, saying, 'I repent,' you shall forgive him."*

> ***The Amplified Bible*** *And [Jesus] said to His disciples, Temptations (snares, traps set to entice to sin) are sure to come, but woe to him by or through whom they come! It would be more profitable for him if a millstone were hung around his neck and he were hurled into the sea than that he should cause to sin or be a snare to one of these little ones [lowly in rank or influence]. Pay attention and always be on your guard [looking out for one another]. If your brother sins (misses the mark), solemnly tell him so and reprove him, and if he repents (feels sorry for having sinned), forgive him. And even if he sins against you seven times in a day, and turns to you seven times and says, I repent [I am sorry], you*

must forgive him (give up resentment and consider the offense as recalled and annulled).

This passage of scripture lets us know that it is impossible to avoid offenses. As we fellowship and advance the kingdom together, we should be looking out for one another. We should care for one another so that we do not cause others to be offended. We must seek to resolve offenses when they occur. The word "*woe*" reveals that offenses can be painful, grievous, afflicting, and troubling. The word "*woe*" places us on alert to be mindful of offenses and to resolve them quickly, as they have dire consequences.

Abuse is a transgression, while violating moral laws and standards, and breaching our spiritual covenant with God and each other. Abuse means, "*to wrongly or improperly misuse, injure, harm, deceive, insult, mislead someone.*" Abuse is "*corrupt, revile, and harsh.*" Abuse can occur physically, emotionally, sexually, or spiritually. It has no care for another person. It is self-focused in its intent, focus, and action.

> **2Timothy 3:1-8** *This know also, that in the last days perilous times shall come. For men shall be lovers of their own selves, covetous, boasters, proud, blasphemers, disobedient to parents, unthankful, unholy, without natural affection, trucebreakers, false accusers, incontinent, fierce, despisers of those that are good, Traitors, heady, highminded, lovers of pleasures more than lovers of God; Having a form of godliness, but denying the power thereof: from such turn away. For of this sort are they which creep into houses, and lead captive silly women laden with sins, led away with divers lusts, ever learning, and never able to come to the knowledge of the truth. Now as Jannes and Jambres withstood Moses, so do these also resist the truth: men of corrupt minds, reprobate concerning the faith.*

Blasphemers in this passage of scripture is *blasphemos* in the Hebrew and although it means to be grossly and obscenely abusive towards God, and to have a lack of reverence for God and religious practices, it also means to be slanderous, malicious, disrespectful, and abusive towards another person. We also discern that whether this has become the nature or the disposition of a person, the entire eighth verse defines the posture of an abuser. We should never be controlling, oppressive, demoralizing, or self-indulged, where we take advantage of those we oversee or fellowship with. Such behavior is not of God or the design for his church. It is an idolatrous counterfeit where we have become our own master. We are seeking to please self rather than pleasing God and esteeming our fellowman.

> *1Peter 5:2-3 Feed the flock of God which is among you, taking the oversight thereof, not by constraint, but willingly; not for filthy lucre, but of a ready mind; Neither as being lords over God's heritage, but being ensamples to the flock.*

> *Jeremiah 5:30-31 The Amplified Bible An appalling and horrible thing [bringing desolation and destruction] has come to pass in the land: The prophets prophesy falsely, and the priests exercise rule at their own hands and by means of the prophets. And My people love to have it so! But what will you do when the end comes?*

> *Jeremiah 6:13-15 For from the least of them even unto the greatest of them everyone is given to covetousness; and from the prophet even unto the priest everyone dealeth falsely. They have healed also the hurt of the daughter of my people slightly, saying, Peace, peace; when there is no peace. Were they ashamed when they had committed abomination? nay, they were not at all ashamed, neither could they blush: therefore they shall fall among them that fall: at the time that I visit them they shall be cast down, saith the Lord.*

Some leaders and saints can be abusive, and some churches have taken on an abusive nature. This does not mean that every offensive experience within a church is abuse. Some offenses can be resolved through effective communication and a willingness to change. We must learn to separate offensive experiences from true church abuse, so we can adequately address, be delivered, and heal from church hurts.

When you remain in offense, the scripture says the offense is like a millstone necklace hanging around your neck.

> *Luke 17:2 It would be better for him if a millstone were hung around his neck, and he were thrown into the sea, than that he should offend one of these little ones.*

A millstone necklace is a heavy emotional or mental burden or hardship that physically feels like a humongous stone.

This stone is so large that you fall into the sea and go straight to the bottom.

The millstone is heavy and cannot float. You are not able to remove it, or swim back up to the top with it around your neck, therefore, you drown. In this case, you drown in the offense. If you are drowning, you are suffocating. You are also rendered inaudible because you cannot talk underwater. You are holding your breath, so you do not die, yet, you are being drained of your life and ability to express your thoughts and feelings effectively, to live life effectively, and to walk with God effectively. His voice in you has been cut off as everything about you is immersed and filtered through offense. **I believe this is the reason people deem some of their experiences as abuse, because the millstone of offense is strangling them.** In cases where no true abuse occurred, but just conflicts that caused offense, they are abusing themselves rather than being abused by leaders, saints or the church. **The refusal to rectify the offense has**

become abuse – a millstone around their neck that has drug them to a place of helplessness and hopelessness where they are drowning in negativity. *"Woe unto offense."* I believe this is also the reason why those who leave the church offended are so negative towards leaders, saints, and the church. The millstone has them stuck in the trauma of their experience. They cannot see past what they are submerged in. The abuse of the millstone becomes the abuse they operate in. Help Us Lord! *"Woe unto offense."*

I in no way want to negate abuse within the church so let's take some time to explore the realities of church abuse. **I believe church abuse is when the millstone of offense has been placed around the neck of a person by the offender – the leader, saint, church doctrine – church system – thus abusing the victim.** The millstone necklace has postured the person in a place of control, oppression, degradation, torment, and even death. The person has been forced to submit to idolatry where they become loyal to the voice and powers of the leader, saint, doctrine, or system, rather than God. The person is stripped of their innocence, purity, identity, covenant with God and the healthy covenant they are to have with their offender. Everything becomes a counterfeit as they are suppressed in a false covenant with the abuser.

In *Jeremiah 5 and 6*, God calls church abuse appalling, horrible, covetous, disgusting, and abominable.

> *Jeremiah 5:30-31 The Amplified Bible An appalling and horrible thing [bringing desolation and destruction] has come to pass in the land: The prophets prophesy falsely, and the priests exercise rule at their own hands and by means of the prophets. And My people love to have it so! But what will you do when the end comes?*
>
> *Jeremiah 6:13-15 For from the least of them even unto the greatest of them everyone is given to covetousness; and from the prophet even unto the priest everyone dealeth falsely. They have healed also the hurt of the daughter of my people slightly, saying, Peace, peace; when there is no peace. Were they ashamed when they had committed abomination? nay, they were not at all ashamed, neither could they blush: therefore they shall fall among them that fall: at the time that I visit them they shall be cast down, saith the Lord.*

The abusive church appears to have his will and purpose at heart, but this is a lie. God is not in it and God is not pleased. This is where we must recognize God's true church from false churches. We keep equating these idolatrous leaders, people, and ministries with God. However, when we or our vision give into a character and nature contrary to God, we are no longer representing him. We can claim that we are his, we are advancing his kingdom, we are establishing his purpose in the earth, but we are just fooling ourselves and one another. God is not fooled and will not take responsibility for our mess. We have become an enemy of God and have positioned ourselves to be judged by him.

In *Jeremiah 5:31*, God is appalled that the people love this idolatry – this abuse. He lets us know that the judgment of such a house is not good. In *Jeremiah 6:14*, God is appalled at his daughters – his beloved – being taken advantage of and made to seem like they are being healed, when really, they are being ravaged and trifled over. Though God wants us to be delivered from offense, he does not want us to remain in abusive relationships, abusive churches, abusive doctrines, and abusive systems. In these situations, separation from these people and entities are good and necessary. As God heals us, we should seek to be restored with his true leaders and his true church.

Church abuse is unfathomable and depending on the experience, it can take some time to overcome these painful experiences. Jesus however, has a cure to break the millstone. Forgiveness is the cure for offense.

> *Luke 17:1-4* Then He said to the disciples, "It is impossible that no offenses should come, but woe to him through whom they do come! It would be better for him if a millstone were hung around his neck, and he were thrown into the sea, than that he should offend one of these little ones. Take heed to yourselves. If your brother sins against you, rebuke him; and if he repents, forgive him. And if he sins against you seven times in a day, and seven times in a day returns to you, saying, 'I repent,' you shall forgive him.

This word *forgive* in this passage of scripture means "*to remit, depart, divorce.*" Divorce is a contract that is legal and binding. When you divorce offense, you are literally divorcing the sin that you did and/or that was done against you, while choosing to fall out of agreement with being offended. Any conscious, emotional, and justifiable contract you had with being offended is relinquished by your choice to breech the transgression with forgiveness, and revoke its authority to lord over and between you and that person. Though some abusive experiences can be addressed with the offender, most of them can be taken care of with God alone. When Jesus was crucified and rose again, he rectified some situations with those that offended him such as Peter (*John 21:13-*

18) and Thomas (*John 20:24-26*), but he did not appear to those who abused him on the cross. You may not be able to have a resolution meeting with your abuser, but you can still forgive, release the millstone, and be healed through your relationship with God.

> *Matthew 11:28-30 Come unto me, all ye that labour and are heavy laden, and I will give you rest. Take my yoke upon you, and learn of me; for I am meek and lowly in heart: and ye shall find rest unto your souls. For my yoke is easy, and my burden is light.*

Resist remaining bound to the millstone of abuse, and equating God's true church and leaders to an idolatrous counterfeit. He has need of you, loves you, and never wants you in bondage to abuse and wickedness. SHIFT!

Healing Activation:
1. Examine whether you have truly experienced church abuse or offense.
2. Examine whether the offense has become a millstone around your neck. Journal the effects of this, and what you learned from this chapter regarding the consequences of a millstone.
3. If you have experienced offense, explore with God whether it is necessary or even possible to have a conflict resolution meeting with the person you had the challenge with. Do as the Lord leads concerning this situation.
4. If this is a church abuse experience, seek a Christian Counselor or a mature leader to help you explore with God on how to handle the situation.
    a. Some abusive situations may require legal action where the authorities are involved. A Christian Counselor or mature leader will be able to assist you if this is what God is leading you to do.
    b. Even if legal matters are not considered or necessary, a process to deliverance and wholeness is necessary. A Christian Counselor or mature leader will be able to assist you in acquiring the proper strategies from God, while keeping you accountable as you process to wholeness.
5. Here are some suggestions should you seek healing without the assistance of a counselor or leader.
    a. Divorce the spirit of offense.
    b. Break any spiritual, mental or emotional covenants made with offense.
    c. Forgive your offender. You may have to spend time in prayer working out your thoughts and feelings with God where true

forgiveness occurs. Keep going before God until you know you have forgiven and the millstone of offense is annihilated.

d. Use the hammer of God to break every millstone necklace.
e. Cast out any drowning or suffocation spirits that may have attached themselves to you, and spend time decreeing healing restoration to your heart, soul, mind, and spirit.
f. Depending on the experience, offense can be threefold - against the person, against God, against the situation or church body. Assess yourself before God concerning where your offense resides and deal accordingly with offense. Break the two or threefold cord if necessary, cast out all demonic spirits of offense, and allow God to heal every focused area of offense.
g. Cancel every way your voice, ministry, and destiny has been cut off in the spirit and the natural, and assert your authority and right to be who God has ordained you to be, and how he desires you to connect and serve in his true church body.

HINDERANCES TO RECONCILIATION

The major reasons people resist reconciling and returning to church is:
- ✓ Rejection and fear of rejection
- ✓ Fear that there will be no change
- ✓ Being traumatized and angry to the point of rebellion and refusing to assimilate

When a person is dealing with issues of rejection, they are already in a place of separation before they even begin trying to integrate with another person or entity. They have already ostracized and separated themselves. Even when interacting, they have a wall up or they are engaging from a posture of an outsider. This is because the person has been wounded, has lost faith, is untrusting, is insecure, and thus inadequacy or brokenness has hindered their ability to connect or fear connecting. They therefore, self-reject to protect themselves from being rejected again.

The rejected person is seeking to be validated and justified regarding their wounds. They may attempt to get their needs met for approval and belonging through their giftings and calling, rather than initially trying to truly connect with people or the ministry. Sometimes, the person maybe on a mission to instill change in areas where they have been hurt or violated. They may appear prideful regarding their gifts, ideas, and perceptions. Much of this pride is really a false confidence rooted in a heart not to be hurt again, or to see others hurt by the world, but especially within the church. The challenge with this is, most churches do not acknowledge church hurt, nor are they discerning of those attempting to be reconciled and restored to the church. People who are hurt by the church do not reveal their challenges when they initially seek to give the church another try. And if they do, it is with the main pastor who they may have little to no contact with compared to other department heads and saints of that ministry. Because church hurt is not acknowledged and because there is no spiritual exploration to discern the underlying root of challenging behaviors and situations that occur with those who are not new converts, these people end up being re-offended. Their rejection is reaffirmed as they are given the impression that they are not valued, do not belong, and the church is no different than the world.

As hurtful challenges within the church have become more exposed and prevalent, and as the world is moving farther away from God and biblical standards, people fear being associated with the church. They fear the church will not change and they fear the church is a false system that only seeks to deceive and take from them. Many are traumatized and angry to the point of rebellion and refusing to assimilate. Though there may be some truth to this regarding some people and some churches that are in error, mixture, or are false churches, this is not the truth of the entire body of Christ. It is also important to note that as the world separates more and more from biblical principles, the persecution of the saints and God's church will increase. But holiness does not mean hypocrite. Holiness will always be the standard of God and his church regardless to who exemplifies it or not.

To dissolve the fears regarding reconciling with the church, we must acknowledge the damage hurtful challenges the church has caused, that false and abusive churches have caused, and seek to heal people from these experiences. We cannot keep demanding people change their wicked ways and return to God, yet presenting them with a people and a system that refuse to examine their flaws and pursue transformation. As we admit that we need to address the issues of church hurt and begin to deal with them, people will be more apt to forgive the church, be delivered of their trauma and anger, and consider assimilating again with God's true church. I decree we the body of Christ will become the example of the change we are requiring others to achieve. SHIFT!

SPIRITUAL STOCKHOLM SYNDROME
KIDNAPPED DESTINIES
By: Reenita Keys
Kingdom Shifters Ministries, Muncie, Indiana

There are various saints in the body of Christ who are finding themselves in toxic relationships that involve people, places, or things. It is very common to find ourselves so consumed with the excitement around us that we fail to see the ungodly altars set within our soul. We will continue to feed these ungodly soulties until something goes wrong. Allowing the success of ministries, leadership, or churches to dictate your discernment is a dangerous place. It will cause you to idolize and exalt unhealthy relationships above the name of the Lord unknowingly.

There have been certain movements in this day and age where people find themselves bandwagoning the words of modern-day influences. Bandwagoning will cause you to latch onto leaders, rather than hearing the voice of the Lord for yourself. Do not allow excitement to sift your discernment as wheat. Countless souls fail to recognize the subtle seduction that takes place when they are under the influence of bewitchment. We should continuously aim to destroy places of relational seduction in our soul that causes us to measure our decisions with the feeling of wanting to belong. Leadership seduction will cause an alternative SHIFT to come upon our lives that will ultimately dig our graves and lay our true identity and destiny to rest. This type of seduction in ministry will call you into the bedchambers setting out to birth carbon copies of demonic seed. Inordinancy will cause you to be an erected replica of the ungodly shrine created in your heart for the leader. With each impartation that takes place, you are only getting a quick fix, while conducting your funeral by dismissing intricate - unique places that God knit inside of you. It is imperative to allow the Holy Spirit to mold you rather than the hand of man.

Placing complete faith in the hands of man will position your destiny to be hijacked and abducted. Seductive leaders will claim to be a mirroring image of Jesus Christ. In reality, they are utilizing your gift and calling as a footstool to overstep healthy boundaries. Innocent lives are led astray when they are looking for leaders, ministries, and churches to fulfill voids only God can heal. In today's society, it is effortless to get your needs met with the rapid growth of social media and technology. Those who are wounded want a sense of belonging, even if the abuser beats them countless times. Pew members who know they are to leave become battered men and women who are punched by the hand of defilement because they are bound to their abuser.

The Lord revealed to me that there are sheep in the body of Christ who are hurting by the hands of shepherds they trusted. Although these sheep are aware of the abuse, they have knitted an emotional soultie with the abuser. The Lord went to identify this cycle of spiritual violence as "Spiritual Stockholm Syndrome." If you are unaware of Stockholm Syndrome, it is a psychological complex that stems from a traumatic frightening situation. It is defined as a coping pattern where hostages bond emotionally with their captor. When this happens, the person taken hostage has positive feelings towards their controller. Those held captive, no longer want to be saved, and will have negative feelings towards authorities, friends, or family trying to fight for their release. Hostages will support and justify the behavior of the person abusing and controlling them. In certain cases, the stronghold is so strong that it creates a trust deep enough to send the hostage out publicly to recruit more potential hostages. We have people like this in the body of Christ that go to unhealthy, dead, and even abusive churches. Yet, they recruit others to submit under this unhealthy covering.

Those who suffer from Spiritual Stockholm Syndrome will sit in the pew week after week justifying the abuse of their leader. Although members are dying spiritually, their false sense of loyalty will keep them bound. Psychologically, they have entered a slave mentality that is set up by a demonic system to sabotage their advancements. The enemy will tell them that they are going to be shunned, cast into the pit of hell, be viewed as rebellious, and will regret their decision. Staying at a church just because they have "phenomenal worship" is not a good excuse to stay in a place where God's presence is not dwelling in the actions or behaviors of the leadership. This does not make you any different than a battered man or woman who takes prescription pills, drugs, and alcohol just so the abuse does not feel "as bad." When you are choosing to stay in this place, you are jeopardizing each business, prophetic word, ministry, opportunity, and many more things the Lord has in store for you. Even if the ministry, church, or platform is well-known around the world does not make it a God decision. Any connection that you are submitting to outside of the will of the Lord has the potential to kidnap your destiny. Selah.

WOULDA SHOULDA COULDA
DEALING WITH REGRETS

Church hurt is baffling. You are trying to process how this could happen, how can people still stay and support this, how can there be no conviction or compassion for your hurt, how can a Godly people do this, why did you not see it sooner, how did you get into this situation, how could God let you experience this, not wanting to miss the lesson, fears of the future, fears of whether the pain will ever stop and on and on. It is all hitting you at once, along with the principalities and powers that have ganged around you in the spirit realm.

As you process towards healing with God, a lot of *"woulda, shoulda, couldas"* manifest. These are regrets we tend to have after a traumatic or challenging situation occurs. This occurs because there are times that our church hurt is not just about those that hurt us, but ways we may have put ourselves under the wrong leadership or in unhealthy situations. It is important to address regrets and to be honest about what decisions and choices we could have made that would have caused a different outcome. As we deal with regrets, we can repent for our actions and heal where necessary, while gaining insight and tools to make better future decisions. Let's examine some *"woulda, shoulda, couldas,"* to further expose the truths and myths regarding church hurt, heal, and move forward in healthiness.

Choosing The Unhealthy Leadership & Ministry
Some of us need to admit that the reason we were a part of a ministry was because we idolized the leader. The relationship may or may not have been of God. Infatuation was the greatest drawing to that leader or ministry. In these cases, we must admit that we have some responsibility for what we are drawn to. Sometimes, God will even tell us to be a part of that ministry or submit to that leader, even though it is not his true will for our lives. Or it is his will but we are not ready for what he is releasing. There was something in us that God was revealing to us by letting us attend that church or submitting to that leader. In our hurt, we will think God is exposing that leader or ministry, and there could be some truth to this. God exposing us to us is the complete truth; he wants to rid those ungodly attributes out of us, so we can see how susceptible we can be if our desires are greater than his desires and purpose for us. God did not set you up to be hurt. He allowed his permissive will to unfold so you would want and trust his original will and purpose for your life. It is important that our leadership choices are God focused and God led in the future. It is also essential to address what inadequacies, voids, needs, and

desires were in us that drew us to believing we were to sit under this leader or be a part of this church. As we examine this, we will recognize that the signs regarding the unhealthiness of the leader and the church was their all along, we just did not see or acknowledge them. Our issues of validation and mesmerism blinded the reality of that leader and ministry. Church hurt and challenges opened our eyes, as drama tends to expose truth about ourselves and others. We can now repent, heal inadequacies, fulfill voids in a Godly manner, and SHIFT under a healthy leadership and ministry. It is okay to search yourself, receive truth, heal and SHIFT!

False or Fantasy Relationships
Some of us need to admit that we left a church because:
- We wanted a relationship with the leader or position in the church that God did not ordain
- We were not mature, healed and healthy enough to have that relationship or position
- Our love was more for the leader and the ministry than for God

It was not that the leader or church hurt us per say, but we had unmet expectations of a leader that refused to be more than God said.
- We overstepped boundaries that caused challenges when that leader rejected the unhealthiness in us
- We positioned ourselves through our idolatry to be taken advantage of by a perverted or unhealthy leader
- We were not able to have the personal relationship or position we dreamed (fantasized) about with that leader or ministry because it was a mega church with mega folks

I have had people leave my life because they wanted to be spiritual children, but God had not reveal that yet. Or they were so infatuated with me that God wanted them to be mentored first, healed, and balanced in him being their head before he released that level of relationship. These people could not handle the process of healing they needed personally, and that we needed to take in our interactions where a spiritual parenting relationship would be healthy. They saw my need to be only what God was requiring as rejection, and no matter how much I tried to empower and assure them to stick with the process, they aborted it, left my life and the ministry. It is unfortunate and disheartening because I knew our relationship was of God. Many of them have taken paths that have led them outside of the will and destiny of God as they sought people and things to fulfill areas within them that only God can fulfill.

Please know this is not real church hurt. This is self-inflicted hurt. Your desires placed you in this position. To really heal, take responsibility for your idolatry - YES IDOLATRY - get delivered, put God first, and let him lead you to the church and leader you are to connect to. Search yourself. It is a regret, but the fantasy is over. Well it is over if you acknowledge and accept truth, commit to living, and allow God to make his reality a fulfilling truth for you.
I have had people reject me for platform ministers that really do not have the time, character, or vision to journey with them in the level of mentorship they need; or who were not called to mentor them. My love for them and knowing what God has said regarding our relationship has kept some of the connections. Yet, there tends to be a delay in their destiny unfolding because their first submission is to that leader, and rightfully so as this is biblically correct order. It however, hinders their growth and release because they are waiting for that leader to see, confirm and release them in what I am readily able to bring to their lives. Because that relationship has usurped the position of our mentoring relationship, there is a delay in some of their destiny endeavors. Sigh!!!!

There is a leader that God has ordained to closely journey with you. There is a position in ministry for you, whether in a church, community, or market place. That is the truth. The leader God has ordained for you may not be famous or have a huge platform. They however, are huge to God, mighty in their sphere, and need their divine connection with you to further advance the kingdom of God. As you connect with them, they will be a greater blessing than you ever thought possible in your imagination with a famous preacher. That is because you all were designed to walk together. It is not forced, and it is not illegal. It is the will of God, and when he blesses you with divine connections, it adds exceedingly to your life and destiny. Get ready to be blessed. Repent, heal, and SHIFT!

Leadership Identification
Some of us should admit that the reason we became a part of a ministry is because there were somethings about the leader that reminded us of ourselves, what God has spoken to us, and that we wanted to be that leader. It is okay to want to be under a leader that reminds us of ourselves and that has like qualities, mantles, and destiny paths. It is okay to glean from such leaders and to receive revelation and tools to empower and advance in our destiny path. We still have to make sure it is God if we are to sit under that leader. We also

must make sure our motives are in order regarding decisions we make about that leader. We are never trying to be anyone else, even those that may have like mantles and ministries. We are never seeking to be a clone or to be so infatuated that we want to be that person, while rejecting the uniqueness of who we are in God.

It is important to make sure we address if we crossed boundaries in our emotions, souls, and intent regarding our motives for sitting under a leader. We must take responsibility for how our infatuation overrode healthy identification and we became more or received more than God intended from that leader. Church hurt and challenges ensued, and now we have a chance to cleanse unhealthy motives and infatuation and SHIFT with God. Search yourself. It is a regret, but you are only condemned if you remain in the hurt and victimization of it. Repent, heal, and SHIFT!

Stayed Too Long
Some of us need to admit that the reason we stayed so long at that unhealthy church that we knew deep down was not ever going to equip and release us into destiny, or that was not good for us, was because:
- We were hiding from our calling
- Scared to leave for fear of failing or making the wrong decision
- Fear of missing out on things that may have been spoken about that leader or ministry
- Were bound by familiarity, false loyalty, and false honor, bewitched by doctrine or people
- Fear hurting people or being hurt and abandoned
- Fear giving up the platforms and positions we have established
- Have been just plain ole' disobedient in harkening to the voice and will of the Lord

I remember a time God was leading me to follow through with what he was asking of me regarding ministry and the position I was in. He told me if I did not SHIFT I would endure horrible warfare. My heart so wanted to stay because I cared about the people. I did not want them to be angry with me, but I had to trust God and SHIFT where God was taking me. I will be honest and say I lost a whole lot of supports and relationships due to my obedience and it hurt something terrible. But I healed, and I am living a vibrant fulfilled life in God.

When we stay too long, it was not the churches' or the leaders' fault we have not SHIFTED into destiny. It is our fault. Let's just admit the fear today, release it, forgive ourselves, let go of the perceived church hurt, familiarity, and obligation. Let's get free and SHIFT with God. I LOVE YA'LL! Truth packaged in love and a desire to see you repent, heal, and SHIFT!

Ecclesiastes 3:1 declares *"To everything there is a season, and a time to every purpose under the heaven."* Some of us need to admit that the leadership and ministry was right, but our timing was wrong. Maybe we SHIFTED to that church or under that leadership too soon or too late. I will use myself for example. There is a person I believe is to mentor me. I asked her to pray about it. She has been very busy, but is praying and following up with me when she can. I have not pressed her, and I have not taken off running the other way for fear of rejection, or that the relationship will not unfold. In God's timing, the fellowship and mentorship will begin. If I press her:
- She might think I am unhealthy and reject the mentorship
- The relationship might become a burden to her already heavy schedule and cause complications in our interactions
- The relationship could become inordinate and result in interactions that are not in alignment with God's will

We are living in a "right now" world. We must not allow this mentality to cause us to move ahead of God or outside his will. Yet, we must make sure we move with God, so we do not hinder or abort our progress or destiny process. I believe this is the reason God only shows us things in measure. We are so quick to rush to the end result without fulfilling the in between work, or processing into a vision or endeavor. Or we can be delayed in our SHIFT and risk missing the timing of God or redoing a season over again. I decree NO REGRETS FROM THIS DAY FORWARD and that you shall know the timing and move of GOD and SHIFT accordingly. I decree you shall not allow fear, insecurity, and negative voices from people or the enemy to cause you to move ahead or behind God. I decree you shall rest in the will and purpose of God, and operate in his momentum, while seeing his purpose come to pass for you in every season of your life. YOU GOT THIS! Repent, heal, and SHIFT!

Exposing Leadership Or Ministries
Some of us would benefit from admitting that we sounded the alarm on an unhealthy leader or ministry out of spite and hurt, and not at God's leading.
- It caused more harm, pain, and chaos to us and others than we expected.

- The justice we thought we would receive or thought would heal us did not manifest.
- Instead of us being vindicated, we looked like and were viewed as the offender, rather than the victim. SIGH!!!

Sometimes we can equate waiting on God regarding when to address or expose a leader or ministry, to us being shamed to tell our story, or to us being silenced by the enemy or those who hurt us. I understand the drive of wanting to blast someone that hurt you, or vindicate your name. I also understand the importance of waiting on God and even being healed before you speak on a matter. Waiting on God is sure to bring retribution to you. No one can hinder God's will from coming to pass for you. And speaking through a healed well is sure to expose truth, while SHIFTING you into the resurrection power of your identity and purpose. You will be able to share without remorse or additional warfare. I speak grace, deliverance and healing to you if you "jumped the gun" in sharing before God's timing. I decree the grace of God is rectifying any additional drama and warfare that ensued and anyway the truth concerning your experience was misconstrued. As the grace of God clears the airways and cleanses messiness, I decree a clean slate for you. I decree that as you heal, and share as God leads, you will do it with pure intent, his intent, and where the good of who you are, and the good of his kingdom, can be made manifest for his glory. Repent, heal, and SHIFT!

Healing Activation:
1. Spend time with God searching out the regrets you may have regarding your church hurt experiences.
2. Accept responsibility for your actions and repent where necessary.
3. Forgive yourself and those that hurt you.
4. Seek God for the reasons you made the choices you did.
5. Work with God to heal areas in your soul, heart, mind, and identity that subjected you to those choices. This will be a focused daily effort where it may take a season to SHIFT into healing.
6. Activate what God says and commit to wellness regarding what he requires of you.
7. Ask God for revelations and tools so that you will not make these choices in the future.

RECKLESS WISDOM!
DISPLACING THE SHEEP!

It is error for leaders to declare to people to leave their churches, as we should not want people leaving unless God is requiring it of them. This has become a huge fad at conference events and on social media. Some ministers preach at different conferences and events proclaiming to people that they should have been released years ago, they are ready to go forth in the things of God, should leave from under that leader who will not release them, and on and on they preaaaaaach. These proclamations have some validity and are empowering. Yet, there is no regard for the rejection and hurt that person endured for not being released, and for where their mental and spiritual capacity is regarding ministry, church, or God. The people are left charged with what comes across as revelation, prophecy, and confirmation, but it was really rebellion that strengthened the hurt inside their souls and hearts. Such reckless rhetoric without providing wisdom for resolving conflicts in a healthy manner, searching God as to whether it is his will to leave, or wisdom on how to leave properly, feeds into church hurt and church division. It breeds rebellion, division, promotes renegade mentalities, and incites leadership and church bashing.

- There is no regard for where the people are personally and whether it is time for them to go.
- These rhetorical rants are given with excitement or as if they are of God, without providing people with strategy in how to search God for whether it is time to go, what type of new church they need to be looking for, how to search for that new church, and how to properly leave where even if the leader does not want them to go, they can still exit with honor for what they have gained from that ministry and for what others can still receive from that ministry.
- The person is not given advice to examine themselves to determine if they are utilizing what is already within their church or what God has already instilled in them. Many have not honored or walked in what is already in them; yet they are encouraged to pursue and be spiritual gluttons, rather than assistants in advancing the kingdom of God.
- There is no advice given as to whether people need to activate and release what they have learned within the church and from God before they leave as this could be a time of pouring out rather than transitioning.

- There is no consideration for those who have church hurt and how to bring healing to them before they connect to another ministry. Hurting people hurt people so they take their pain and drama elsewhere. They are equipped in their gifts, but are wounded or have caused woundedness. They still lack skills to deal with conflict within and outside of the church.
- If they are being abused or taken advantage of, there is no wisdom of how to pursue help, guidance to handle the situation, and healing from the experience.

Many of these leaders believe folks are "catching it in and through the spirit of God," and will act accordingly. But they are catching it through their emotions and acting through their wounds. Such rhetoric and unthought out wisdom causes further division and church hurt within the body of Christ. I say this because people are caught up in the hype of the moment, and they are only focused on their challenges, what they believe they are not getting, and what they think they can get somewhere else. When done through this well, the focus is more about gratifying self, than being in God's will, exalting God, and advancing his body. Though not always the case, people who follow this advice also tend to leave messy. They leave focused on what leaders and the church did not do. They bash leaders and churches who have poured into them for years. There is no regard that even though they may have outgrown the ministry, that ministry is still viable and important to God and to people who still are being empowered and equipped through that ministry. The leader and the ministry become the enemy even though we all should be one body, empowering and supporting one another for the good of God's kingdom.

A varied number of people leave abruptly with no plan.

- Some end up sitting at home and even start to backslide because they are not able to sustain without a church body.
- Some are so focused or bound in their challenges or hurt, they fear going to another church, so they leave, but resist integrating into another ministry.
- Some go on bashing sprees against the leader and ministry they left and even build a fleshly ordained ministry around their crusade. They end up pulling others out of position as they rally and draw folks of like experiences to their woundedness.

- Some become rebels and renegades. They become the parking lot - bathroom preachers - you talk about. Though you empowered them in one area, you helped to unleash or feed rebellion in another area.
- Some church hop, and because they do not know what they want or need - lack strategy - they waste time in the limbo of their transition.
- Some take their drama and challenges to the other church and because there was no closure, strategy, or healing entertained in their transition, these issues just manifest wherever they go. So even if they are not the initiator of the church hurt, some challenges seem to follow them because they have not learned new tools needed to make better choices, not pick the same type of ministry environments, or close doors where the enemy attacks them through leaders and ministries.
- They may not have a mature mentor or accountability partner that can help them. When they start reaching out to you, you may not have the time or do not want to make the time to help walk them through their transition. Do not break people if you are not willing to really help fix them.

We should not want people to be uprooted, scattered, further wounded, and misaligned. We want people to be aligned with God and in their rightful place. We need to be more accountable in how we use our platforms as we influence others:

- Good wisdom with no strategy results in reckless wisdom
- We cause division amongst ourselves
- We contribute to church hurt, drama, and discord
- We displace sheep
- We cause and breed rebellion within the church body

If God gives you a word that people need to leave their ministry, then make sure you acquire specifics regarding that word, so you can reach the people he is speaking to. Ask God for a strategy or encourage them to pursue him for guidance regarding how to leave, when to leave, and what their next steps are. Search out if these people are broken and need healing. Take a moment to pray for them and to activate them in pursuing God for further healing and direction.

> ***Proverbs 4:7*** *Wisdom is the principal thing; therefore get wisdom: and with all thy getting get understanding.*

New International Version *The beginning of wisdom is this: Get wisdom. Though it cost all you have, get understanding.*

Your word about leaving may have been wisdom, but the people need understanding, so they will not error in the Lord. You must receive wisdom and understanding so you can impart it into the people.

Matthew 9:37 *Then saith he unto his disciples, the harvest truly is plenteous, but the labourers are few.*

A laborer is not just one who makes proclamations across platforms. A laborer is a toiler. You must toil for a clear word, strategy for that word, to impart that word, bring guidance to further activate that word, walk with people to see that word come to pass, or direct people to others who can help them manifest the harvest of that word in their lives. Be accountable to all areas of your ministry. It may cost you more time with God to get understanding, but that is better than the cost of another person's soul or destiny. SHIFT!

HOW TO LEAVE A MINISTRY

Some of this revelation is from my "Leaving & Cleaving" chapter of "Healing The Wounded Leader Manual."

If you experience church hurt and God leads you to leave a ministry, it is important to do so honorably. You want to be in order with God and you want him to be pleased with you no matter what other people do or do not do. It does not matter if the leader wants you to stay, if people want you to stay, and even if you are hesitant about whether you should go or stay, if God is unctioning you to leave, be obedient and follow the plan he gives you regarding leaving. When you remain in a church due to familiarity or fear of backlash, slander, etc., it causes unnecessary challenges. Emoting drama usually manifests due to you being out of alignment with what God is saying and where he desires you to be as you are uncovered. This opens a door for the enemy to wreak havoc in an already challenging transitional situation.

Reasons God will have a person leave a ministry:

- The person has received all they can under that ministry.
- The person needs to connect or be under the covering of another ministry to further align with God, and the calling and destiny on his or her life.
- The person needs to receive greater training and equipping.
- The person has a specific assignment somewhere else; some people are sent into ministries to raise up or cover a specific remnant within that ministry, or to impart or govern a specific area of that ministry, community, region, nation.
- It is time for the person to independently focus on their own life and ministry vision.
- The leader and/or church is operating in somethings contrary to God, and he is requiring the person to separate themselves from the reproach, consequences, and judgment that may come upon that ministry.
- The person was only to be there for a season, a particular work, or for specific training. Some ministries are not your lifetime ministry. God is a SHIFTING God. He never plateaus. He is always focused on upward mobility and success. He is always seeking to do the exceeding, abundant, and beyond. What we deem as success could be just the beginning for God. He may be elevating you or allowing you to experience different facets of his glory and kingdom. Remain a life learner so you can SHIFT with God.

- The person has experienced hurt within that church and need to SHIFT to adequately work on his or her healing process and further align in their destiny.

It is important to understand that:

- We are not one church, but a body of believers.
- We are one kingdom under God.
- We are not in competition with one another.
- We are all ONE church with different assignments and functions.
- If someone leaves and goes to another church or starts a ministry, they are still your brother and sister in Christ. They are an extension of God's work through you, and of the body of Christ as a whole.

Romans 12:4 For just as each of us has one body with many members, and these members do not all have the same function.

1Corinthians 12:12 For as the body is one, and hath many members, and all the members of that one body, being many, are one body: so also is Christ.

If someone decides to leave your church, you must respect their decision. Slandering and betraying them causes church hurt. If they are leaving due to church hurt, then this just caused more harm to their soul, and potentially made it more complicated for them to bond with their new ministry assembly.

Reasons people do not leave when God says:

- False loyalty
- False obligation
- Fear of being betrayed or being viewed as a renegade
- Fear of not being supported
- Fear of being abandoned and ostracized
- Fear of leaving the familiar
- Fear of going alone
- Fear of being alone, losing supports, and friendships
- Fear of failing
- Fear that there is no one to step in and do their work, or the lack of raising up a successor
- Feeling like they are letting down the leaders or ministry

- Bound by ungodly or unhealthy soulties with the leader, people, and the ministry
- Bound in religion and tradition
- Rebellious; self-focused rather than God focused
- Bound and used to being hurt while contending it is persecution for the gospel
- Traumatized to a point of not being able to make an effective decision

There is a general population of people that does not leave as God required because they have difficulty dealing with the grief and loss of leaving. Sometimes just the thought of leaving causes an influx of emotions. Anytime you leave or lose something, whether good or bad, there are emotions to process through. Loss creates a void in our soul and lives. Now we must learn to live without that person, place, or thing.

> *2Corinthians 5:17 Therefore if any man be in Christ, he is a new creature: old things are passed away; behold, all things are become new.*

The "*new*" can be exciting, but it also can be scary. It is an unfamiliar place where we trust and learn God, and ourselves at a new dimension. What we learned in previous seasons has prepared us for the new, but may not necessarily be our survival mechanism, spiritual tools, and supports, for sustaining in the new place. Our focus should be on this truth of *Ephesians 3:20*, "*Now unto him that is able to do exceeding abundantly above all that we ask or think, according to the power that worketh in us.*" God has greater for you in the new place. SHALL YOU NOT KNOW IT?

> *Isaiah 43:19 Behold, I will do a new thing; now it shall spring forth; shall ye not know it?*

When God is requiring a person to leave, even if it is due to church hurt and a need for healing in a fresh environment, we must view this as elevation for the entire body of Christ. We must bless and support people, so they can be obedient to the will of God, and transition in the healthiest manner possible.

If people do not support your transition, you must SHIFT with God regardless of ill treatment. Some people either are not meant to go with you to your "next" or abort their position in your "next." You must take on the mindset that you are going to be exactly where God wants you to be and do whatever he is requiring, no matter who likes it or not; no matter who joins you on your journey or not.

Today I encourage you to:
- Let the familiarity with your leader, the people, your positions, and the ministry go!
- Let the false expectations you have for your leader and the ministry go!
- Let the anger, hurt, disappointment, and resentment of not being empowered or validated go!
- Let the fear of the unknown go!
- Let the excuses, laziness, disobedience and rebellion go!
- Let the lie that you are waiting on God and to hear from God go!
- Let the unhealthiness and drama go!
- Let the fear that you cannot heal without these people or this ministry go!
- Let the fear that you are aborting your inheritance if you leave this leader or ministry go!

Stop toiling a ground that is bringing pain and death to your destiny. God is waiting to further align you with the "new!" SHIFT!

Wisdom Keys for Shifting with God!

Leave Honorably
Schedule a meeting with your leader/s and share with them what God has spoken to you. Be respectful and honoring no matter how they respond. Let them know that you are simply being obedient to God, but do not defend what God has led you to do. Speak honestly, and do not add more to what God has said. If you do not know everything God has prepared, be honest in sharing that, and let them know you are open to sharing as God further reveals information to you. Give a date of departure, and tie up any ministry duties, etc., say your goodbyes to those you have done ministry with, bless them in their continued endeavors, and move forward with God.

It is always good to equip successors while you are in a leadership position. However, if you did not do this, seek God on what day you are to leave, then share this with your overseer, and encourage them to find a replacement for you. If you know of those within the ministry that are equipped to replace you, then recommend them to your leader. If the leader agrees in them replacing you, ask them if they are open to taking your place. If they accept the position, pray a blessing impartation over them, release all duties to them, and encourage them and those under them in being able to carry the vision further. Share any revelation and duties that will enable their transition to be smooth and successful. If there is no one to take your place, then move forward, while trusting God to provide for the ministry.

Avoid Gossip
If people become messy and gossipy regarding your transition, do not get into this type of conversation with them. Do not have conversations about flaws and issues regarding the leader and the ministry, or regarding your hurtful challenges and any concerns you may have relating to your experience. Simply focus on the fact that it is your time to go and SHIFT, while dealing with your hurts and challenges in prayer with God, a Christian Counselor, or a mature saint who can keep you focused on where God is taking you. Shut down all conversations that will try to draw you into dishonor as even if it is true, when you yield to gossip and slander, it is dishonor to God, and to the fact that he SHIFTED and separated you to steer you away from mess. Tell the gossipers you have nothing to say, and if cutting ties with them is necessary, then do that. When I left my previous church, I shut the gossipers down by blessing the leadership and the ministry, and simply contending that it was just time for me to transition and therefore, I was being obedient to God. There was no room to entangle me in their gossip, so they hushed with trying to engage me in conversation.

If you are being slandered by gossip and betrayal due to the leader and/or the ministry because of leaving, do not seek to defend yourself, and do not try to have others within that ministry to comfort and support you in your time of transition. Those that would try to comfort and support you from that ministry are going to be torn between you and that ministry. Any assistance they give you will be mixed with confusion and turmoil, and will still connect you to something God has brought you out of. You can be cordial and friends, but receive your support and healing from people who are not attached to the situation, and that can focus you on healing and SHIFTING with God. When I left my previous ministry, my God sister and brother still attended that ministry. They are like blood family to me, and my God sister is one of my main life supports. But for this situation, I did not go to her to help me with this transition. I did not want to put her in a position to choose, be torn, or draw her from what God was still requiring her to do in the ministry. I also did not want her to feel like she had to fix or defend how others were responding to my transition. That was not her responsibility as I simply was doing what God was leading me to do. Though she and I remained close, and she was in my everyday life, I went to my overseer, my mentor, and two close friends who lived in other states, to help me process through my thoughts, feelings, and experiences with the SHIFT that had taken place in my life.

Avoid The Victim Mentality
Do not go to broken saints and saints who are still wounded by church hurt for support and counsel when you are transitioning out of a church. I mention this because even if you do not seek them out, they will find you. I do not know if the devil sends them or if it is because you are in a vulnerable place, and possibly even wounded that they smell the blood of your wounds and flock to you. But whatever the case, when they come, do not rely on them for support. Give up your need to have people understand you for the sake of just healing in a healthy manner and SHIFTING with God. You do not need a support group of wounded folks who only want to drown in their pain, and validate that leaders and the church are a farce. Such people are out for revenge, and to tear down leaders and the church, thus becoming an enemy of God and his will to advance his kingdom in the earth. Your focus should be to build up the kingdom, so do not attach to this crowd.

Do not get stuck in rehearsing your pain that it drowns out your ability to be healed and to hear God for the next revelation and moves he has for your life. When you constantly rehearse your pain, you are stuck in a victim mentality. You have become your own offender, because you are now the one continuing to reopen and inflict pain upon wounds that God has healed or wants to heal.

You do not need to talk to 700,894,842 folks about what has happened to you. Especially when all they are doing is agreeing with you, and validating that it should not have occurred. True encouragers sympathize with you, while seeking to bring healing so your pain will end. They do not feed into your pain where it continues or deepens. If you continuously need attention and validation for your wounds, then you are bound by a victim mentality and have become your own offender. Get a few accountable, mature, healthy people that can be sympathetic to you, yet SHIFT you to being delivered, healed, and advancing forward with God.

Draw Nigh Unto God
Though it is important to have a few mature supports who can encourage you, support you, provide deliverance, healing, and wise counsel, everyone is not going to understand your transition. Even people that support you and provide

guidance, will not fully understand your SHIFT. Transitions are supernatural. They are a time of really treading in the truth, power, faith, and encouragement of God. He is the only one who can FULLY comfort, support, instruct, guide, and help you comprehend what is happening to you and for you. Transition is a time of drawing near to him. Those who are supports will confirm what he personally does in, through, and for you. Study the story of Jesus as he transitioned from leading the disciples to dying on the cross. It will provide significant keys and revelation of how to draw near to God and transition with him.

Break Soulties
Break soulties with anything that will try to keep you stuck or focused on your past ministry or church season, where it is a hindrance to you being focused on the "new." Lots wife looked back because her soul was still tied to Sodom and Gomorrah (***Genesis 19:26***).

You may have to break soulties with:

- Your leader/s.
- The people in the ministry. You may have to break soulties with friends and acquaintances. Sometimes it is difficult to leave when we are tied to people we love. The soultie is unhealthy if it is hindering or causing a struggle where we cannot SHIFT with God. The soultie may need to be broken and then re-established in the new place you are in.
- The ministry itself.
- Prophecies or promises you believe you have aborted due to leaving. Declare they will come to pass in your future seasons.
- Drama and messiness that you were a part of or that was present within the ministry.
- False promises and promotions that never came to pass or that was only given in measure. Declare they will come to pass in your future seasons.
- The potential you saw in the ministry and hoped would manifest.
- Disappointments, pains, and hurts that you endured from the leader, the ministry, and during your transition.
- The community and region if you were SHIFTED to a new community and region to minister in.
- Ministry positions and platforms you held that may be pulling on your heart and soul.

Deliverance and Healing:
If you are going to be a progressive person, it is necessary to focus on SHIFTING forward. That means anything that is going to keep you stuck or bound in the past should be removed. As much as you will be justified and want to hold on to your emotions, do not do it. Use the strategies and revelations throughout this book so you can be delivered and healed. SHIFTING comes with its own set of emotions that you have to conquer. Do not confound your transition by holding onto unhealthy or challenging emotions that will keep you bound and stifled. Work through them and commit to being made well of anything from your past. Please understand that when a SHIFT has occurred, the foundation has been cracked. When your emotions are driving you, you are subject to fall into one rather than having the focus to jump over hurdles and obstacles. Transitions display your maturity and faith in God. You will learn where your character is strong, and where you need improvement and further development.

> ***2Timothy 2:3-4*** *Take [with me] your share of the hardships and suffering [which you are called to endure] as a good (first-class) soldier of Christ Jesus. No soldier when in service gets entangled in the enterprises of [civilian] life; his aim is to satisfy and please the one who enlisted him.*

Endure the trials of SHIFTING with integrity and character, while taking your pains and hurts to God so he can deliver and heal you. Seek your close support system for further deliverance and healing of areas that may be difficult to heal or be free from. Some areas will require a continual battering and release unto God before breakthrough occurs. This is a transition, so it is a process that is occurring. Therefore, you will have to be processed to wholeness even as you are being processed to your "next." God is also doing some new things in your mind, heart, and soul to build you in your "new." Some things will happen quickly, and some will happen over time. Let God lead you in the process of transitioning into the "new" with him. As you surrender your process to God, receive deliverance, and healing in the following areas:

- Forgive anyone who hurts you, does not understand you, or betrays you.
- Cleanse and heal from all bitterness, anger, rage, resentment, retaliation, murder, slander, and gossip.
- Release all expectations and hurt from not being supported, being overlooked, not being understood, and being betrayed.
- Break powers of shame, guilt, condemnation, accuser of the brethren, gossip, slander, and word curses against your "next".
- Cast out and break powers of fear, inadequacy, insecurity, and feeling

unworthy of what God has for you. Consistently declare out who you are, and what God is requiring of you. Command the earth, region, and new place to receive you as God's chosen vessel (*See Romans 8:22*). Refuse to be denied, and know that you deserve to be where God is taking you.

- Have your personal confidants praying and covering you as you SHIFT. Be specific in what they should pray for, so they can agree with what God is saying.
- Deal with the grief and loss of your transition. Do not stuff your grief, ignore it, or wallow in it. Typically, the stages of grief are denial, anger, bargaining, depression, and acceptance. It is very easy to get stuck in one of these stages during transition. The main reason is because we expect everything about the new to be glorious and easy. We assume that there will not be challenges, hardship, new things to learn and conquer, etc. We quote "*new level - new devils,*" but we expect blessings and overflow. We become challenged and fixated on all that we loss and have given up. Such a focus plagues us with grief. Your feelings are real and understandable, and God cares about how you feel. Tell the Lord exactly how it hurts and sucks, but be willing to let the feelings go. Receive his deliverance and healing when he strives to exchange your grief for comfort, peace, joy, love, and healing.
- Immediately complete and implement whatever God tells you. Some of it will sound farfetched. Remember that God uses the foolish to confound the wise. His methods are not of this world. They are conventional. Some matters you will not understand until you implement them, or until future seasons of your life. I am still learning and understanding things that God had me do in a major SHIFT that occurred years ago. I had to give up my need to understand so I could flow with God. It was totally worth it. You will not regret trusting God.
- Embrace your new relationships and connections. They will be different, and some will not be what you are used to and expected. But God is not trying to establish the old, he is about the "new." Trust who he has put in your life and do not make them be responsible for what others have done and have not done in your life. Just because they are new, it does not guarantee that you will not be hurt again. Neither does you putting up walls and being resistant to embracing these relationships. God does not control our freewill to be messy. But as you go through this transition, it is important to accept people for exactly who they are, flaws and all. Learn to engage people from the truth of who they are, as then you will be able to accept and heal from challenges you will encounter in

your relationships. This helps in discerning drama and challenges before they occur, and dealing with them quickly so you can keep it moving with God.

Addressing the Congregation During Transitions

A lot of times we move forward and act like nothing happened when people leave the ministry, however, the challenges that occur when people transition out of the ministry need to be addressed. We must be open and available to discussing, and bringing healing to the people and the ministry organizations, as regardless of whether people leave in a healthy or unhealthy manner, it is still a loss. Addressing the loss especially needs to be done if the person was a major leader within the ministry or if offense occurred with various people within the ministry. Be open to the following:

- Meet with the congregation, and or members of specific ministries, and deal with feelings and issues of abandonment, grief, and loss. People will feel abandoned because of unresolved issues of abandonment in their personal lives. People will not even know that these unresolved issues are there, and will feel voided and hurt due to the person's transition. A lot of slander and gossip can be avoided simply by dealing with this area, and helping people to process their feelings. As I transitioned out of my previous church, I had several meetings with my leaders before leaving. I believe people would have handled my transition better if this information was shared with them by leadership.
- Pray for the entire congregation, and for people who may need more personal processing in the areas of abandonment, grief, and loss, and provide people with healthy tools and supports to process their thoughts and feelings.
- Demonstrating genuine support of the person that is leaving is key to helping members transition in a healthy manner. If leaders are silent regarding a transition, it leaves room for the enemy to cause division and confusion, and for people to form their own interpretation about that person's transition. When people see leaders giving genuine blessings despite challenges of losing that person, they are apt to deal with their feelings in a healthy manner.
- Do not preach about the issue over the pulpit, or make public remarks regarding your challenges with the person's transition. This provokes gossip and slander, and causes people to take sides.

- Do not lend to gossip and slander, and discourage people from engaging in such negativity. Promote unity and respect of the person's right to make their own decisions.
- Provide people with wise counsel regarding their own thoughts and feelings concerning being challenged by the person leaving, or them feeling they should leave.
- Be kingdom minded and not church focused. Kingdom minded leaders recognize that we are all one body advancing the kingdom of God. Church minded leaders are focused on building their own little kingdom and gathering people unto themselves.

Decreeing that transitions will be smoother as people learn to respect God's will and flow in the process of SHIFTING with him. SHIFT!

FORSAKE NOT THE ASSEMBLY

I truly understand the desire to be separated from the church when you have experienced church hurt. There was a time I experienced church hurt while God was leading me into another dimension of ministry. I shared what God was requiring of me and the training I needed to achieve his will. It was not received. As the situation unfolded, I realized that God had a greater purpose regarding me sharing his desired endeavors. As this purpose unveiled, God led me to fully transition out of that ministry. Though he was using me to manifest revelation, he said it was not my ground to toil. I was so challenged by how I had been treated, that I did not want to attend anybody's church. I even completed a bible study on how God was my covering and head, how I did not need an overseer, and how I did not need to assimilate with a church body. I was committed to completing the work that God was granting to my hands, but I did not want to have anything to do with church people and the church. Like many of you, I started contending I was *"spiritual"* and *"kingdom."* I refused to associate with what was considered *"religious"* or *"the church;"* and even though I had a ministry, I did not even want to be considered *"nondenominational."* I felt that too had become a religious doctrine in and of itself. I did not want any association with what I had decided was bondage. There very well were some justifications and truths to my perceptions, but nothing warranted forsaking the assembly of myself with other believers.

My other commitment was to being healed. I knew I was wounded and wanted to be healed and healthy. I, therefore, sought God relentlessly for deliverance and healing of church hurt. It was the worst pain I ever experienced, and I did not want to live with it nor did I want it to be my identity. As God worked on my heart, I realized that it was my wounds talking and causing me to reject a part of God – his church, and his people – my fellow brothers and sisters. Even my bible study on spiritual covering and not having to be a part of a church, was an accumulation of scriptures I used in error to justify my hurts and fears. I had come up with my own doctrine that was binding me to self-idolatry due to church hurt. Had I not been committed to healing and the truth that came with my healing process, I would have succumbed to a different pathway of error that would have taken me further away from destiny and God. That is what forsaking the assembly does. It SHIFTS us into a paradigm that is no different than the religious or traditional paradigm we are running from. One that is manmade and flawed in its beliefs and doctrines.

It is very difficult to separate yourself from God's people and his church body, but still try to fully be in the will of God and in covenant relationship with God. When God enters covenant with us, he receives all of us – the good – the bad – the ugly – and the greatness he knows we can be. When we enter covenant with him, he desires the same regard of love and sacrifice, which includes him, his church body and all its flaws and potential. God knew the church needed work. I believe that is the reason he said, *"upon this rock I will build my church"* (***Matthew 16:18***). When something is built, it is being constructed, confirmed, emboldened, edified, and established. It is also being repaired, reconstructed, rebuilt, and remodeled when and where necessary. There is a day when the church will fashion into the unspotted perfection that God desires. But we are working towards that day. No matter what challenges go on within certain church ministries, God will never change his mind about the church body. He will expect for us to be a part of it, honor it, and love it as he does. It is a part of him. He is not going to reject a part of him, and does not want us rejecting any part of him.

> ***Hebrews 10:24-25*** *And let us consider one another to provoke unto love and to good works: Not forsaking the assembling of ourselves together, as the manner of some is; but exhorting one another: and so much the more, as ye see the day approaching.*

As I processed to wholeness regarding church hurt, I learned that being a part of the assembly of God was a heart matter. I claimed to love people and even though I was willing to do the work of my destiny, I did not want to socialize, be affiliated with, or even be in fellowship with those I was claiming to save, deliver, and heal. More importantly, I did not value how important being in relationship and fellowship with the church and with God's people was a vital part of my covenant with him. God is the overseer of a kingdom and is seeking to establish and advance a kingdom. Yes, he loves personal relationship with each of us, but he is seeking to restore his kingdom the way it should have been before the fall of man. All of us being in our rightful place in his kingdom and being in his kingdom is valuable to him. So is the structure of family, generational inheritance, and the healthy assembly of a body of people that glorifies, honors, and lives through and for him. We cannot provoke one another to live through and for him, and receive the edification of that, if we are all having our own little private churches in the back of some closet temple we made at home because we were hurt in the church. Or we are tired of the challenges within church, but have not done anything within our own souls and through our destiny to help bring changes to the church.

I remember times when I was fed up with church. Even before I experienced the church hurt that caused me to not want to go to church anymore. I would have times in my walk where I just did not want to do church anymore. I would take a month off to refresh and refocus. I would then return revived in the new vision and clarity God had given me. As I think about this now, I wonder whether there were times that God thought about giving up on me. Has God taken time off because he was fed up with me? When considering this, I am saddened. Though I was probably burned out from giving my life to ministry, I should never get to a place of wanting to be done with God's church assembly. I am happy I had the mind to take time off and refocus. I am even happier that my perspective has changed in this area and church and ministry is no longer a burden. I believe what made it a burden is operating in works. When I grasped a destiny mentality, I began to understand that it was a part of my inheritance as a believer, a part of my covenant, and a part of my lifestyle.

As God was processing me to wholeness regarding church hurt, I had to realize that I could not keep my hurt and purely love God or do his work. I also was expecting others to change, yet I had to be willing to relinquish my wounds, so I could be transformed and be an effective ambassador in the body of Christ. The desire to never want to hurt anyone the way I was hurt, was greater than the bondage of pain and to forsake the assembly of the body. Just as you want those who hurt you to take responsibility for hurting and disappointing you, you too must take responsibility for the transformation you need, and for the SHIFT in your perspective concerning the church assembly.

Like me, some of you have justifiable church hurt. You were molested, raped, pimped, betrayed, abused, used, overlook, stifled, delayed, bewitched, led astray, by church people, and/or leaders. I had a right to be angry and unforgiving. The only thing I did was be obedient to God. But even in that, it did not justify forsaking the assembly. It did not justify launching an all-out assault on Christians, leaders, the church, and the body of Christ. It did not justify living through unforgiveness, operating in rebellion, and refusing to be in alignment with God and his word regarding being a part of his church - his bride. It did not justify finding a healthy church assembly to connect to or justify planting a church work when God led me to do so. God does not work in this manner. Just as he held me and those who hurt me accountable, he is holding you and those accountable that hurt you. He is holding you accountable to your response and further breeding of reproach upon his church and his name by refusing to be healed and fully aligned with his kingdom. Sigh!!!!

Healing from church hurt was one of the greatest gifts I ever gave myself and my destiny. I say this because it SHIFTED me to embracing the will and purpose of God from a lifestyle of fulfillment and privilege. I no longer operated through religious obligation and erred loyalty to God, people, and ministry. God was not fussing at me about not going to church. He was revealing to me who I was and my purpose within the church and in the world. As I learned about who I was to God, his people, his church, the body of Christ and the world at large, I understood that it was an honor to serve God, advance his kingdom with the body of Christ, and to be in fellowship and relationship with those who would live eternally with him. I learned that church assembly was not a choice, but my privilege. I understood that it was unhealthy to pick and choose parts of God that I wanted to accept and choose to follow, while rejecting parts I could not make perfect; for the perfecting of the saints and the church was God's job not mines. I was trying to do God's job and mines. I could not be my own God and journey in a surrendered lifestyle of his ordained destiny at the same time. That was like saying I knew what was best for me, yet trying to take credit and implement the best life God had ordained for me at birth. See how allowing church hurt to rule you makes you double minded and even a bit schizophrenic???

I learned that my picking and choosing what I want to accept about God, made me no different than the religious folks I claimed I did not want to be like. I was dictating to God and people what being a Christian should be like, while setting a religious standard that I myself could not attain. I was a work in progress too. I was working out my salvation just like everyone else. I needed the empowerment that came from the assembly of the saints just like everyone else. My liberation from religion and any bondage was in being exactly who God designed me to be and striving to obtain it through his leading, not binding myself to a paradigm that restricted me and him in our destiny journey. Such bondage hindered me from learning and experiencing a greater facet of God, even though my soul's cry was *"teach me all about you Lord."* Either I wanted all of God and trusted him with my heart, my experiences, my life, or I needed to stop declaring God was a savior, a deliverer, a healer, while walking bound in church hurt that I did not want to relinquish; as to do so meant I had to be accountable to the healthiness, truth, and liberty that accompanied it. And truth is, there is no perfect assembly. God is perfecting us.

> ***Ephesians 5:25-27*** *Husbands, love your wives, even as Christ also loved the church, and gave himself for it; That he might sanctify and cleanse it with the washing of water by the word, that he might present it to himself a glorious*

church, not having spot, or wrinkle, or any such thing; but that it should be holy and without blemish.

God is sanctifying and cleansing us with his word. He is making us glorious. Somewhere we got it twisted that it was our job to make ourselves without spot or wrinkle. God said he was presenting himself a glorious church, so this is what he will do and is doing as we produce his kingdom in the earth. Our job is to surrender to his workings and trust him to perfect us and his body.

I believe the main purpose for the gathering of the assembly is for soul winning, salvation, deliverance and healing. We also need the fellowship of likeminded believers who can keep us rooted and grounded in the truths and standards of God. In addition, we gather to be refreshed, empowered, equipped, and released into the world to do the work of the kingdom. The rules and regulations are necessary to bring order and excellence to the assembly. Are some of these rules and regulations a bit over the top? Yes, some of them are. That is the reason it is important to find a church that is in line with your destiny and that empowers you in your walk with the Lord. This way the rules will not be a burden or a stumbling block, but a blessing to your life and your spiritual walk.

I employ you to:
- Search God for your purpose and destiny, and how it impacts your generations, your region, the church body, and the world at large.
- Allow God to cleanse and heal you from your hurts and challenging perspectives of the church, while seeking him for a fresh understanding regarding the church and his body.
- As God delivers and heals you, allow his truth and fresh perspective to operate in your life and destiny. Be open to what he says and to his wisdom becoming your truth, versus focusing on the imperfections of the church and people. Ask God to give you revelation on how he will perfect the church, how this is his job, and how you can trust him to fulfill his will and purpose in his body, even as you take your rightful place as an ambassador in his kingdom.
- Search God for the attributes you would need in a church assembly to empower your identity, equip you in your calling, and release you into your destiny. Be open to visiting churches until God reveals the assembly he has for you.
- As you join an assembly, know that even though that is the ministry for you, they are flawed. But God has given you tools and strategies in his

word to work out challenges with your brothers and sisters where your personal growth in these trials, help to perfect you all personally and the church body.

WHY DO WE GATHER AS THE CHURCH?

By: Apostle David Rodgers
House Of Prayer For All Nations, Chicago, Illinois

Even in soul winning mode, I am infatuated with the mindset of sinners, backslidden saints, and modular "Christians," who have not made the full commitment to Christ and His Kingdom. One of the most asked questions I get is, *"Do I have to go to church to be saved?"* This is not a dumb question nor a question that we can give trite, surface answers to. This question is at the HEART of a spiritual pandemic that is ravaging the culture and future impact of the church.

To help us grasp the weight of this question, I want to make one clear statement: GOING TO CHURCH IS NOT AN OBLIGATION, IT IS A PRIVILEGE! Church membership and attendance is not a SALVATION issue, it is a SANCTIFICATION and RELATIONSHIP ISSUE. Because the divine purpose of the Church has been marred with the traditions of men, bad doctrine and practice, and immature biblical understanding, the "CHURCH" has become more of a social event, instead of a covenant community.

The reason we gather as the Church is because we are THE BODY OF CHRIST. It is within the context of the BODY DYNAMIC that who WE ARE is exalted above personal preferences and desires. Our inner man is strengthened by the preached and taught Word of GOD, impartation is made to empower our ministries, and relationships are fostered to impact the world with LOVE. It is challenging. Learning to trust, LOVE, and commit to others, goes counter to our sensibilities and self-importance philosophies that make us the gods of our own lives. It is in the church where the needs of others are placed above our own and we humble ourselves to stand with those who need our strength, wisdom and maturity to navigate this Christian walk. Each local church has a specific assignment to which GOD has graced you to help accomplish. Understanding your place within that framework helps you to understand the TRUST that GOD placed in you when He placed you in that Church. We violate GOD's trust in us, when we carelessly, lethargically, and selfishly REBEL, REJECT, and RIDICULE, the very entity that HE ORDAINED to perfect and send us, to bring His LOVE to the planet.

I want to encourage you to PRAY and ASK GOD, to lead you to the CHURCH that HE has assigned you to. Like your natural family, the leaders will have flaws and the members will have flaws, but they are assigned to you. And believe it or not, you have flaws as well. But as we unify by the power of the Holy Ghost, WE THE CHURCH, can demonstrate the most dynamic spiritual power on the planet which is LOVE. To remain in COVENANT with those who are FLAWED is the perfect model that JESUS CHRIST demonstrated for us, and expects us to LIVE OUT, in the context of THE CHURCH! So, as you rise today, GO TO CHURCH and do not just become a part of the activity, become a part of the COMMUNITY!!! ADR

> ***Hebrews 10:22-25*** *Let us draw near with a true heart in full assurance of faith, having our hearts sprinkled from an evil conscience, and our bodies washed with pure water. Let us hold fast the profession of our faith without wavering; (for he is faithful that promised;) And let us consider one another to provoke unto love and to good works: Not forsaking the assembling of ourselves together, as the manner of some is; but exhorting one another: and so much the more, as ye see the day approaching.*

IS SPIRITUAL COVERING IMPORTANT?

After people experience church hurt and leave a ministry, they tend to fear or even rebel regarding submitting under a leader that can adequately cover and partner with them to advance their ministry and destiny. In this day and age, where people can start ministries through social media, and other avenues, the resistance of covering has increased. As I studied covering, I found that the art of submission and covering we have had within the body of Christ was more manmade and birthed during the Charismatic Movement, to help bring accountability to falling preachers. Because some overseers who implement this movement have fallen into discrepancies, and because some leaders in general, have abused their position of covering or have provided insufficient covering and accountability, many people have resorted to being resistant to it. Despite the challenges with sufficient covering, I will contend that though we are ultimately accountable to the authority of God and he is our main covering, the importance concerning being connected with a leader and ministry that is mature and can help counsel, train, and advance you in your calling and destiny is beneficial, wise, biblical, and necessary. I refer such relationships as affiliate coverings. This is more of a covenant partnership with an overseer that when done in a healthy manner healthy, manifests inheritance, successorship, accountability, and eternal kingdom fruit that last throughout generations.

After I transitioned from the ministry I was under, I was initially resistant to covering. God said he would send me covering, but I already had reasons that stemmed from my wounds, why I did not need covering. I however, needed training, definition, understanding and guidance regarding my calling, destiny and the ministries and businesses I was to birth in the earth. I also needed prayer partners, support, and someone that recognized who I was in the earth, understood the calling on my life, could provide encouragement, empowerment, and wisdom to the path I needed to take, and could ensure I possessed the character, responsibility and accountability needed to remain consistent in my destiny journey.

Whether we have this or not, or acknowledge that we need this or not, we ALL NEED mature leaders speaking into our lives and help to navigate our destiny. God is all about order and covering which is the entire reason he placed fathers as heads of households (*1Corinthians 11:3, Ephesians 5:23-28*). Many people who have not sufficient covering will tell you that their path has been increasing hard and they have had a lot of hardships and bumpy roads, while experiencing unnecessary mistakes and regrets. Those that have successfully experienced affiliate covering, speak of it with honor, and deem it an essential key to their sustaining success.

When God released my covering to me, I was resistant at first. I was expecting to be rejected, suppressed, boxed in, only defined by what she could handle about me or what benefited her, and silenced in the areas she could not understand or contain regarding me. I realized quickly that these were the very attributes she honored and empowered concerning me. I loved that she stated that we were in covenant partnership with one another and would pour and build up one another. I loved that she did not force a formula or doctrine regarding covering on me. I love that she prayed about the specific covering I needed and allowed me to do the same, so that I would hear from God for myself regarding who she was to be to my life and ministry and vice versa. I loved that she recognized that I was broken, needed healing, and was willing to take time to walk me to wholeness. She did not force covering on me. She allowed me to get to know her, trust her, and to embrace what God was saying about our covenant relationship. Because of her sensitivity to the Holy Spirit and to my needs and wounds, I was able to heal from leadership hurt through our interactions. I learned to trust and submit to leadership again, and to even separate my real church hurt from misperceptions I endeavored due to my experiences.

Examples of healthy affiliate covering relationships in the Bible:
- ❖ Elijah and Elisha
- ❖ Samuel and David
- ❖ Barnabas and Paul
- ❖ Paul and Timothy
- ❖ Jesus and his disciples

Scriptures that suggest the biblical principles, standards, and honor of affiliate covering:

> ***Romans 13:1-2*** *LET EVERY person be loyally subject to the governing (civil) authorities. For there is no authority except from God [by His permission, His sanction], and those that exist do so by God's appointment. Therefore he who resists and sets himself up against the authorities resists what God has appointed and arranged [in divine order]. And those who resist will bring down judgment upon themselves [receiving the penalty due them].*

***1Thessalonians 5:11-13 The Amplified Bible** Therefore encourage (admonish, exhort) one another and edify (strengthen and build up) one another, just as you are doing. Now also we beseech you, brethren, get to know those who labor among you [recognize them for what they are, acknowledge and appreciate and respect them all] – your leaders who are over you in the Lord and those who warn and kindly reprove and exhort you. And hold them in very high and most affectionate esteem in [intelligent and sympathetic] appreciation of their work. Be at peace among yourselves.*

Hebrews 13:17 *Obey them that have the rule over you, and submit yourselves: for they watch for your souls, as they that must give account, that they may do it with joy, and not with grief: for that is unprofitable for you.*

1Peter 2:14-15 *Be submissive to every human institution and authority for the sake of the Lord, whether it be to the emperor as supreme, or to governors as sent by him to bring vengeance (punishment, justice) to those who do wrong and to encourage those who do good service.*

***1Peter 5:1-5 The Amplified Bible**. Even though God told me he would send covering, and I had temporary covering, when I left my previous ministry, I was not trying to hear anything about covering. And because people where speaking curses regarding me failing I was wounded and was suspicious of someone covering me. I kept saying God is my covering and even did an entire biblical study on God being my covering. I had all the biblical reasons why I did not need man to be my covering. of glory. Likewise, you who are younger and of lesser rank, be subject to the elders (the ministers and spiritual guides of the church) – [giving them due respect and yielding to their counsel]. Clothe (apron) yourselves, all of you, with humility [as the garb of a servant, so that its covering cannot possibly be stripped from you, with freedom from pride and arrogance] toward one another. For God sets Himself against the proud (the insolent, the overbearing, the disdainful, the presumptuous, the boastful) – [and He opposes, frustrates, and defeats them], but gives grace (favor, blessing) to the humble.*

As you progress in destiny, and depending on what you are to birth in the earth, you may have a main covenant partner, while other partners come along side of you to help birth, equip, and advance you in other areas of your destiny. I believe this is the reason the scripture says to *"obey them who have rule over you."* God knew there would be different authorities for different areas of your destiny and calling. Keeping this mindset will help you avoid being boxed in to controlling leaders or stagnated in your destiny and calling when you may need more than what your covenant partner can provide in different seasons of your walk. God will let you know if it is time to SHIFT altogether from under that covering, or what other coverings to add to your destiny partnership.

Covering is important because it provides:
- Accountability
- Correction
- Counsel
- Wisdom
- Guidance
- Confirmation
- Deliverance and healing of past and present wounds
- Keeps you doctrinally sound
- Keeps you God focused & submitted to God being the head of the vision, your calling, and your life
- Fortification, support, & prayer against warfare & life challenges
- Undergirding & hands on assistance with carrying, planting, plowing, & building your apostolic walk & ministry vision
- Training and equipping
- A safe place to learn, make mistakes, & grow
- An unconditional display of the love, grace, compassion, & refuge of God
- Fresh prophecy, insight, & enlightenment of vision
- Empowerment to consistently walk in your destiny vision
- Reintegration & confirmation of the work of the Lord, navigation of changes & shifts necessary in your apostolic walk or ministry vision

Do not allow church hurt to hinder you from covering and covenant relationships. Ask God to send you a mature healthy leader who honors who you are and can impart, empower, release, advance, grow and journey with you in your destiny and calling. SHIFT!

POSSESSING MINISTERIAL VISION

It is important that people have a clear understanding of the ministry's vision and purpose, so they will know what to expect from the ministry.

When there is no vision people:
- Implement their own vision
- Become disappointed when their needs and desires are not met concerning what a ministry should provide for them
- Implement what they feel is best or improvise based on the season or situation
- Operate in confusion and discord as different perceptions and personalities tend to clash in effort to create vision

✓ Often there is vision and procedures in place, but people are not informed of what it is.
✓ Often members are not provided with revelation of how important the vision is to the foundation and advancement of the church.
✓ Often the vision will change without being fulfilled and people become confused regarding the vision of the ministry.
✓ Often vision is discussed when a member first joins the church or when a challenge arises, when truly vision should be revisited with members a couple times a year. There should also be a progress report regarding how the ministry is advancing in the vision, what God has said to further expand or advance the vision, and what needs to be changed or implemented to strengthen and process the vision.
✓ Often people know the doctrine of the church and the rules and regulations of the church, but not how these standards significantly impact the vision.
✓ Often people are not cultivated in how their destinies and callings are significant to the vision, therefore, they have minimal to no insight on their purpose in being a vision carrier.

Habakkuk 2:2-3 And the Lord answered me, and said, Write the vision, and make it plain upon tables, that he may run that readeth it. For the vision is yet for an appointed time, but at the end it shall speak, and not lie: though it tarry, wait for it;

Proverbs 29:18 And the Lord answered me, and said, Write the vision, and make it plain upon tables, that he may run that readeth it. For the vision is yet for an appointed time, but at the end it shall speak, and not lie: though it tarry, wait for it;

Perish is *pâra* in the Hebrew. When we consider the definition of *para*, we find that without vision the people will be:

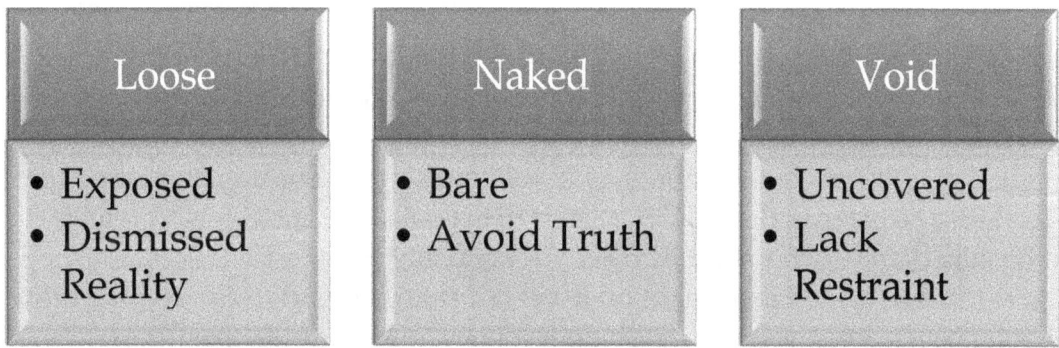

Loose	Naked	Void
• Exposed • Dismissed Reality	• Bare • Avoid Truth	• Uncovered • Lack Restraint

A lack of ministry vision causes people and the ministry to be:
- Loose in their ideas, and actions
- Unrestrained in their morals and standards
- Susceptible to dismiss or avoid reality and truth
- Naked, bare, and uncovered
- Void of the uniqueness and identity of God

A lack of ministry vision causes unnecessary conflicts, while also giving room for the enemy to wreak havoc in our assemblies. We tend to be defensive rather than offensive in this area, where we strive to clean up messes and resolve conflicts that could have been avoided if people initially had clear ministry vision.

When I say vision, I am referring to the purpose to which God planted the assembly you are integrated with. This is not about doctrines and systems. Every ministry should have a specific mandate for why they have been established in the earth. We can have the same doctrines and be a part of the same denominational system, but have different visions. Usually a vision is tailored to the unique gifting and calling on a leader's life, or in alignment with the needs or purpose of a community or region. Some leaders have planted ministries through doctrines and systems, but lack vision. Doctrines and systems have their place, but as the people mature in their walk with God, they grow weary and restless in having no specific purpose for attending a ministry. If they are not provided vision and are only used through works, they will find a purpose to pursue. This can cause confusion and even church hurt as they will appear to be usurping authority, or trying to implement unorthodox paradigms and suggestions that are rejected by the leader/s and the system itself. As the person is rejected, conflicts and challenges arise that result in church hurt. Leaders must have vision so that people can be clear on the purpose of the assembly and even whether they are in the assembly that is aligned with their destiny.

Some leaders plant a ministry based on need, but God did not tell them to start that work. They saw the heart of the people or community and decided to provide that ministry to the people. God will honor this, but it is important for the leader to be clear in their purpose and to even search out a person who is God ordained and equipped to further advance that work once it is established in the earth. Many leaders remain overseers of such ministries out of obligation or they have invested so much, they do not want to relinquish the ministry. These perceptions are understandable but if you are not supposed to be over that work, it will start to lose its investment if you stay too long or if you do not start SHIFTING the work under your God ordained mantle. The toiling, weariness, and drainage that comes with investing in a work that God did not ordain will begin to suffocate you like the millstone necklace. As the ministry will feel like a burden than a blessing from God. Therefore, even what you are striving to hold on to will start to be swallowed up and choked out as you strive to remain afloat in a ministry that is good and needful, but is not in alignment with who you are in God. Seek to release those ministries to the people whose mantles match those ministries so that the fullness of the kingdom can be made manifest through what you compassionately established.

As leaders impart vision, it is important to teach people how to discern their purpose in life, so they can align with destiny. Doing this properly positions people within the ministry where they are not just doing works, but walking in destiny. It also reveals the equipping and training people need to walk in destiny. If the church is not able to provide training, they will know the needs of the people and be able to bring in ministers that can train and equip people. They can also provide ministry suggestions where people can receive training. When people have a clear identity and are working destiny, they are more fulfilled and less likely to engage in petty and mindless situations or conflicts. As they are being trained and empowered, providing platforms and avenues for people to walk in their calling is essential. One of the biggest challenges we have at present in the body of Christ, is there is a lot of equipping and training, but minimal releasing. People are spiritually dying on the pews, while becoming restless and rebellious. As time has been wasted and regret has set in, some have become complacent in the pews and lost hope, or stopped going to church altogether, while others are being uprooted by internet preachers and conference ministers who are training them in how to start their own ministries, businesses and organizations. While I have nothing against internet and conference ministers, I do believe that our destinies are connected to the communities and regions God leads us to live in.

> *Isaiah 49:1-5 Listen, O isles, unto me; and hearken, ye people, from afar; The Lord hath called me from the womb; from the bowels of my mother hath he made mention of my name. And he hath made my mouth like a sharp sword; in the shadow of his hand hath he hid me, and made me a polished shaft; in his quiver hath he hid me; And said unto me, thou art my servant, O Israel, in whom I will be glorified. Then I said, I have laboured in vain, I have spent my strength for nought, and in vain: yet surely my judgment is with the Lord, and my work with my God. And now, saith the Lord that formed me from the womb to be his servant, to bring Jacob again to him, Though Israel be not gathered, yet shall I be glorious in the eyes of the Lord, and my God shall be my strength.*

The word *"isles"* in this passage of scripture means *"region."* LISTEN O REGION! I am called from my mother's womb to do a work in this sphere. YESSSSSS!

As people are equipped, the focus has been more on being international, while building your business and ministry online and through social media opportunities. People are not encouraged or given revelation of searching out how their destiny impacts their region. The lack of connection to a local assembly, and/or the lack of release in these destiny endeavors through a local assembly, causes regions to be void of the establishment and advancement of the kingdom of God that is to occur in one's own sphere. Churches need to awaken to the revelation of releasing people in their destiny and connecting their destinies to the vision of the assembly, so people can be strategically aligned with what God is saying for their lives and regions. I decree a SHIFT in realizing the importance of ministry vision, and how to make people vision carriers and destiny bearers for the kingdom of God. SHIFT!

HEAL THEN RELEASE

Members need healing from church hurt just as much as they need equipping as an apostle, prophet, teacher, preacher, evangelist, pastor, intercessor, deliverance worker, healer, leader, etc. Now that we have the revelation and the consistency of imparting, training, activating and releasing within the body of Christ, we need to make sure we send people to the highways and byways healthy, where they will not be manifesting their issues and releasing subtle fiery darts against the church and people through their works, all because of unhealed church hurts in their hearts. We need to heal first, then impart, train, activate, and release.

There is a fashion of saints who are hurt because they were not released in their ministry by the church, were not validated in their gifting and callings, and were not equipped in their gifting and calling. This hurt is valid and needs to be dealt with first, so when they are sent out, they can sustain in their destiny. We need to ACKNOWLEDGE AND HEAL CHURCH HURT FIRST, then impart, train, activate, and release.

The body is not equipped or perfected if it is not healthy.

> ***Ephesians 4:11-12 The Amplified Bible*** *And His gifts were [varied; He Himself appointed and gave men to us] some to be apostles (special messengers), some prophets (inspired preachers and expounders), some evangelists (preachers of the Gospel, traveling missionaries), some pastors (shepherds of His flock) and teachers. His intention was the perfecting and the full equipping of the saints (His consecrated people), [that they should do] the work of ministering toward building up Christ's body (the church).*

Perfecting means fully *furnish*.

<u>Saints</u> in this scripture is *hagios* and means:
1. sacred (physically, pure, morally blameless or religious, ceremonially, consecrated)
2. (most) holy (one, thing), saint

You are not perfected if you are bound in church hurt and unresolved wounds. Your motives for ministry cannot remain consistently pure if you are not healed, healthy and well in your soul. We are trying to make a broken saint preach holiness and commit to holiness. We are trying to make a unconsecrated vessel carry a vision that their womb has not birthed, and is not well enough to carry. This can cause us to be a kingdom divided within ourselves, as we have become a part of our own demise. Stop operating in extremes and balance in our ability to equip, such that we save and heal first, then impart, train, activate, and release. We need to acknowledge the wounds and unresolved issues, while providing tools and avenues to heal our broken within the church. As we heal and equip them, they can sustain in the calling that is on their lives.

Please know that sending them unhealed will not heal many of them. Many of them have buried their wounds and do not know they need healing. You - the preacher – the mentor - did not fill them with the knowledge or desire to be healed, or they did not have a desire or focus to be healed. And not just to be healed, but to be made whole.

> *Luke 17:11-19 And it came to pass, as he went to Jerusalem, that he passed through the midst of Samaria and Galilee. And as he entered into a certain village, there met him ten men that were lepers, which stood afar off: And they lifted up their voices, and said, Jesus, Master, have mercy on us. And when he saw them, he said unto them, Go shew yourselves unto the priests. And it came to pass, that, as they went, they were cleansed. And one of them, when he saw that he was healed, turned back, and with a loud voice glorified God, And fell down on his face at his feet, giving him thanks: and he was a Samaritan. And Jesus answering said, were there not ten cleansed? but where are the nine? There are not found that returned to give glory to God, save this stranger. And he said unto him, Arise, go thy way: thy faith hath made thee whole.*

A great number of people attend conferences and events, hoping to get equipped, confirmed and released into their destiny and calling. And rightfully so. Because God is always in the midst of a praising and worshipping people, they are healed as they go. But much of the time, healing is not the main intent of the event. It is the afterthought. Therefore, the people are not equipped regarding how to maintain their healing. As a result, they do not SHIFT to a place of sustaining wholeness. They return home, and just like the nine lepers, they are focused on activating their prophecy, word of knowledge, etc., while their soul is still in a place where the enemy can steal their healing. They are not focused on consecrating in devotion and relationship unto God like the one leper, so they can be made well. They take their initial healing and go forth in the works of God. Prayerfully, the priest can provide the lepers with strategies to remain healed and even empower them to pursue a sustaining relationship with God. However, some people who attend the events and conference are coming because they have no priest to be mentored by or accountable to. We unfortunately see them years later bleeding all over the sheep that they are ministering to. Regardless to whether we recognize it or not, we are partly responsible for them not being equipped in maintaining their healing. Heal the people and equip them with strategies to maintain their healing, so as they SHIFT into the things of God, wholeness can be their portion.

SURVIVAL IS NOT HEALING

Survive means:
- To remain alive after a death or trial
- To succeed something
- To remain or continue in existence or use
- To endure or live through

It also can mean to get along or remain healthy, happy, and unaffected despite some occurrence: although most people are just living after they survived a situation. They are not happy, well, and are still challenged by what happened to them.

- Just because you survived an ordeal does not necessarily mean you are healed.
- Just because you can talk about a challenging ordeal does not necessarily mean you are healed.
- Just because you do not cry anymore regarding a situation does not necessarily mean you are necessarily healed.
- Putting distance between you and the situation does not necessarily mean you are healed.

Survival means you got through it and we thank God you did.

- Being able to talk about it means you are giving voice to your experience and we thank God you can do that.
- Not crying anymore could mean your emotions are no longer responding to the impact of the ordeal and we thank God for that.
- Putting distance between yourself and the situation is great, and we thank God that you recognize it was unhealthy for you.

However, healing means you have been made healthy, whole, sound, and restored in your soul, heart, mind, identity, perspective, and actions concerning that situation. You not only survived it, you conquered it, such that it no longer has any control over you. Where it no longer dictates your responses, where you do not need unhealthy walls and mindsets to protect you from it, where you no longer fear succumbing to it again, and where you possess applicable - healthy wisdom and tools to not to succumb to it again. And if experiencing it again becomes unavoidable, you possess the tools to conquer it.

- ❖ You have healed from it.
- ❖ Have a balanced perspective regarding it.
- ❖ Your every life action demonstrates the wellness that you have prevailed over it.

Revelation 12:11 *And they overcame him by the blood of the Lamb, and by the word of their testimony; and they loved not their lives unto the death.*

Overcome is *nikao* in the Hebrew and means to:
1. subdue (literally or figuratively): — conquer, overcome, prevail, get the victory
2. to conquer, to carry off the victory, come off victorious
3. of Christ, victorious over all His foes
4. of Christians, that hold fast their faith even unto death against the power of their foes, and temptations and persecutions
5. when one is arraigned or goes to law, to win the case, maintain one's cause

When we overcome an experience, we have killed its presence in our lives. Jesus not only survived the cross, he put death to death. He made sure that life, living, and wellness were the only factors that existed. The shedding of his blood allowed such an annihilation. Periodically, we apply the blood to our situation, but the motive and/or account does not exemplify victory. We survived but we have not killed that thing in our life where we are the only thing that is living and where Jesus is the only thing that is testifying. Many times:
- ❖ Our pain and wounds are still testifying and getting glory
- ❖ Our anger, bitterness and unforgiveness are still testifying and getting glory
- ❖ Our fears and insecurities are still testifying and getting glory
- ❖ Our walls and suspicions are still testifying and getting glory
- ❖ Our desire for revenge and justice is still testifying and getting glory

True deliverance and healing is so vital, especially currently where we are quick to share our experiences, while declaring we are testifying. There are a plethora of saints who build platforms, ministries, their identities, and even make money from survival experiences disguised as testimonies. Our experiences bless people, draw people, validate people, give people a voice or words to their hurts and pains, but because we have not truly overcome, we do not possess the resurrection power to deliver and transform peoples' lives.

I also want to point out that having integrity in how you handle a situation does not necessarily mean you are healed either. I state this because a lot of us tend to do the right thing and make the right choices because we want to please God and be viewed as honorable. Though this is important and necessary, and helps you to align with healing, it does not mean we are healed. We can publicly present one way, while still be writhing with pain in our hearts. This is still a form of survival. It is like being out to sea in a boat that you realize has a hole in the bottom. Turning back to shore and rowing quickly does not fix the hole. It merely changes the direction of your sinking process. In our effort to be integral, we are seeking to remain politically correct with God and people, so we do not sink in our experience, but our soul still needs to process into alignment with true healing.

Apostle Ursula Wright of The Fusion Center in Miami, Florida, stated in a sermon that, "*Just surviving makes you overlook the seeds that are inside of you.*"

I decree this will not be your testimony; that the true healing testimony of God will be your portion as every seed is revealed as harvest in your life. I decree a SHIFT where every unhealthy attribute and every unhealed wound is exposed and healed. I decree a processing to wholeness where true prevailing with Jesus manifests and makes you free, while being endued with resurrection power to set others free!

There is a difference between surviving and healing. Heal us Jesus. SHIFT!

HOW DO I KNOW IF I AM REALLY HEALED?

By: Dr. Apostle Kathy Williams
New Day Ministries, Muncie, Indiana

You know when you are healed of church hurt when:

- ✓ Remembering or conversing about your experiences no longer triggers hurtful or negative emotions.
- ✓ When remembering the experience is more of a victorious memory from the past than a specific point of relevancy in your life.
- ✓ The point of hurt no longer becomes a point of reference for your life and identity.
- ✓ You do not view the church and church people through a negative or contaminated well.
- ✓ You no longer need to tear the church or church people down to get your point across regarding your experiences or challenges. Even if you have challenges and concerns, they do not flow from a well of death, doom, degradation, belittlement, bitterness, strife, or division. You can express your concerns from a place of hope and empowerment.
- ✓ You no longer have any expectations for an apology, justice, retaliation, or validation.
- ✓ You can hear or see your offender and though you may be conscious in your interactions, you do not have any ill will.
- ✓ You no longer feel you need the opinions or actions of others to heal. You know that God is your healer and he is more than enough to make you whole.
- ✓ You no longer believe or question whether or why God allowed this to happen to you.
- ✓ You are no longer angry or questioning your belief in God for what happened to you.
- ✓ You can pray for the people that hurt you and desire the best of God for them.
- ✓ You are not fearful that you will be hurt again. You trust your healing process and the revelation and tools you have learned, to handle situations better in the future.

NUGGETS FOR DETERRING CHURCH HURT

- Teach members healthy conflict resolution skills, communication skills, anger management skills, interpersonal skills, and social skills.
- Have a counseling center within the church so that counselors, social workers, mentors, and coaches can assist people with church and life problems, and provide guidance and practical tools for dealing with life situations.
- Leaders live the same lifestyle in public that you have in private so people will know your true character, nature, and identity.
- Leaders be accountable when you fall, repent, and display a true processing towards healing and transformation.
- Be consistent with resolving conflicts quickly and promote an atmosphere of love, empowerment, reconciliation, and restoration.
- Promote an atmosphere of quick repentance and forgiveness.
- Be conscious of the principalities and powers that hang around the atmosphere of your assembly. Displace them in warfare and intercession, while maintaining an open heaven where the kingdom of God reigns in your midst.
- Make a conscious effort to acknowledge, address and deliver people from church hurt just as you would any other sin or tribulation.
- Implement guidelines to address possible church hurt in members that are transitioning from other ministries.
- Address the truths and myths regarding the church so people will know God's purpose for the church and his truth about the church.
- Teach people to have realistic expectations for the leaders, members, and the church.
- Consistently train your elders, deacons, and department heads how to be healthy and productive leaders.
- Have a clear working ministerial vision aside from doctrines and systems.
- Help people identify their calling and how their destiny impacts the vision, the ministry, the region, the body of Christ, and the world at large.
- Train, equip, and release people in their destinies and callings.
- Have connections within the body of Christ where people can go for further training and equipping when it is not available in the ministry.
- Implement rules regarding social media pages and internet ministry to bring accountability to these platforms.

- Implement accountability measures where people are responsible for the teachings, trainings, prophecies, revelations, and guidance they are receiving within the church and from those within the body of Christ.

ANNIHILATING THE POWERS OF CHURCH HURT CHARGE

I decree that whatever extent you were negatively impacted by the church, that through the revelation of this book, you will be delivered, healed, and SHIFTED in Jesus name. I decree that your hurt matters to God and that breakthrough is your portion in Jesus name.

I decree that even as church hurt has become a popular fad and that rebelling against the church, leaders, and God has become the style, that this will not be your fashioned testimony. I decree you will not get stuck in a system that rejects a part of God by rejecting the church.

I decree you understand that God loves the church, is coming back for the church, and that you will process through your pain to being healed and set free from the principality webbing of church hurt.

I decree that as you SHIFT into wellness, you will be able to testify, encourage, and empower others not to reject God because of man or challenging experiences.

I decree that you will annihilate the powers of church hurt by SHIFTING into your true identity of loving God, loving people, loving the church, being sold out to God, and being a representative of his character, nature, integrity, compassion, love, and forgiveness.

I decree you triumph and church hurt is demolished. The demonic kingdom that once tried to divide you from being God's bride and being a part of God's bride, is dung under your feet, as church hurt has become your eternal footstool. Decreeing it is your portion in Jesus name! SHIFT!

BOOK REFERENCES

- *Blueletterbible.com*

- *Biblestudytools.com*

- *Dictionary.com*

- *Healing The Wounded Leader Manual By Taquetta Baker*

- *Millstone photo is from http://kingsenglish.info/wp-content/uploads/2011/09/millstone-232x300.jpg*

- *Millstone drowning photo is from http://www.destinywordoftheday.com/wp-content/uploads/2013/03/millstone.jpg*

- *Olivetree.com*

- *Strongs Exhaustive Bible Concordance Online Bible Study Tools*

- *Wikipedia*

- *Cover photo by Latasha Hyatt. Connect with her via Facebook.*

Kingdom Shifters Books & Apparel
Available at Kingdomshifters.com

BOOKS FOR EVERYONE

Healing The Wounded Leader
Kingdom Shifters Decree That Thang
There Is An App For That
Kingdom Watchman Builder On the Wall
Embodiment Of A Kingdom Watchman
Dismantling Homosexuality Handbook
Releasing The Vision
Feasting In His Presence

Kingdom Heirs Decree That Thing
Let There Be Sight
Atmosphere Changers (Weaponry)
Apostolic Governing
Apostolic Mantle
Dancing From Heaven to Earth
Annihilating Church Hurt

BOOKS FOR DANCERS

Dancers! Dancers! Decree That Thang
Spirits That Attack Dance Ministers & Ministries
Dance & Fivefold Ministry
Dancing From Heaven To Earth

TEE SHIRTS

Kingdom Shifters Tee Shirt
Let The Fruit Speak Tee Shirt
Releasing The Vision Tee Shirt
Kingdom Perspective Tee Shirt

Stand in Position Tee Shirt
No Defense Tee Shirt
My God Rules Like A Boss Tee Shirt
Destiny Blueprint Tee Shirt

CD'S

Decree That Thing CD
Kingdom Heirs Decree That Thing CD
Teachings & Worship CD's

www.ingramcontent.com/pod-product-compliance
Lightning Source LLC
Chambersburg PA
CBHW080334170426
43194CB00014B/2564